WORKBOOK/STUDY GUIDE

for use with

MANAGERIAL ACCOUNTING

CONCEPTS FOR PLANNING, CONTROL, DECISION MAKING

Eighth Edition

Ray H. Garrison
Eric W. Noreen

IRWIN

Chicago • Bogotá • Boston • Buenos Aires • Caracas
London • Madrid • Mexico City • Sydney • Toronto

Printed in the United States of America.

ISBN 0–256–23569–4

4 5 6 7 8 9 0 EB 3 2 1 0 9 8 7 6

Preface

To The Student

This study guide is designed to supplement the eighth edition of *Managerial Accounting* by Ray H. Garrison and Eric W. Noreen. Each chapter of the study guide contains three major sections:

1. *Chapter Study Suggestions* to help you to study more efficiently.
2. *Chapter Highlights* that summarize in outline form the essential points in a chapter.
3. *Review and Self Test* questions and exercises that test your knowledge of the material in the chapter. Solutions are provided. *Caution:* If you want to score well on exams, you *must* work out each solution on your own and *then* check to see whether your solution is correct by comparing it to the solution in the study guide. You cannot learn the material by simply reading the solution provided in the study guide. This does not work.

This study guide can be used as an integral part of the process of learning the material in a chapter. When used for this purpose, we recommend that you follow the steps below:

1. Before reading the chapter in your textbook, read the *Chapter Study Suggestions* in this study guide.
2. Read the textbook chapter.
3. Read the outline in the *Chapter Highlights* section of the study guide. If you run across anything in the outline you don't understand, refer back to the textbook for a more detailed discussion.
4. Work the questions and exercises in the study guide and then compare your answers to those given in the study guide. If you find something you don't understand, refer to the textbook for help.
5. Work the homework problems assigned by your instructor.

Alternatively, the study guide can also be used as a very effective way to study for exams. Before reading the chapter in your textbook, read the *Chapter Study Suggestions* in this study guide. Then lay the study guide aside until it is time to prepare for an exam. The *Chapter Highlights* section of the study guide can then be used to review the essential material covered in the chapter. The *Review and Self Test* provides lots of questions and exercises that can be used to practice for the exam. The questions and exercises in the study guide are particularly effective used in this way since they are likely to be similar to the questions and exercises your instructor will ask on an exam.

Remember, the study guide is not a substitute for the textbook. Rather, its purpose is to *supplement* the textbook by helping you to learn the material.

We welcome your suggestions and comments. You can write to us at the following address:

Prof. Eric Noreen
Box 353200
University of Washington
Seattle, WA 98195-3200

Ray H. Garrison
Eric W. Noreen

Contents

Contents

Chapter 1

Managerial Accounting and the Business Environment

Chapter Study Suggestions

The chapter describes the work that managers do and the kinds of information they need in order to do this work effectively. The chapter also describes important aspects of the contemporary business environment. The chapter is unusual in that there are almost no numerical problems to be worked. However, there are many new terms to be learned. Study these new terms with care.

CHAPTER HIGHLIGHTS

A. An organization is a group of people united for a common purpose. Organizations are run by managers who carry out three major activities: planning, directing and motivating, and controlling. All three of these activities involve making decisions.

1. *Planning* involves identifying alternatives and selecting the alternative that best furthers the organization's objectives.

2. *Directing and motivating* involves mobilizing people to carry out the plans and overseeing day-to-day activities.

3. *Controlling* involves obtaining feedback to ensure that all parts of the organization are following the plans.

B. There are at least six major differences between financial and managerial accounting. In contrast to financial accounting, managerial accounting:

1. Focuses on providing data for internal uses.

2. Places more emphasis on the future.

3. Emphasizes relevance and flexibility rather than precision.

4. Emphasizes the segments of an organization, rather than just looking at the organization as a whole.

5. Is not governed by Generally Acceptable Accounting Practice.

6. Is not mandatory.

C. In many industries today, a company that does not continually improve will find itself quickly overtaken by competitors. The text discusses five major approaches to improvement—Just-In-Time (JIT), Total Quality Management (TQM), Process Reengineering, Automation, and the Theory of Constraints (TOC). These approaches can be combined—using one does not preclude using another as well.

D. The Just-In-Time (JIT) approach is based on the insight that reducing inventories—particularly work in process inventories—can be the key to improving operations. Companies have work in process inventories to protect against disruptions in the production process and as a consequence of using large batch sizes; however, they have a number of drawbacks:

1. Work in process inventories tie up funds and take up space.

2. Work in process inventories increase the *throughput time*, which is the amount of time required to make a product. If there is an average of two weeks of work in process inventories, then it takes two weeks longer to complete a unit than if there were no work in process inventories. Long throughput time makes it difficult to respond quickly to customers and can be a major competitive disadvantage.

3. When work in process inventories are large, units sit idle for long periods of time before being passed to the next work station. Therefore, defects may not be noticed for quite some time. If a machine is out of calibration, many defective units will be produced before the problem is discovered. And when the defects are discovered, it may be very difficult to track down the source of the problem since it may have occurred long ago.

4. Because of the long throughput time, units may be obsolete or out of fashion by the time they are finally completed.

5. Large work in process inventories encourage sloppy procedures and mask inefficiencies and problems in the production process. When inventories are reduced, these problems are uncovered and can be identified and dealt with.

E. *Just-In-Time (JIT)* seeks improvement by reducing inventories to the absolute minimum levels possible.

1. "Just in time" means that raw materials are received just in time to go into production, subassemblies are completed just in time to be assembled into products, and products are completed just in time to be shipped to customers.

2. In JIT, the flow of goods is controlled by a "pull" approach.; work is initiated only in response to customer orders.

a. At the final assembly stage, a signal is sent to preceding workstations as to the exact amounts of parts and materials that will be needed over the next few hours to assemble products ordered by customers.

b. In contrast, under conventional systems parts and material are "pushed" forward to the next workstation regardless of need. The result is a needless buildup of inventory.

F. A successful JIT system involves five key elements.

1. A company must learn to rely on a few suppliers who are willing to make frequent (even daily) deliveries in small lots.

2. A company often must improve its product flow lines by creating an individual flow line for each separate product. This may involve setting up a *focused factory* in which all the machines needed to make a particular product or family of products are brought together in one location. This is in contrast to a conventional, "functional plant layout" in which similar machines are grouped together in one location. When a functional plant layout is used, units must be moved long distances between work centers to be completed.

3. A company must reduce the setup time that is required between production runs. *Setups* consist of the activities that must be performed whenever production is switched over from making one type of unit to another.

4. A company should strive for zero defects. If any units in an order are defective, the whole production process would have to be restarted in order to replace the defective units. This would make it impossible to deliver the order on time. In a JIT system, suppliers are required to deliver defect-free parts and production workers are given responsibility for continuously monitoring the quality of units they work on.

5. A company must develop a multi-skilled and flexible work force that is capable of operating many different machines and of performing routine maintenance on the machines.

G. Many benefits result from a JIT system. The most important are:

1. Working capital is bolstered by recovering funds that were tied up in inventories.

2. Usable space is increased. Areas previously used to store inventories are made available for other, more productive uses.

3. Throughput time is reduced, resulting in greater potential output and quicker response to customer needs.

4. Defect rates are reduced, resulting in less waste and greater customer satisfaction.

H. *Total Quality Management (TQM)* is an approach to continuous improvement that focuses on the customer and that involves systematic problem-solving using teams of front-line workers. A variety of specific tools are available in TQM to aid teams in their problem solving. Two of these tools are benchmarking and the Plan-Do-Check-Act Cycle.

1. *Benchmarking* involves studying how a successful "world-class" company runs a particular operation. For example, a company trying to improve its customer service might study the employee training program of a company that is well-known for customer satisfaction such as Disney.

2. The *Plan-Do-Check-Act (PDCA) Cycle* is a systematic, fact-based approach to continuous improvement that resembles the scientific method. Exhibit 1-6 in the text illustrates the PDCA Cycle.

a. In the Plan phase, the current process is studied, data are collected, and possible causes of the problem at hand are identified. A plan is developed to deal with the problem.

b. In the Do phase, the plan is implemented and data are collected. This is done on a small scale if possible since at this point the team is rarely sure that the plan will work.

c. In the Check phase, the data collected in the Do phase are analyzed to verify whether the expected improvement actually occurred.

d. In the Act phase, the plan is implemented on a large scale if it was successful. If the plan was not successful in eliminating the problem, the cycle is started again with the Plan phase.

3. Perhaps the most important characteristics of TQM are that it empowers front-line workers to solve problems and it focuses energy on solving problems rather than on finger-pointing.

I. *Process Reengineering* is a more radical approach to improvement than TQM. It involves completely redesigning business processes and it is often implemented by outside consultants.

1. In Process Reengineering, the process under examination is thoroughly diagrammed in the form of a process flowchart. The flowchart, when completed, usually reveals unnecessary steps, called *non-value-added activities*.

2. The process is then completely redesigned from the ground up, eliminating non-value-added activities.

3. If successful, Process Reengineering will result in a streamlined process that will get the job done using fewer resources in less time and with fewer errors.

4. However, there is a trap that some managers fall into. If Process Reengineering results in laying off workers who are no longer needed, employees will resist further Process Reengineering efforts.

J. *Automation* may be used to improve processes.

1. While automation is expensive, there can be substantial benefits in terms of reductions in setup time, flexibility, reductions in defects, and increases in the rate of output.

2. A *flexible manufacturing system (FMS)* is a product flow line controlled by a central computer in which automated machines are linked together by an automated material-handling system. Setup times are minimal since the machines are computer controlled.

K. *The Theory of Constraints (TOC)* is based on the idea that every organization has at least one constraint that prevents it from obtaining more of its objective. For example, a machine that is slower than other machines on an assembly line will prevent the company from increasing its rate of output. To improve (in other words, increase its rate of output), the company must focus its improvement efforts on the constraint. Improvement efforts focused on machines that are not constraints will be largely wasted.

L. *Organizational Structure.*

1. Almost all organizations are decentralized to some degree. *Decentralization* involves delegating decision making authority to lower levels in the organization.

2. An *organization chart* shows the levels of responsibility and formal channels of communication in an organization. In other words, it shows who reports to who in the organization. There is an example of an organization chart in Exhibit 1-8 in the text.

3. A manager may occupy either a line position or a staff position.

a. *Line positions* are directly related to achieving the basic objectives of the organization.

b. *Staff positions* provide service, assistance, and specialized support to the line positions. They do not have direct authority over line positions. Accounting is a staff position.

4. The *controller* is the manager of the accounting department and often acts as a key adviser to top management.

M. Ethics plays a vital role in an advanced market economy.

1. If people were generally dishonest, it would become more difficult for companies to raise investment funds, the quality of goods and services would decline, fewer goods and services would be available for sale, and prices would be higher.

2. The Institute of Management Accountants has issued The Standards of Ethical Conduct for Management Accountants. This is a useful, practical guide for general managers as well as management accountants. The Standards for Ethical Conduct are reproduced in Exhibit 1-10 in the text. You should study this exhibit carefully.

Jackie Cochran

REVIEW AND SELF TEST
Questions and Exercises

True or False

For each of the following statements, enter a T or an F in the blank to indicate whether the statement is true or false.

F 1. Managerial accounting is as concerned with providing information to stockholders as it is with providing information to managers.

T 2. When carrying out their control function, managers obtain feedback to ensure that each part of the organization is following the plan.

F 3. When carrying out their planning function, managers mobilize the organization's resources and oversee day-to-day operations.

F 4. The planning, directing and motivating, and control activities of a manager are kept separate from the manager's decision-making responsibilities.

T 5. Managerial accounting focuses more on the segments of an organization than on the organization as a whole.

T 6. Managerial accounting need not follow Generally Accepted Accounting Principles.

T 7. An objective of a JIT inventory system is to complete products just in time to ship to customers.

F 8. Under JIT, partially completed units are "pushed" from one workstation to another to ensure all workstations have enough work to keep busy.

F 9. The maintenance of large work in process inventories helps reduce the number of defective units that are produced.

T 10. A company will typically have fewer suppliers under JIT than under a conventional system.

F 11. For JIT to operate successfully, all similar pieces of equipment (such as lathes or drill presses) must be grouped together.

F 12. JIT requires an increase in funds to finance additional inventories.

T 13. Total Quality Management involves a focus on serving the customer and systematic problem-solving using teams made up of front-line workers.

F 14. The Plan-Do-Check-Act Cycle is used in the Theory of Constraints to eliminate constraints.

T 15. In the plan phase of the Plan-Do-Check-Act Cycle, data are analyzed to identify the possible causes of a problem and a solution is proposed.

F 16. Process Reengineering is less likely to result in employee resistance than Total Quality Management.

F 17. Non-value-added activities are the constraints in the system.

T 18. Efforts that are designed to improve the rate of output of a work station should generally be focused on the constraint.

F 19. The Standards of Ethical Conduct for Management Accountants promulgated by the Institute of Management Accountants specifically states, among other things, that a management accountant should refuse all gifts and hospitality offered by one of the company's suppliers.

Multiple Choice

Choose the best answer or response by placing the identifying letter in the space provided.

d 1. Staff positions: a) are not shown on the organization chart; b) are superior in authority to line positions; c) are subordinate in authority to line positions; d) none of these.

a 2. The controller: a) occupies a staff position; b) occupies a line position; c) has little influence in the decision-making process; d) none of these.

c 3. Managerial accounting: a) is governed by Generally Accepted Accounting Principles; b) places more emphasis on precision of data than does financial accounting; c) is not mandatory; d) is geared primarily to the past rather than to the future.

b 4. Financial and managerial accounting are similar in that: a) both emphasize reporting the performance of the entire organization rather than segments of the organization; b) both rely on the same accounting database; c) both focus on providing data for internal uses; d) none of these.

c 5. In a decentralized organization, decisions are made: a) only by top management; b) only by managers occupying staff positions; c) at the lowest managerial level possible in the organization; d) none of these.

b 6. In large part, "control" in an organization is achieved through: a) decentralization of decision making authority; b) obtaining feedback on how well the organization is moving toward its objectives; c) preparing an organization chart that shows both line and staff functions; d) none of these.

b 7. Under JIT: a) the plant floor is laid out in a functional format with similar machines grouped together; b) focused factories are used; c) the plant floor is laid out in a single flow line through which all products pass; d) work in process inventories are maximized in order to ensure that all work stations have enough work to stay busy.

b 8. Which of the following involves systematic problem-solving by teams consisting of front-line workers? a) The Theory of Constraints; b) Total Quality Management; c) Process Reengineering; d) Automation.

a 9. The Plan-Do-Check Act Cycle is used to: a) solve problems in Total Quality Management; b) manage constraints in The Theory of Constraints; c) redesign processes in Process Reengineering; d) none of these.

Exercises

1-1. Mary Karston was hired by a popular fast-food restaurant as an order-taker and cashier. Shortly after taking the job, she was shocked to overhear an employee bragging to a friend about short-changing customers. She confronted the employee who then snapped back: "Mind your own business. Besides, everyone does it and the customers never miss the money." Mary didn't know how to respond to this aggressive stance.

What would be the practical consequences if cashiers generally short-changed customers at every opportunity?

Eventually customer's would become aware of the situation & be reluntant to purchase meals at those establishments. If this was wide-spread, businesses would start losing sales which in turn would lose profits.

Answers to Questions and Exercises

True or False

1. F The central purpose of managerial accounting is to provide information to managers. The information needs of stockholders are provided through financial accounting.

2. T This is what is meant by control.

3. F Planning involves deciding on the actions to be taken in order to achieve the organization's objectives; it does not involve overseeing day-to-day activities.

4. F Decision making is an integral part of the planning, organizing, and controlling functions.

5. T The primary concern of managerial accounting is with the segments of an organization, rather than with the organization as a whole.

6. T There is no requirement that managerial accounting follow GAAP.

7. T Under JIT, goods are produced and shipped only as needed to satisfy customer orders.

8. F JIT operates under a "pull" approach in which partially completed units are passed to the next work station only as needed to fill customer orders.

9. F Large work in process inventories increase defect rates. Because of delays in passing units on to the next work station, problems are not detected until after many units have been affected.

10. T Under JIT, a company uses only a few suppliers who are bound under firm contracts to deliver materials on a frequent basis.

11. F Typically under JIT, all of the different pieces of equipment needed to manufacture a product are placed on a single flow line, thus breaking up groupings of similar equipment.

12. F JIT reduces inventories and the need for funds to finance them.

13. T These are common characteristics of TQM.

14. F The Plan-Do-Check-Act Cycle is used in TQM, not TOC.

15. T This statement correctly describes the plan phase of the PDCA Cycle.

16. F The reverse is true. Process Reengineering tends to be imposed from above using outside specialists and it may lead to loss of jobs.

17. F A non-value-added activity is an activity that consumes resources or takes time that adds nothing of value. It may or may not be a constraint.

18. T The rate of output of the constraint determines the output of the entire system. Therefore, improvement efforts should ordinarily be focused on the constraint.

19. F The Standards state that the management accountant should "refuse any gift, favor, or hospitality that would influence or would appear to influence their actions." There is no absolute prohibition. For example, it would be okay to let a supplier pay for one's dinner while on a fact-finding trip to the supplier's plant. This is a common courtesy and it is extremely unlikely that this small favor would influence the management accountant's judgment in matters relating to the supplier.

Multiple Choice

1. d Staff positions (such as Accounting) do appear on the organization chart, but they are neither superior nor equal in authority to line positions. They serve the needs of line positions by providing essential services.

2. a The controller occupies a staff position that provides support to other positions within the organization.

3. c Managerial accounting is not required by any external law or regulation.

4. b Since it would be a waste of money to have two data collecting systems existing side by side, managerial accounting largely uses the data generated by the financial accounting system.

5. c The purpose of decentralization is to move all decisions to the lowest managerial level possible in an organization.

6. b By obtaining feedback, management can see how well an organization is moving toward its objectives and thus control is maintained.

7. b Under JIT, the plant floor is laid out into many product flow lines—one for each family of products.

8. b Total Quality Management involves systematic problem-solving by teams consisting of front-line workers.

9. a The Plan-Do-Check-Act Cycle is used to solve problems in TQM.

Exercises

1-1. If cashiers routinely short-changed customers whenever the opportunity presented itself, most of us would be careful to count our change before leaving the counter. Imagine what effect this would have on the line at your favorite fast-food restaurant. How would you like to wait in line while each and every customer laboriously counts out his or her change? Additionally, if you can't trust the cashiers to give honest change, can you trust the cooks to take the time to follow health precautions such as washing their hands? If you can't trust anyone at the restaurant would you even want to eat out?

Generally, when we buy goods and services in the free market, we assume we are buying from people who have a certain level of ethical standards. If we could not trust people to maintain those standards, we would be reluctant to buy. The net result of widespread dishonesty would be a shrunken economy with a lower growth rate and fewer goods and services for sale at a lower overall quality level.

Chapter 2

Cost Terms, Concepts, and Classifications

Chapter Study Suggestions

This chapter introduces general cost terms that will be used throughout the remainder of the book. The chapter also gives a broad outline of the flow of costs in a manufacturing company. (Chapter 3 covers cost flows in more depth.) As you read the chapter, note each new term and be sure you understand its meaning. It is important to keep in mind that costs are classified in many ways, depending upon how the costs will be used. This is the reason for so many different cost terms. To fit the cost terms into a framework, you should frequently refer to Exhibit 2-7 as you go through the chapter.

Exhibit 2-3 presents the *schedule of cost of goods manufactured.* You should memorize the format of this schedule, as well as the material in Exhibit 2-5. Learning this material will help you in Chapter 3 and will also lay a foundation for many chapters that follow.

CHAPTER HIGHLIGHTS

A. *Manufacturing costs* are the costs involved in making a product. Manufacturing costs can be subdivided into three basic elements: direct materials, direct labor, and manufacturing overhead.

1. *Direct materials* include those materials that become an integral part of a finished product, and can be conveniently traced into it.

a. An example of direct materials would be the steel used to make a file cabinet.

b. Small material items, such as glue, are classified as *indirect materials* rather than as direct materials. It is too costly and inconvenient to trace such small costs to the individual units that are produced.

2. *Direct labor* consists of those labor costs that can be easily (i.e., physically and conveniently) traced to the creation of products. Direct labor is sometimes called touch labor.

a. An example of direct labor cost would be a worker on a manufacturing assembly line.

b. Other labor costs, such as supervisors and janitors, are treated as *indirect labor* rather than as direct labor. These costs cannot be traced to individual units of product since these individuals do not directly work on the product.

3. *Manufacturing overhead* consists of all manufacturing costs except direct materials and direct labor.

a. Manufacturing overhead includes indirect materials, indirect labor, and other manufacturing costs such as factory rent, factory utilities, and depreciation on factory equipment and facilities.

b. Synonyms for manufacturing overhead include factory overhead, factory burden, and indirect manufacturing costs.

4. Sometimes the terms prime cost and conversion cost are used.

a. *Prime cost* consists of direct materials plus direct labor.

b. *Conversion cost* consists of direct labor plus manufacturing overhead.

B. *Nonmanufacturing costs* are those costs involved with selling and administrative activities.

1. *Selling, or marketing, costs* include all costs associated with marketing finished products, including commissions, depreciation of delivery equipment, depreciation of finished goods warehouses, and advertising.

2. *Administrative costs* include all costs associated with the general administration of an organization, including secretarial salaries, depreciation of general administrative facilities and equipment, and executive compensation.

C. For purposes of external financial reports, costs can be classified as product costs or period costs.

1. *Period costs* are expensed on the income statement in the period in which they are incurred.

2. *Product costs* are matched with units of product and are recognized as an expense on the income statement only when the units are sold. Until that time, product costs are considered to be assets and are recognized on the balance sheet as inventory.

3. In a manufacturing company, product costs include direct materials, direct labor, and manufacturing overhead. Thus, in a manufacturing company, product costs and manufacturing costs are synonymous.

4. In a manufacturing company, period costs and nonmanufacturing costs are synonymous terms. Thus, the period costs are selling and administrative costs.

5. In a merchandising company such as Macy's or K-mart, product costs consist solely of the costs of products purchased from suppliers for resale to customers. All other costs are period costs.

D. The income statements and balance sheets prepared by manufacturing firms differ in important respects from those prepared by merchandising firms.

1. The balance sheet of a manufacturing firm contains three inventory accounts: Raw Materials, Work in Process, and Finished Goods. By contrast, the balance sheet of a merchandising firm contains only one inventory account—Merchandise Inventory.

a. *Raw Materials* consists of materials on hand that will be used to make products.

b. *Work in Process* consists of unfinished products.

c. *Finished Goods* consists of units of product that are completed and ready for sale.

2. The income statement of a manufacturing firm contains an element termed *cost of goods manufactured.* You should study the schedule of cost of goods manufactured in Exhibit 2-3 in the text very carefully. If you have difficulty understanding this exhibit, look at Exhibit 2-4, which shows the same information in a different format.

E. Manufacturing costs (direct materials, direct labor, and overhead) are also known as *inventoriable costs.*

1. The term inventoriable costs is used since direct materials, direct labor, and overhead go into Work in Process and Finished Goods, which are inventory accounts. Therefore, direct materials, direct labor, and overhead can end up on the balance sheet as part of these inventory accounts (as assets) if goods are either not completed or not sold at the end of a period.

2. You should study Exhibit 2-5 in the text with great care. It shows the flow of manufacturing costs through inventory accounts and the way these costs become an expense (cost of goods sold) on the income statement. *This is a key exhibit for Chapter 2.*

3. We can summarize manufacturing and nonmanufacturing cost terms as follows:

Synonymous Cost Terms	*Costs Involved*
• Manufacturing costs • Product costs • Inventoriable costs	• Direct materials, direct labor, and manufacturing overhead
• Nonmanufacturing costs • Period costs	• Selling and administrative expenses

F. For purposes of describing how costs behave in response to changes in activity, costs are often classified as variable or fixed. For example, one might be interested in describing how the costs of admitting patients to a hospital behave in response to changes in the number of patients admitted. Or, one might be interested in how much it would cost for paint in a furniture factory if the output of the factory were increased by 10%.

1. *Variable costs* are those costs that vary, in total, in direct proportion to changes in the volume or level of activity within the relevant range. Exhibit 2-8 illustrates variable cost behavior. Examples of variable costs include direct materials, (usually) direct labor, commissions to salespersons, and cost of goods sold in a merchandising company such as a shoe store.

2. *Fixed costs* are those costs that remain constant in total amount within the relevant range. They include, for example, depreciation, supervisory salaries, and rent. Exhibit 2-8 illustrates fixed cost behavior.

3. The *relevant range* is the range of activity within which the assumptions about cost behavior can be considered valid. If there is a big enough change in activity (for example, a ten-fold increase in volume), even the "fixed" costs are likely to change.

G. For purposes of assigning costs to objects, costs are classified as direct or indirect.

1. Managers often want to know how much something (e.g., a product, a department, or a customer) costs. The item for which a cost is desired is called a cost object.

2. A *direct cost* is a cost that can be conveniently traced to the cost object under consideration. For example, if the cost object under consideration is a unit of product, then the materials and labor involved in its manufacture would both be direct costs.

3. An *indirect cost* is a cost that cannot be conveniently traced to the cost object. For example, if the cost object is a unit of product, then the manufacturing overhead involved in its manufacture would be an indirect cost.

H. For purposes of making decisions, the following cost terms are often used: differential costs, opportunity costs, and sunk costs.

1. Every decision involves choosing from among at least two alternatives. A difference in cost between two alternatives is called a *differential cost.*

2. An *opportunity cost* is the potential benefit given up by selecting one alternative over another.

a. Every alternative facing a manager has opportunity costs attached to it.

b. Opportunity costs are not recorded in the accounting records. They represent a lost benefit rather than an out-of-pocket cost.

3. A *sunk cost* is a cost that has already been incurred and that cannot be changed by any decision made now or in the future. Sunk costs are never differential costs and should always be ignored when making decisions.

Appendix 2A: Further Classification of Labor Costs

A. Labor costs can be broken down into five main categories: direct labor, indirect labor, idle time, overtime premium, and labor fringe benefits.

1. As mentioned earlier, direct labor consists of those factory labor costs that can be easily traced to products.

2. Indirect labor consists of factory labor costs that are supportive or supervisory in nature. These include the costs of supervisors, superintendents, custodians, maintenance persons, and others whose services are essential to factory operations, but who do not work directly on the product.

3. *Idle time* represents the costs of direct labor workers who are unable to perform their assignments due to material shortages, power failures, and the like. Idle time is treated as part of manufacturing overhead.

4. *Overtime premium* consists of any amount paid above an employee's base hourly rate.

a. For example, if the base rate is $6 per hour and the employee is paid time-and-a-half for overtime, then the overtime premium would be $3 per hour (not $9 per hour).

b. Overtime premium is ordinarily not charged to specific jobs, but rather is included as part of manufacturing overhead. An exception is when a customer specifically requests a rush job that results in having to work overtime. In such a case, the overtime premium may be charged directly to that job.

5. *Labor fringe benefits* include employment related costs paid by the employer, such as insurance programs, retirement plans, etc.

a. Many firms include all such costs as part of manufacturing overhead.

b. Other firms include only the labor fringe benefits relating to indirect labor as part of manufacturing overhead and treat those benefits relating to direct labor as added direct labor costs. This is the preferred method.

REVIEW AND SELF TEST
Questions and Exercises

True or False

For each of the following statements, enter a T or an F in the blank to indicate whether the statement is true or false.

____ 1. Raw materials consist of basic natural resources, such as iron ore.

____ 2. A supervisor's salary would be considered direct labor if the supervisor works directly in the factory

____ 3. Nonmanufacturing costs consist of selling costs and administrative costs.

____ 4. All selling and administrative costs are period costs.

____ 5. The terms product cost and manufacturing cost are synonymous.

____ 6. The cost of goods manufactured is an expense in a manufacturing firm.

____ 7. Part of a cost such as factory depreciation can end up on the balance sheet as an asset if goods are uncompleted or unsold at the end of a period.

____ 8. Inventoriable costs and product costs are synonymous terms in a manufacturing firm.

____ 9. Total variable cost will change in proportion to changes in the level of activity.

____ 10. A fixed cost is constant per unit of product.

____ 11. Manufacturing overhead is an indirect cost with respect to units of product.

____ 12. Sunk costs can be either variable or fixed.

____ 13. Property taxes and insurance on a factory building are examples of manufacturing overhead.

____ 14. (Appendix 2A) Overtime premium should be charged to the specific jobs worked on during overtime periods.

Multiple Choice

Choose the best answer or response by placing the identifying letter in the space provided.

____ 1. If the activity level increases, one would expect the fixed cost per unit to: a) increase; b) decrease; c) remain unchanged; d) none of these.

____ 2. Which of the following costs would not be a period cost? a) indirect materials; b) advertising; c) administrative salaries; d) shipping costs; e) sales commissions.

____ 3. The term used to describe the cost of goods transferred from work in process inventory to finished goods inventory is: a) cost of goods sold; b) raw materials; c) period cost; d) cost of goods manufactured.

____ 4. Manufacturing cost is synonymous with all of the following terms except: a) product cost; b) inventoriable cost; c) period cost; d) all of the above are synonymous terms.

____ 5. If the activity level drops by 5 percent, one would expect the variable costs: a) to increase per unit of product; b) to drop in total by 5 percent; c) to remain constant in total; d) to decrease per unit of product.

____ 6. All of the following would be product costs except: a) indirect materials; b) advertising; c) rent on factory space; d) idle time; e) all of the above would be product costs.

____ 7. Walston Manufacturing Company has provided the following data concerning its raw materials inventories last month:

Beginning raw materials inventory	$80,000
Purchases of raw materials......................	$420,000
Ending raw materials inventory.............	$50,000

The cost of the raw materials used in production for the month was: a) $500,000; b) $450,000; c) $390,000; d) $470,000.

___ 8. Juniper Company has provided the following data concerning its manufacturing costs and work in process inventories last month:

Raw materials used in production	$270,000
Direct labor	$140,000
Manufacturing overhead	$190,000
Beginning work in process inventory	$50,000
Ending work in process inventory	$80,000

The cost of goods manufactured for the month was: a) $730,000; b) $630,000; c) $600,000; d) $570,000.

___ 9. Vonder Inc. has provided the following data concerning its finished goods inventories last month:

Beginning finished goods inventory	$110,000
Cost of goods manufactured	$760,000
Ending finished goods inventory	$70,000

The cost of goods sold for the month was: a) $800,000; b) $720,000; c) $950,000; d) $280,000.

___ 10. (Appendix 2A) A machinist earns $10 per hour. During a given week he works 40 hours, of which he is idle 5 hours. For the week: a) $400 cost should be charged to direct labor, b) $50 cost should be charged to overtime premium; c) $50 cost should be charged to overhead; d) $425 cost should be charged to direct labor, and $25 cost should be charged to overhead.

Exercises

2-1. Classify each of the following costs as either period costs or product costs. Also indicate whether the cost is fixed or variable with respect to changes in the amount of output sold.

	Period Cost	*Product Cost*	*Variable Cost*	*Fixed Cost*
- Example: Rent on a sales office	X	___	___	X
- Example: Direct materials	___	X	X	___
a. Sales commissions	___	___	___	___
b. Rent on a factory building	___	___	___	___
c. Headquarters secretarial salaries	___	___	___	___
d. Assembly line workers	___	___	___	___
e. Product advertising	___	___	___	___
f. Cherries in a cannery	___	___	___	___
g. Top management salaries	___	___	___	___
h. Lubricants for machines	___	___	___	___
i. Shipping costs via express service	___	___	___	___
j. Executive training program	___	___	___	___
k. Factory supervisory salaries	___	___	___	___

2-2. Using the following data and the form that appears below, prepare a schedule of cost of goods manufactured.

Lubricants for machines MO	$ 4,500
Rent, factory building M.O	16,000
Direct labor	90,000
Indirect materials M.O	2,000
Sales commissions S+M	24,600
Factory utilities MO	5,800
Insurance, factory MO	2,000
Purchases of raw materials	120,000
Work in process, beginning	16,000
Work in process, ending	11,500
Raw materials, beginning	15,000
Raw materials, ending	5,000
Depreciation of office equipment	4,000

Schedule of Cost of Goods Manufactured

Direct materials:		
Raw materials inventory, beginning	$ 15,000	
Add: Purchases of raw materials	120,000	
Raw materials available for use	135,000	
Deduct: Raw materials inventory, ending	5,000	
Raw materials used in production		130,000
Direct labor		90,000
Manufacturing overhead:		
Lubricants for machines	$ 4500	
Rent, factory building	16000	
Indirect materials	2000	
Factory utilities	5800	
Insurance factory	2000	
Total overhead costs		30,300
Total manufacturing costs		250,300
Add: Work in process, beginning		16000
		266300
Deduct: Work in process, ending		- 11500
Cost of Goods Manufactured		$ 254 800

2-3. Harry has decided to produce and sell surfboards in his spare time. He has a garage that was constructed at a cost of $4,000 several years ago, and which will be used for production purposes. The garage will be depreciated over a 20-year life. Harry has determined that each surfboard will require $30 in wood. He will hire students to do most of the work and pay them $35 for each surfboard completed. He will rent tools at a cost of $200 per month. Harry has drawn money out of savings to provide the capital needed to get the operation going. The savings were earning interest at 6 percent annually. An ad agency will handle advertising at a cost of $100 per month. Harry will hire students to sell the surfboards and pay a commission of $20 per board.

Required:

From the foregoing information, identify all the examples you can of the following types of costs (a single item may be identified as more than one type of cost):

Variable cost: ....

....

Fixed cost: ....

....

Selling or administrative cost: ....

....

Product cost: ....

....

Manufacturing overhead cost: ....

....

Sunk cost: ....

....

Opportunity cost: ....

....

Differential cost (between the alternatives of producing or not producing surfboards): ....

....

....

2-4. (Appendix 2A) Sally Anderson worked 47 hours last week. She was idle 3 hours and spent the remaining 44 hours working directly on the manufacture of finished products. Sally is paid $8 per hour and time-and-a-half for work in excess of 40 hours per week. Allocate her week's wages between direct labor and manufacturing overhead using the form that appears below.

Direct labor		$______
Manufacturing overhead:		
Idle time	$______	
Overtime premium...............................	______	______
Total earnings		$______

2-5. Mary has just been hired by Acme Company. Mary's duties are such that the company is unsure whether to classify her salary as a period cost or as a product cost. From the point of view of the company's annual reported net income, explain why it does or does not matter how her salary cost is classified.

....

....

....

....

....

....

....

....

Answers to Questions and Exercises

True or False

1. F Raw materials consist of any materials used to make a product, and the finished goods of one company can become the raw materials of another company.

2. F Direct labor is labor that can be physically traced to products in a "hands on" sense. Supervisors do not work directly on products and therefore are not direct labor.

3. T Nonmanufacturing cost is synonymous with selling and administrative costs.

4. T Selling and administrative costs are period costs because they are charged against income in the period in which they are incurred, rather than being added to the cost of manufactured or purchased goods.

5. T These two terms are synonymous.

6. F Cost of goods manufactured is not an expense. It is the amount transferred from work in process to finished goods inventory when goods are completed. This is a subtle, but important point.

7. T Manufacturing costs are assigned to units during production. If these units are not complete or not sold at the end of a period, then the manufacturing costs incurred to date are included as part of Work in Process or Finished Goods inventories which are assets on the balance sheet.

8. T These two terms are synonymous.

9. T Since a variable cost is constant per unit, it will change in total in proportion to changes in the level of activity. If activity increases by 25 percent, then the total variable cost will also increase by 25 percent.

10. F A fixed cost is constant in total amount; on a per unit basis, it varies inversely with changes in the level of activity.

11. T Manufacturing overhead cost is an indirect cost since it must be allocated in order to be assigned to units of product.

12. T A sunk cost is a cost that has already been incurred, and can be variable or fixed. If direct materials have already been purchased, for example, then the cost of the materials is a sunk cost.

13. T Manufacturing overhead consists of all production costs except direct materials and direct labor.

14. F Overtime premium should be added to manufacturing overhead cost and spread over all jobs worked on during the period.

Multiple Choice

1. b The fixed cost per unit should drop since a constant amount is spread over more units.

2. a Indirect materials would be part of manufacturing overhead, and thus it would be a product cost.

3. d Goods that are completed and ready for sale move out of work in process and into finished goods. The cost of such goods is termed cost of goods manufactured.

4. c A period cost represents a cost charged against the period in which the cost is incurred; it has nothing to do with the manufacture of a product and therefore it is not synonymous with manufacturing cost.

5. b By definition, total variable cost changes in proportion to changes in the activity level.

6. b Advertising is a period cost, rather than a product cost.

7. b The computations are as follows:

Beginning raw materials inventory	$ 80,000
Add: Purchases of raw materials............	420,000
Raw materials available for use..............	500,000
Deduct: Ending raw materials inventory....................................	50,000
Raw materials used in production	$450,000

8. d The computations are as follows:

Raw materials used in production	$270,000
Direct labor	140,000
Manufacturing overhead	190,000
Total manufacturing costs	600,000
Add: Beginning work in process inventory	50,000
	650,000
Deduct: Ending work in process inventory	80,000
Cost of goods manufactured	$570,000

9. a The cost of goods sold is computed as follows:

Beginning finished goods inventory	$110,000
Add: Cost of goods manufactured	760,000
Goods available for sale	870,000
Deduct: Ending finished goods inventory	70,000
Cost of goods sold	$800,000

10. c All of the cost of idle time is charged to manufacturing overhead. Thus, $10 per hour x 5 hours = $50.

Exercises

2-1.

	Period Cost	*Product Cost*	*Variable Cost*	*Fixed Cost*
a. Sales commissions	X		X	
b. Rent on a factory building		X		X
c. Headquarters secretarial salaries	X			X
d. Assembly line workers		X	X	
e. Product advertising	X			X
f. Cherries in a cannery		X	X	
g. Top management salaries	X			X
h. Lubricants for machines		X	X	
i. Shipping costs via express service	X		X	
j. Executive training program	X			X
k. Factory supervisory salaries		X		X

2-2.

Direct materials:		
Raw materials inventory, beginning	$ 15,000	
Add: Purchases of raw materials	120,000	
Raw materials available for use	135,000	
Deduct: Raw materials inventory, ending	5,000	
Raw materials used in production		$130,000
Direct labor		90,000
Manufacturing overhead:		
Lubricants for machines	4,500	
Rent, factory building	16,000	
Indirect materials	2,000	
Factory utilities	5,800	
Insurance, factory	2,000	
Total overhead costs		30,300
Total manufacturing costs		250,300
Add: Work in process, beginning		16,000
		266,300
Deduct: Work in process, ending		11,500
Cost of Goods Manufactured		$254,800

Note: Sales commissions and depreciation on office equipment are not manufacturing costs.

2-3. Variable cost: wood, $30; labor, $35; commission, $20.
Fixed cost: garage depreciation, $200; tool rent, $200; advertising, $100.
Selling or administrative cost: advertising, $100; commission, $20.
Product cost: garage depreciation, $200; wood, $30; labor, $35; tool rent, $200.
Manufacturing overhead cost: garage depreciation, $200; tool rent, $200.
Sunk cost: original $4,000 cost of the garage.
Opportunity cost: interest on the savings withdrawn.
Differential cost: all costs, except possibly the garage depreciation, are differential costs since they could be avoided by not producing surfboards. The garage depreciation is not a differential cost if the real, physical, depreciation on the garage will be the same whether the garage is used for making surfboards or not.

2-4.

Direct labor (44 hours x $8)		$352
Manufacturing overhead:		
Idle time (3 hours x $8)	$24	
Overtime premium (7 hours x $4)	28	52
Total earnings		$404

2-5. From the point of view of the company's annual reported net income, it does matter how Mary's salary cost is classified. If her salary is classified as a period cost, the entire amount of salary will appear as an expense on the company's income statement each year. If her salary is classified as a product cost, then it will go into Work in Process along with other production costs. If any goods are not completed at the end of the year, part of Mary's salary will remain in the Work in Process inventory account as part of the cost of these uncompleted goods. That portion of her salary that is attached to completed goods will go into the Finished Goods inventory account. If any of these goods are not sold at year-end, part of Mary's salary will remain in the Finished Goods inventory account as part of the cost of these unsold goods. Only that portion of Mary's salary that is attached to the goods that are completed and sold during the year will appear as an expense on the income statement (as part of Cost of Goods Sold).

Chapter 3

Systems Design: Job-Order Costing

Chapter Study Suggestions

This chapter expands on the concepts introduced in Chapter 2 by showing how costs are accumulated in manufacturing organizations for purposes of computing unit costs. The costing method illustrated in the chapter is known as *job-order costing*. Using this method, costs are first assigned to jobs and then to units within jobs. Exhibit 3-5 provides a bird's eye view of the overall flow of cost and documents in a job-order cost system. Pay particular attention to the section in the chapter titled "Application of Manufacturing Overhead." *Overhead application is a key concept in the chapter.*

Exhibits 3-6, 3-7, and 3-8 show how direct materials, direct labor, and overhead costs are assigned to jobs. Study these exhibits with particular care—the concepts they contain will show up often in the homework material. Exhibits 3-10 and 3-11 summarize these concepts. Notice from Exhibit 3-11 that the Schedule of Cost of Goods Manufactured has been expanded from that given in Chapter 2. *You should memorize this schedule.* Study and then *restudy* the section titled "Underapplied and Overapplied Overhead," paying particular attention to how the under- and overapplied overhead figures are computed.

CHAPTER HIGHLIGHTS

A. There are two basic costing systems in manufacturing organizations: process costing and job-order costing.

1. *Process costing* is used in those situations where manufacturing involves making a single homogeneous product, such as bricks, for long periods at a time.

2. *Job-order costing* is used in those situations where many different products are produced each period. Examples include special order printing and furniture manufacturing. Such products are typically made in small batches. For example, fifty units of a particular type of sofa might be made in one batch. Each batch is called a "job."

3. Regardless of whether one is dealing with process costing or job-order costing, determining unit costs involves averaging of some type. The essential difference between the two costing methods is the way this averaging is carried out.

B. We will begin our discussion of job-order costing with raw materials. When materials are purchased, their costs are recorded in the Raw Materials inventory account, which is an asset.

1. Materials are withdrawn from storage using a *materials requisition form* as authorization. The form lists all the materials required to complete a specific. The journal entry to record withdrawal of raw materials from storage for use in production is:

Work in Process (direct materials)	XXX	
Manuf. Ovhd. (indirect materials)	XXX	
Raw Materials		XXX

Materials that are traced directly to jobs are classified as *direct materials* and are debited to Work in Process. Any materials that are not directly traced to jobs are classified as *indirect materials* and are debited to a special account called *Manufacturing Overhead.*

2. When materials are placed into production, they are recorded on a *job cost sheet,* which summarizes all production costs assigned to a particular job. Exhibit 3-2 in the text illustrates a job cost sheet. Exhibit 3-6 provides a T-account view of materials costs.

C. Labor costs are accumulated on *time tickets* or *time sheets* that are filled out by employees. These documents list the amount of time each employee works on specific jobs and tasks.

1. Labor time spent working directly on specific jobs is termed *direct labor.* Labor time spent working on supportive tasks (maintenance, janitorial) is termed *indirect labor.* The entry to record labor costs is:

Work in Process (direct labor)	XXX	
Manuf. Ovhd. (indirect labor)	XXX	
Salaries and Wages Payable		XXX

2. Direct labor costs are recorded on individual job cost sheets at the same time they are recorded in the formal accounts. This is illustrated in Exhibits 3-4 and 3-7 in the text.

D. As explained in Chapter 2, manufacturing overhead is an *indirect* cost and therefore must be allocated in order to be assigned to units of product. This allocation is carried out with a *predetermined overhead rate.*

1. The predetermined overhead rate is computed *before* a year begins and is based entirely on estimated data. Ordinarily, the rate is computed for an entire year to eliminate seasonal fluctuations. The formula is:

$$\text{Predetermined Overhead Rate} = \frac{\text{Estimated manufacturing overhead cost}}{\text{Estimated base (e.g., direct labor–hours)}}$$

An *allocation base* is some measure of activity, such as direct labor-hours, direct labor cost, or machine-hours. Ideally, a base should be selected that causes overhead. Such a base is called a *cost driver.* It is most common, however, to use direct labor hours or cost as an allocation base even though it is no longer clear that direct labor has much to do with causing overhead costs.

2. To assign overhead costs to a job, the predetermined overhead rate is multiplied by the number of direct labor hours worked on the job. This figure is entered on the job cost sheet and is recorded with the following journal entry:

Work in Process	XXX	
Manufacturing Overhead		XXX

Turn to Exhibit 3-8 in the text to see how overhead costs flow through the accounts and onto the job cost sheets.

3. Assigning overhead to jobs is known as the application or absorption of overhead.

4. Notice from Exhibit 3-8 that applying overhead to jobs and the incurrence of actual overhead costs represent two separate and distinct processes. *This is a key concept that you must understand in order to figure out the material in this chapter.*

a. When incurred, actual overhead costs are *not* charged to Work in Process. Instead, they are charged to the Manufacturing Overhead account. Exhibit 3-8 in the text illustrates this process with entries (2) through (6). Note that *actual overhead costs all appear as debits to Manufacturing Overhead.*

b. Entry (7) in Exhibit 3-8 illustrates applying overhead to jobs. Note that the *applied overhead is debited to Work in Process and credited to Manufacturing Overhead.*

E. After direct materials, direct labor, and overhead costs have been added to jobs and the jobs are completed, they are transferred from Work in Process to Finished Goods to await sale.

1. The entry to record completed jobs is:

Finished Goods	XXX	
Work in Process		XXX

2. When completed jobs are sold, the entry is:

Cost of Goods Sold	XXX	
Finished Goods		XXX

3. Exhibits 3-10, 3-11 and 3-12 are key exhibits that summarize much of the material in the chapter. Study these exhibits with care. Note particular how the manufacturing overhead costs are handled. The net effect of all the calculations is to include in the Cost of Goods Sold only the "Manufacturing Overhead Applied to Work in Process."

F. Generally there will be a difference between the amount of overhead cost *applied* to Work in Process and the amount of *actual* overhead cost for a period. This difference will be reflected in a debit or credit balance in the Manufacturing Overhead account. Note that in Exhibit 3-10, there is a $5,000 debit balance in the Manufacturing Overhead account. This occurred because actual manufacturing overhead costs totaled $95,000, but only $90,000 of overhead costs were applied to Work in Process.

1. If less overhead cost is applied to Work in Process than has actually been incurred, then overhead has been *underapplied* and there is a debit balance in the Manufacturing Overhead account.

2. If more overhead cost is applied to Work in Process than has actually been incurred, then overhead has been *overapplied* and there is a credit balance in the Manufacturing Overhead account.

3. The formula for computing under- or overapplied overhead is:

Actual overhead costs	$XXX
Less overhead costs applied to Work in Process:	
Actual amount of allocation base x predetermined overhead rate	XXX
Under- or overapplied overhead	$XXX

The "actual amount of the allocation base" is the actual amount of whatever the allocation base (e.g., direct labor hours, direct labor cost, or machine hours) incurred during the period.

4. At the end of a period, under- or overapplied overhead is usually closed out to Cost of Goods Sold. Less commonly, under- or overapplied overhead is allocated between Work in Process, Finished Goods, and Cost of Goods Sold.

a. Closing any balance out to Cost of Goods Sold is simpler, since only one account is involved.

If overhead has been underapplied, the entry would be:

Cost of Goods Sold	XXX	
Manufacturing Overhead		XXX

This entry increases the Cost of Goods Sold figure that will appear on the income statement. This makes sense since underapplied overhead means that not enough overhead cost was applied to jobs during the period and therefore costs were understated in the accounts. The journal entry adjusts costs so that they are no longer understated.

If overhead has been overapplied, the journal entry would be:

Manufacturing Overhead	XXX	
Cost of Goods Sold		XXX

This entry decreases the Cost of Goods Sold figure that will appear on the income statement. This makes sense since overapplied overhead means that too much overhead cost was applied to jobs during the period and therefore costs were overstated in the accounts. The journal entry adjusts costs so that they are no longer overstated.

b. Allocating any under- or overapplied overhead among inventory accounts and Cost of Goods Sold is more complex, but it is considered to be more accurate. The allocation is based on the ending balances in the Work in Process, Finished Goods, and Cost of Goods Sold accounts.

Assuming that overhead is underapplied, the entry would be:

Work in Process	XXX	
Finished Goods	XXX	
Cost of Goods Sold	XXX	
Manufacturing Overhead		XXX

G. In large companies, *multiple overhead rates* are often used rather than a single, "plant wide" rate. As a job moves through the production process, overhead cost is applied in each separate department using its own predetermined overhead rate.

REVIEW AND SELF TEST
Questions and Exercises

True or False

For each of the following statements, enter a T or an F in the blank to indicate whether the statement is true or false.

___ 1. A company producing furniture would probably use a job-order cost system.

___ 2. Process costing systems are used in those situations where output is basically homogeneous.

___ 3. Both job-order and process costing systems use averages in computing unit costs.

___ 4. Most factory overhead costs are direct costs and therefore can be easily identified with specific jobs.

___ 5. The predetermined overhead rate is computed using estimates of cost and activity.

___ 6. The predetermined overhead rate is generally computed on a monthly basis rather than on an annual basis to increase the accuracy of unit costs.

___ 7. The cost of indirect materials used in production is added to the Manufacturing Overhead account rather than added directly to Work in Process.

___ 8. The job cost sheet is used to accumulate the costs chargeable to a particular job.

___ 9. Actual manufacturing overhead costs are charged directly to the Work in Process account as the costs are incurred.

___ 10. Selling and administrative expenses should be added to the Manufacturing Overhead account.

___ 11. If more overhead is applied to Work in Process than is actually incurred, then overhead will be overapplied.

___ 12. All the raw materials purchased during a period are included in the cost of goods manufactured figure.

___ 13. A debit balance in the Manufacturing Overhead account at the end of a period would mean that overhead was underapplied for the period.

___ 14. Any balance in the Work in Process account at the end of a period should be closed to Cost of Goods Sold.

___ 15. Allocating any under- or overapplied overhead cost between Work in Process, Finished Goods, and Cost of Goods Sold is a more accurate costing approach than closing the entire under- or overapplied amount to Cost of Goods Sold.

___ 16. Under- or overapplied overhead is computed by finding the difference between actual overhead costs and the amount of overhead cost applied to Work in Process.

Multiple Choice

Choose the best answer or response by placing the identifying letter in the space provided.

___ 1. Last year, a company reported estimated overhead, $100,000; actual overhead, $90,000; and applied overhead, $92,000. The company's overhead cost for the year would be: a) underapplied, $10,000; b) underapplied, $8,000; c) overapplied, $2,000; d) overapplied, $10,000.

___ 2. In a job-order cost system, the basic document for accumulating costs by individual job is: a) the materials requisition form; b) the job cost sheet; c) the Work in Process control account; d) the labor time ticket.

___ 3. The most common treatment of under- or overapplied overhead is to close it out to: a) Work in Process; b) Retained Earnings; c) Cost of Goods Sold; d) Finished Goods.

___ 4. Jurden Company bases its predetermined overhead rates on machine hours. At the beginning of the year, the company estimated its manufacturing overhead for the year would be $60,000 and there would be a total of 40,000 machine hours. Actual manufacturing overhead for year amounted to $65,100 and the actual machine hours totalled 42,000. Manufacturing overhead for the year would be: a) underapplied by $2,100; b) overapplied by $3,000; c) underapplied by $3,000; d) overapplied by $5,100.

___ 5. On January 1, Hessler Company's Work in Process account had a balance of $18,000. During the year, raw materials costing $40,000 were purchased, and raw materials costing $35,000 were placed into production. Direct labor cost for the year was $60,000. The predetermined overhead rate for the year was set at 150 percent of direct labor cost. Actual overhead costs for the year totaled $92,000. Jobs costing $190,000 to manufacture were completed during the year. On December 31, the balance in the Work in Process inventory account would be: a) $13,000; b) $18,000; c) $15,000; d) $8,000.

___ 6. On the Schedule of Cost of Goods Manufactured, the final Cost of Goods Manufactured figure: a) represents the amount of cost charged to Work in Process during the period; b) represents the amount transferred from Work in Process to Finished Goods during the period; c) represents the amount of cost placed into production during the period; d) none of these.

___ 7. If overhead is overapplied for a period, it means that: a) the predetermined overhead rate used to apply overhead cost to Work in Process was too low; b) the company incurred more overhead cost than it charged to Work in Process; c) too much cost has been assigned to units of product; d) none of these.

___ 8. Malt Company's Manufacturing Overhead account showed a $10,000 underapplied overhead balance on December 31. Other accounts showed the following balances on that date:

Raw Materials	$ 50,000
Work in Process	40,000
Finished Goods	60,000
Cost of Goods Sold	100,000

If the company allocates the underapplied overhead among Cost of Goods Sold and appropriate inventory accounts, the amount allocated to Work in Process would be: a) $2,000; b) $4,000; c) $1,600; d) $1,800.

Exercises

3-1. Bartle Company uses a job-order cost system. Estimated cost and activity data for the current year were: manufacturing overhead, $150,000; direct labor hours, 100,000. At the end of the year, cost records revealed that actual overhead costs of $160,000 had been incurred and that 105,000 direct labor hours had been worked.

a. The predetermined overhead rate for the year was.. $____________

b. Manufacturing overhead cost applied to work in process during the year was .... $____________

c. The amount of underapplied or overapplied overhead cost for the year was .... $____________

3-2. The following selected account balances are taken from the books of Pardoe Company as of January 1 of the most recent year:

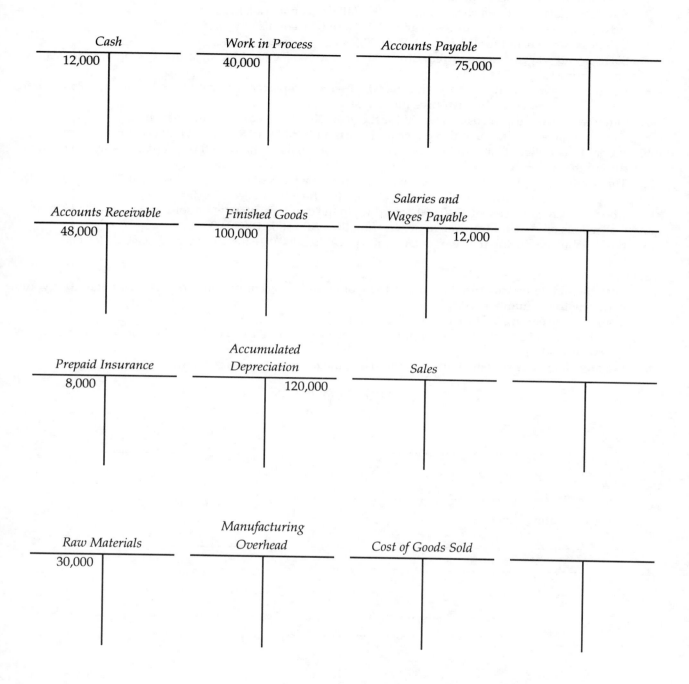

Cash		*Work in Process*		*Accounts Payable*			
12,000		40,000			75,000		

Accounts Receivable		*Finished Goods*		*Salaries and Wages Payable*			
48,000		100,000			12,000		

Prepaid Insurance		*Accumulated Depreciation*		*Sales*			
8,000			120,000				

Raw Materials		*Manufacturing Overhead*		*Cost of Goods Sold*			
30,000							

The following data relate to the activities of Pardoe Company during the year:

1. Raw materials purchased on account, $150,000.
2. Raw materials issued to production, $145,000 (all direct materials).
3. Advertising cost incurred for the year, $50,000 (credit accounts payable).
4. Utilities cost incurred for the factory, $35,000 (credit accounts payable).
5. Salaries and wages costs incurred: direct labor, $250,000 (30,000 hours); indirect labor, $75,000; selling and administrative, $140,000.
6. Depreciation recorded for the year, $20,000, of which 75 percent related to the factory and 25 percent related to selling and administrative functions.
7. Other factory overhead costs incurred for the year, $30,000 (credit accounts payable).
8. Other selling and administrative expenses incurred for the year, $25,000 (credit accounts payable).
9. Prepaid insurance relates to factory operations. One-half of the $8,000 of prepaid insurance expired during the current year.
10. The company applies overhead cost to production on a basis of direct labor hours, at $5.50 per hour.
11. Goods completed (cost of goods manufactured) for the year totaled $550,000.
12. Goods which had a cost of $540,000 according to the costing system were sold on account for $800,000.
13. Collections on account from customers during the year totaled $790,000.
14. Cash disbursed during the year: on accounts payable, $300,000; for salaries and wages, $460,000.

Required:

a. Post the above entries directly to Pardoe Company's T-accounts on the previous page. Key your entries with the numbers 1-14.

b. Compute the ending balance in each T-account.

c. Is overhead underapplied or overapplied for the year? Close the balance to Cost of Goods Sold. (Key the entry as #15.)

d. Prepare an income statement for the year using the form that appears below.

PARDOE COMPANY
Income Statement

Sales		$_______
Less cost of goods sold		_______
Gross margin		_______
Less operating expenses:		
_______________	$_______	
_______________	_______	
_______________	_______	
_______________	_______	_______
Net Income		$_______

3-3. The following data were taken from the Precision Milling Machine, Inc., cost records for the current year. Compute the amount of raw materials used in production during the year:

Direct labor cost	$240,000
Raw materials inventory, 12/31	15,000
Indirect labor cost	90,000
Raw materials inventory, 1/1	10,000
Work in process inventory, 12/31	75,000
Work in process inventory, 1/1	60,000
Purchases of raw materials	145,000

3-4. **Critical thought writing exercise:** Quality Foods, Inc., is a major producer of canned vegetables, fruits, and other goods. This year the company planned a normal year of producing canned goods and set its predetermined overhead rate the same as in other years. However, during the year a major freeze in key growing areas wiped out much of the expected fruit crop and the company was able to do little canning of fruit. A large amount of the manufacturing overhead cost associated with producing canned goods consists of depreciation and other fixed costs. Would you expect Quality Foods, Inc., to have underapplied or overapplied manufacturing overhead cost this year? Explain.

Answers to Questions and Exercises

True or False

1. T Job-order costing is used in those situations where units of product are not homogeneous.

2. T Process costing is generally used when output is homogeneous.

3. T Averaging is involved in both costing systems, since common costs such as depreciation, rent, and salaries must be allocated to products.

4. F Only direct materials and direct labor are direct costs; manufacturing overhead, which may be the largest category of cost, is indirect.

5. T Estimates are used since a rate must be developed before the period begins.

6. F The predetermined overhead rate is computed on an annual basis in order to smooth out month-by-month variations in cost and activity.

7. T Indirect costs are charged to the Manufacturing Overhead account.

8. T A separate job cost sheet is prepared for each job entered into production, and used to accumulate costs as they are charged to the job.

9. F Actual manufacturing overhead costs are charged to the Manufacturing Overhead account—not to Work in Process.

10. F Selling and administrative expenses are period costs, not product costs; thus, they are deducted as expenses on the income statement in the period they are incurred.

11. T If more overhead is applied to Work in Process than is actually incurred, then a credit balance will exist in the Manufacturing Overhead account. A credit balance represents overapplied overhead.

12. F Only the raw materials used in production are included in the cost of goods manufactured figure. Some materials purchased during a period may remain in the Raw Materials inventory account.

13. T A debit balance in Manufacturing Overhead would mean that more overhead cost was incurred than was applied to Work in Process. Thus, manufacturing overhead would be underapplied.

14. F Any balance in the Manufacturing Overhead account (not Work in Process) should be closed to Cost of Goods Sold. Work in Process is an inventory account that appears on the balance sheet.

15. T Allocation is more accurate, since it shows where the overhead cost would have gone if overhead rates had been completely accurate.

16. T By definition, this is how under- or overapplied overhead cost is computed.

Multiple Choice

1. c Under- or overapplied overhead represents the difference between actual overhead cost and applied overhead cost (see Exhibit 3-11). Thus, the computation in this case would be:

Actual overhead cost	$90,000
Applied overhead cost	92,000
Overapplied overhead cost	$(2,000)

2. b The job cost sheet is used to accumulate direct materials, direct labor, and overhead costs.

3. c Since under- or overapplied overhead represents a cost adjustment item, it must eventually flow through Cost of Goods Sold. The simplest procedure is to close any under- or overapplied balance directly to the Cost of Goods Sold account at the end of a period.

4. a The predetermined overhead rate would be: $60,000 ÷ 40,000 hours = $1. 50/ hr.

Actual overhead cost	$65,100
Applied overhead cost ($1.50 X 42,000 hours)	63,000
Underapplied overhead cost	$ 2,100

5. a The solution would be:

	Work in Process		
Balance	18,000	190,000	Goods completed
Direct materials	35,000		
Direct labor	60,000		
Overhead applied*	90,000		
Balance	13,000		

*$60,000 x 150% = $90,000

6. b The cost of goods manufactured represents goods completed during a period; thus, it is the amount transferred from Work in Process to Finished Goods.

7. c If overhead is overapplied, then more overhead cost has been added to products than has been incurred. Therefore, too much overhead cost will have been assigned to units of product.

8. a The computations would be:

Work in Process	$ 40,000	20%
Finished Goods	60,000	30
Cost of Goods Sold	100,000	50
Total cost	$200,000	100%

20% x $10,000 = $2,000.

Exercises

3-1. a. $\frac{\$150{,}000}{100{,}000 \text{ DLHS}} = \$1.50 / \text{DLH}$

b. 105,000 DLHS X $1.50 = $157,500 applied

c.

Actual overhead cost	$160,000
Applied overhead cost	157,500
Underapplied overhead cost	$ 2,500

3-2. The answers to parts (a) and (b) are on the following page.

c. Overhead is overapplied by $6,000.

d.

PARDOE COMPANY
Income Statement

Sales		$800,000
Less cost of goods sold		534,000
Gross margin		266,000
Less operating expenses:		
Advertising expense	$ 50,000	
Salaries expense	140,000	
Depreciation expense	5,000	
Other expenses	25,000	220,000
Net Income		$ 46,000

Chapter 3

3-2. a. & b.

Cash

Debit	Credit
Bal. 12,000	760,000 (14)
(13) 790,000	
42,000	

Work in Process

Debit	Credit
Bal. 40,000	550,000 (11)
(2) 145,000	
(5) 250,000	
(10) 165,000	
50,000	

Accounts Payable

Debit	Credit
(14) 300,000	75,000 Bal.
	150,000 (1)
	50,000 (3)
	35,000 (4)
	30,000 (7)
	25,000 (8)
	65,000

Advertising Expense

Debit	Credit
(3) 50,000	

Accounts Receivable

Debit	Credit
Bal. 48,000	790,000 (13)
(12a) 800,000	
58,000	

Finished Goods

Debit	Credit
Bal. 100,000	540,000 (12b)
(11) 550,000	
110,000	

Salaries and Wages Payable

Debit	Credit
(14) 460,000	12,000 Bal.
	465,000 (5)
	17,000

Salaries Expense

Debit	Credit
(5) 140,000	

Prepaid Insurance

Debit	Credit
Bal. 8,000	4,000 (9)
4,000	

Accumulated Depreciation

Debit	Credit
	120,000 Bal.
	20,000 (6)
	140,000

Sales

Debit	Credit
	800,000 (12a)

Depreciation Expense

Debit	Credit
(6) 5,000	

Raw Materials

Debit	Credit
Bal. 30,000	145,000 (2)
(1) 150,000	
35,000	

Manufacturing Overhead

Debit	Credit
(4) 35,000	165,000 (10)
(5) 75,000	
(6) 15,000	
(7) 30,000	
(9) 4,000	
(15) 6,000	6,000

Cost of Goods Sold

Debit	Credit
(12b) 540,000	6,000 (15)

Other Selling and Administrative Expenses

Debit	Credit
(8) 25,000	

3-3.

Raw materials inventory, 1/1	$ 10,000
Add purchases of raw materials	145,000
Total	155,000
Deduct raw materials inventory, 12/31	15,000
Raw Materials Used in Production	$140,000

3-4. Quality Foods, Inc. would probably have underapplied manufacturing overhead cost for the year. Since a large amount of the manufacturing overhead cost associated with producing canned goods is fixed, the company's *actual* manufacturing overhead costs would be about as planned. However, the company's *applied* manufacturing overhead costs would be less than planned since less productive activity would take place in the plant due to the loss of the fruit crop. Thus, with a large amount of *actual* overhead cost and less than planned *applied* overhead cost, the company would end the year with an underapplied balance in its Manufacturing Overhead account.

Chapter 4

Systems Design: Process Costing

Chapter Study Suggestions

The chapter is divided into six main parts. The first part is a comparison of job-order and process costing. Exhibit 4-1, which outlines the differences between the two costing methods, is the key item in this part. The second part gives a perspective of cost flows in a process costing system. Study Exhibit 4-4 carefully, as well as the journal entries that follow. The third part deals with a concept known as equivalent units of production. This part will require special effort. Pay particular attention to the computations in Exhibits 4-6 and 4-7.

The fourth part illustrates the preparation of a production report under the weighted-average method. The production report is the single most important concept in the chapter and is the most complex. Thus, you will need to focus a large portion of your time on learning how it is constructed. Exhibit 4-10 provides a detailed example. The fifth part of the chapter provides a discussion of a hybrid system called operation costing, which is widely used in actual practice.

Appendix 4A illustrates the preparation of a production report under the FIFO method. If your instructor assigns this appendix, pay particular attention to Exhibit 4A-3 which shows the format of a FIFO production report, and Exhibit 4A-4 which compares the weighted-average and FIFO methods.

CHAPTER HIGHLIGHTS

A. Process costing is used in industries that produce homogeneous products such as bricks, flour, and cement. It is also used in assembly-type operations, as well as in utilities producing gas, water, and electricity.

B. Process costing is similar to job-order costing in three ways:

1. The same basic purposes exist in both systems, which are to assign material, labor, and overhead costs to products and to provide a mechanism for computing unit costs.

2. Both systems maintain and use the same basic manufacturing accounts: Manufacturing Overhead, Raw Materials, Work in Process, and Finished Goods.

3. Costs flow through these accounts in basically the same way in both systems.

C. Process costing differs from job-order costing in four ways:

1. A single product is produced on a continuous basis, and each unit is identical.

2. Costs are accumulated by department, rather than by job.

3. The department production report (rather than the job cost sheet) is the key document showing the accumulation and disposition of cost.

4. Unit costs are computed by department (rather than by job). This computation is made on the department production report.

D. A *processing department* is any work center where work is performed on a product and where materials, labor, or overhead costs are added.

1. Processing departments have two common features. First, the activity carried out in the department is performed uniformly on all units passing through it. And second, the output of the department is homogeneous.

2. Processing departments can be organized in either a sequential or a parallel pattern. A sequential pattern is where all units go through all departments in the same order. A parallel pattern is where not all units go through all departments. Some units go through one department while other units go through other departments, in a parallel fashion.

E. Cost accumulation is usually simpler in a process costing system than in a job-order costing system. The reason is that costs only need to be identified with a few processing departments rather than with hundreds (or even thousands) of individual jobs.

F. Exhibit 4-4 provides a T-account model of cost flows in a process costing system. A separate work in process account is maintained for each processing department. Materials, labor, and overhead costs are entered directly into each processing department's work in process account.

G. Once costs have been totaled for a department, the department's output must be determined so that unit costs can be computed. Units that have only been partially completed pose a problem. A unit that is only 10% complete with respect to the work done in the department should not count as much as a unit that has been completed and transferred on to the next department.

1. *Equivalent units* consist of completed units and the equivalent, in terms of complete units, of partially completed units. In other words, equivalent units are the number of whole, complete units one could obtain from the materials and effort contained in completed and partially completed units.

2. The *equivalent units of production* refers to the total equivalent units used to compute unit costs in a process costing system. Under the weighted-average method discussed in the text, the equivalent units of production are determined as follows:

Units completed and transferred out	XXX
+ Equivalent units in ending inventory	XXX
= Equivalent units of production	XXX

H. Separate unit costs are computed within each processing department for: 1) costs of prior departments associated with units transferred into the department; 2) materials costs; 3) direct labor costs; and 4) manufacturing overhead costs. However, direct labor costs and manufacturing overhead costs are often combined into one cost category called *conversion costs.*

1. Since separate unit costs are computed for each cost category, an equivalent units of production figure must be computed for each category.

2. Units transferred out of the department to the next department—or, in the case of the last department, to finished goods—are considered to be 100% complete with respect to the work done by the transferring department.

3. The first processing department will not have a cost category for the costs of units transferred in, but subsequent departments will have such a cost category. Units in process in a department are considered to be 100% complete with respect to the costs of the prior department.

I. The purpose of the *production report* is to summarize all the activity that takes place in a department's work in process account for a period. This activity includes the units which flow through the work in process account as well as the costs which flow through it. A production report has three parts:

1. A quantity schedule, which shows the flow of units through a department, and a computation of equivalent units.

2. A statement showing computation of total and unit costs.

3. A reconciliation of all cost flows into and out of a department during a period.

J. The purpose of a *quantity schedule* is to show the flow of units through a department. The schedule shows the number of units to be accounted for in a department and it shows how those units have been accounted for.

1. The format of the schedule under the weighted-average method is:

Units to be accounted for:	
Work in process, beginning	XXX
Started into production	XXX
Total units to account for	XXX
Units accounted for as follows:	
Transferred out*	XXX
Work in process, ending	XXX
Total units accounted for	XXX

*Transferred to the next department or to finished goods.

2. The quantity schedule deals with whole units, not with equivalent units, although the stage of completion is shown parenthetically.

3. The equivalent units for the units transferred out and for the ending work in process inventory are listed next to the quantity schedule.

K. The second step in preparing a production report is to compute *unit costs* for each cost category. This involves summing the costs from the beginning inventory with any costs added during the period to arrive at total cost. This figure is then divided by the equivalent units for the cost category to determine the unit cost per equivalent unit.

L. The final step in a production report is to prepare a *reconciliation* of all costs for the period.

1. Costs are accounted for as being either (a) transferred out during the period or (b) assigned to the ending work in process inventory.

2. Costs are determined as follows:

a. Units transferred out. These units are presumed to be 100% complete (If they were not complete with respect to all the work done in the department, they would not be transferred out of the department.) The cost of units transferred out is computed by multiplying the number of units transferred out by the sum of the unit costs for the various cost categories.

b. Units in ending work in process inventory. The costs of these units are computed separately for each cost category and then summed together. Within each cost category, the number of equivalent units is multiplied by the unit cost for that cost category.

M. Careful study of Exhibit 4-10 will reveal how the weighted-average method works. It is important to note that this method combines costs from the beginning inventory with costs from the current period. It is called the weighted-average method because it averages together costs from the prior period with costs of the current period.

N. *Operation costing* is a hybrid system containing elements of both job-order and process costing. It is used when products have some common characteristics and some individual characteristics.

1. Products are typically handled in batches, with each batch charged with the specific materials

used in its production. In this sense, operation costing is similar to job-order costing.

2. Labor and overhead costs are accumulated by department and these costs are assigned to batches on an average per unit basis as in process costing.

Appendix 4A: FIFO Method

A. The *FIFO method* is a bit more complex than the weighted-average method, but is often considered more accurate. The FIFO method keeps units and costs from the prior period separate from the units and costs of the current period.

B. The production report under the FIFO method is similar to the production report under the weighted-average method. There are, however, important differences in the reports that are easy to overlook.

C. The format of the quantity schedule under the FIFO method follows:

Units to be accounted for:	
Work in process, beginning	XXX
Started into production	XXX
Total units to account for	XXX
Units accounted for as follows:	
Transferred out:	
Units from beginning inventory	XXX
Units started and completed	XXX
Work in process, ending	XXX
Total units accounted for	XXX

D. Under the FIFO method, the equivalent units of production are determined as follows:

Equivalent units to complete the beginning inventory	XXX
+ Units started and completed this year	XXX
+ Equivalent units in ending inventory	XXX
= Equivalent units of production	XXX

The difference between the equivalent units of production under the FIFO method and under the weighted-average method is that the weighted-average method includes the equivalent units in beginning inventory whereas the FIFO method does not.

E. After preparing the quantity schedule and computing the equivalent units, unit costs must be computed. Unit costs under the FIFO method are computed using *only* costs added during the period.

F. The final step in the production report is to prepare a reconciliation of all costs for the period.

1. Costs are accounted for as being either (a) transferred out during the period or (b) assigned to the ending work in process inventory.

2. In computing the cost of units transferred out under the FIFO method, the units in beginning work in process inventory are kept separate from the units started and completed during the current period. Exhibit 4A-3 provides an example of a completed FIFO production report. Study this exhibit with great care.

G In comparing the weighted-average and FIFO methods, four points should be noted:

1. In most situations, the two methods will produce unit costs that are nearly the same.

2. From a standpoint of cost control, the FIFO method is superior to the weighted-average method since it separates the costs of the prior period from the costs of the current period.

3. Although the FIFO method is more complex to apply than is the weighted-average method, this complexity is no longer a significant factor because of the power of computers.

4. Any difference in costs reported using the FIFO and weighted-average methods must be due to the existence of beginning work in process inventories. As work in process inventories are reduced in a JIT program, the differences between the two methods will diminish.

REVIEW AND SELF TEST
Questions and Exercises

True or False

For each of the following statements, enter a T or an F in the blank to indicate whether the statement is true or false.

___ 1. A utility such as a water company would typically use a process costing system.

___ 2. Under process costing it is important to identify the materials, labor, and overhead costs associated with a particular customer's order just as under job-order costing.

___ 3. In a process costing system, the production report replaces the job cost sheet.

___ 4. Costing is more difficult in a process costing system than it is in a job-order costing system.

___ 5. In a process costing system, a work in process account is maintained for each department.

___ 6. Operation costing employs aspects of both job-order and process costing systems.

___ 7. Since costs are accumulated by department, there is no need for a finished goods inventory account in a process costing system.

___ 8. In process costing, costs incurred in a department are not transferred to the next department.

___ 9. If beginning work in process inventory contains 500 units that are 60 percent complete, then the inventory contains 300 equivalent units.

___ 10. (Appendix 4A) Under the FIFO method of computing equivalent units of production, costs in the beginning work in process inventory are kept separate from costs of the current period.

___ 11. (Appendix 4A) Under the FIFO method, units in beginning work in process inventory are treated as if they were completed before any new units are completed.

___ 12. (Appendix 4A) Under the FIFO method, units transferred out are treated in separate blocks—one block consisting of the units in the beginning inventory, and the other block consisting of the units started and completed during the period.

___ 13. (Appendix 4A) The weighted-average and FIFO methods will typically produce widely different unit costs—particularly when there are no beginning work in process inventories.

___ 14. (Appendix 4A) From a standpoint of cost control, the weighted-average method is superior to the FIFO method.

___ 15. (Appendix 4A) Reducing the size of work in process inventories will tend to reduce the difference between FIFO and weighted-average method unit costs.

Multiple Choice

Choose the best answer or response by placing the identifying letter in the space provided.

___ 1. Deerdon Company started 4,800 units into process during the month. Five hundred units were in the beginning inventory and 300 units were in the ending inventory. How many units were completed and transferred out during the month? a) 5,000; b) 4,600; c) 5,300; d) 5,100.

___ 2. Last year Eager Company started 8,000 units into production. The company had 2,000 units in process on January 1 of that year, which were 60 percent complete with respect to conversion, and 3,000 units in process on December 31 which were 50 percent complete. 7,000 units were completed and transferred to the next department during the year. Using the weighted-average method, the equivalent units of production for conversion for the year would be: a) 8,200: b) 8,500; c) 9,200; d) 9,500.

___ 3. (Appendix 4A) Refer to the data in question 2 above. Using the FIFO method, the equivalent units of production for conversion costs for the year would be: a) 8,300; b) 7,700; c) 7,300; d) 6,700.

___ 4. A company uses the weighted-average method in its process costing. At the beginning of the month, there were 200 units in process in the stamping department which were 70 percent complete with respect to materials. During the month 2,000 units were transferred to the next department.

At the end of the month, 100 units were still in process and they were 60 percent complete with respect to materials. The materials cost in the beginning work in process inventory was $2,721 and $39,200 of materials costs were added during the month. What is the cost per equivalent unit for materials costs? a) $19.06; b) $20.35; c) $20.42; d) $19.60.

___ 5. Dolly Company uses the weighted-average method. It had $8,000 of conversion cost in its beginning work in process inventory and added $64,000 of conversion cost during the year. The company completed 37,000 units during the year and had 10,000 units in the ending work in process inventory that were 30 percent complete as to conversion cost. The amount of cost assigned to these units would be: a) $12,600; b) $4,800; c) $11,200; d) $5,400.

___ 6. The heat treatment department at Northern Pipe is the third department in a sequential process. The work in process account for the department would consist of: a) costs transferred in from the prior department; b) materials costs added in the heat treatment department; c) conversion costs added in the heat treatment department; d) all of the above.

___ 7. Dominion Products uses the weighted-average method in its process costing system. Last month in the milling department the cost per equivalent unit for conversion cost was $105. A total of 540 equivalent units of conversion cost were used to compute this unit cost. The total conversion cost added during the month was $54,500. What was the amount of conversion cost in the beginning work in process inventory? a) $0; b) $2,200; c) $4,200; d) $3,000.

___ 8. (Appendix 4A) Mercer Corp. uses the FIFO method in its process costing system. The company had $6,000 of materials cost in its beginning work in process inventory and the company added $75,000 in materials cost during the period. The equivalent units of production for materials was 20,000. The unit cost per equivalent unit for materials would be: a) $3.75; b) $4.05; c) $0.30; d) $3.30.

___ 9. (Appendix 4A) Costs in the beginning work in process inventory are added to the costs of the current period when making unit cost calculations by: a) the FIFO cost method; b) the weighted-average cost method; c) the quantity schedule method; d) none of these.

Exercises

4-1. Diebold Company has a process costing system. Data relating to activities in the Mixing Department for March follow:

		Percent Completed	
	Units	*Materials*	*Conversion*
Work in process, March 1	5,000	100	60
Units started into production	80,000		
Work in process, March 31	2,000	100	50

Using the weighted-average method, fill in the following quantity schedule and a computation of equivalent units for the month:

	Quantity Schedule		
Units to be accounted for:			
Work in process, beginning (all materials; ______% conversion cost added last month)	______		
Started into production	______		
Total units to account for	______		
		Equivalent Units	
		Materials	*Conversion*
Units accounted for as follows:			
Transferred out during the month	______	______	______
Work in process, ending (all materials; ______% conversion cost added this month)	______	______	______
Total units accounted for	______	______	______

4-2. Minden Company has a process costing system and uses the weighted-average method. Complete the cost reconciliation section of the production report below for the company's Mixing Department.

Production Report, Mixing Department

Quantity schedule and equivalent units

	Quantity Schedule			
Units to be accounted for:				
Work in process, beginning (all materials, 20% labor and overhead added last month)	5,000			
Started into production	75,000			
Total units	80,000			
		Equivalent Units		
Units accounted for as follows:		*Materials*	*Labor*	*Overhead*
Transferred out	72,000	72,000	72,000	72,000
Work in process, ending (all materials, 75% labor and overhead added this month)	8,000	8,000	6,000	6,000
Total units	80,000	80,000	78,000	78,000

Total and unit costs

	Total Cost	*Materials*	*Labor*	*Overhead*	*Whole Unit*
Cost to be accounted for:					
Work in process, beginning	$ 9,500	$ 4,500	$ 3,000	$ 2,000	
Cost added by the department	460,500	75,500	231,000	154,000	
Total cost (a)	$470,000	$ 80,000	$234,000	$156,000	
Equivalent units (b)		80,000	78,000	78,000	
Unit cost (a)÷(b)		$1.00	+ $3.00	+ $2.00	= $6.00

Cost reconciliation

		Equivalent Units		
		Materials	*Labor*	*Overhead*
Cost accounted for as follows:				
Transferred out	$______	______	______	______
Work in process, ending:				
Materials	______	______		
Labor	______		______	
Overhead	______			______
Total work in process, ending	______			
Total cost	$ 470,000			

4-3. (Appendix 4A) Sinclair Company uses the FIFO method in its process costing system. Complete the cost reconciliation section of the production report for the company's Cooking Department that appears below.

Production Report, Cooking Department

Quantity schedule and equivalent units	*Quantity Schedule*			
Units to be accounted for:				
Work in process, begin. (all materials; 25% labor and overhead added last month)	8,000			
Started into production	62,000			
Total units	70,000			
		Equivalent Units		
		Materials	*Labor*	*Overhead*
Units accounted for as follows:				
Transferred out:				
Units from the beginning inventory	8,000	—	6,000	6,000
Units started and completed this month	57,000	57,000	57,000	57,000
Work in process, ending (all materials; 80% labor and overhead added this month)	5,000	5,000	4,000	4,000
Total units	70,000	62,000	67,000	67,000

Total and unit costs	*Total Cost*	*Materials*		*Labor*		*Overhead*		*Whole Unit*
Cost to be accounted for:								
Work in process, beginning	$ 16,800							
Added by the department (a)	260,500	$93,000		$134,000		$33,500		
Total cost	$277,300							
Equivalent units (b)		62,000		67,000		67,000		
Unit cost, (a) ÷ (b)		$ 1.50	+	$ 2.00	+	$ 0.50	=	$ 4.00

Cost reconciliation		*Equivalent Units*		
		Materials	*Labor*	*Overhead*
Cost accounted for as follows:				
Transferred out:				
Units from the beginning inventory:				
Cost in the beginning inventory	$________			
Cost to complete these units:				
Materials	________	________		
Labor	________		________	
Overhead	________			________
Total cost	________			
Units started and completed	________	________	________	________
Total cost transferred out	________			
Work in process, ending:				
Materials	________	________		
Labor	________		________	
Overhead	________			________
Total work in process, ending	________			
Total cost	$ 277,300			

Answers to Questions and Exercises

True or False

1. T Process costing is widely used by utilities since their output (water, gas, electricity) is homogeneous.

2. F Since units are indistinguishable from each other, there is no need to identify costs by customer order.

3. T See the discussion in Exhibit 4-1.

4. F Costing is usually easier in a process costing system since costs are accumulated by department rather than by individual job.

5. T In a process costing system a work in process inventory account is maintained for each department.

6. T In operation costing, materials are often handled as in job-order costing while labor and overhead costs are handled as in process costing.

7. F A finished goods inventory account is needed in a process costing system for unsold finished units, just as in a job-order costing system.

8. F As units move from one department to another, the costs that have been incurred to that point are transferred forward with the units.

9. T The computation is:

   500 units x 60% = 300 equivalent units.

10. T Costs in the beginning work in process inventory are kept separate from costs of the current period so that unit costs will reflect only current period activities.

11. T The FIFO method assumes that the units that are first in (i.e., in beginning inventory) are the first out (i.e., completed).

12. T This point is illustrated in Exhibit 4A-3.

13. F Unit costs will tend to be close.

14. F The reverse is true—from a standpoint of cost control, the FIFO method is superior to the weighted-average method.

15. T The only difference between the FIFO and weighted-average methods is how they treat the costs in beginning work in process inventory. As inventories shrink, the differences in unit costs between the two methods also shrink.

Multiple Choice

1. a The computations are:

Beginning inventory	500
Add: Units started into process	4,800
Total units	5,300
Less ending inventory	300
Completed and transferred	5,000

2. b. The computations are:

Units completed and transferred	7,000
Work in process, ending:	
3,000 units x 50%	1 500
Equivalent units of production	8,500

3. c. The computations are:

Work in process, beginning:	
2,000 units x 40%*	800
Units started and completed**	5,000
Work in process, ending:	
3,000 units x 50%	1,500
Equivalent units of production	7,300

*100% - 60% = 40%
**7,000 units - 2,000 units = 5,000 units.

4. b The computations are:

Cost in beginning work in process	$ 2,721
Cost added during the month	39,200
Total cost (a)	$41,921
Units transferred out	2,000
Equivalent units in ending work in process inventory (100 x 60%)	60
Equivalent units	2,060
Unit cost (a) ÷ (b)	$20.35

5. d The computations are:

Cost in beginning work in process	$ 8,000
Cost added during the year	64,000
Total cost (a)	$72,000
Units transferred out	37,000
Equivalent units in ending work in process inventory (10,000 x 30%)	3,000
Equivalent units (b)	40,000
Unit cost (a) ÷ (b)	$1.80

3,000 units x $1.80 = $5,400.

6. d Costs in the department's work in process inventory account include costs transferred in from the previous department and any costs added in the department itself—including materials, labor, and overhead. Labor and overhead together equal conversion cost.

7. b The computations are:

Unit cost	$105.00
x Equivalent units	540
= Total cost	$56,700
- Cost added	54,500
= Cost in beginning work in process	$ 2,200

8. a The computations are:

$75,000 ÷ 20,000 units = $3.75 per unit.

9. b Under the weighted-average method, costs in the beginning inventory are added to costs of the current period when making unit cost computations.

Exercises

4-1.

	Quantity Schedule	*Equivalent Units*	
		Materials	*Conversion*
Units to be accounted for:			
Work in process, beginning (all materials; 60% conversion cost added last month)	5,000		
Started into production	80,000		
Total units to account for	85,000		
Units accounted for as follows:			
Transferred out during the month	83,000	83,000	83,000
Work in process, ending (all materials; 50% conversion cost added this month)	2,000	2,000	1,000
Total units accounted for	85,000	85,000	84,000

4-2.

	Total Cost	*Equivalent Units*		
		Materials	*Labor*	*Overhead*
Cost accounted for as follows:				
Transferred out: (72,000 units x $6)	$432,000	72,000	72,000	72,000
Work in process, ending:				
Materials cost ($ 1 per EU)	8,000	8 ,000		
Labor cost ($3 per EU)	18,000		6,000	
Overhead cost ($2 per EU)	12,000			6,000
Total work in process, ending	38,000			
Total cost	$470,000			

4-3.

	Total Cost	*Equivalent Units*		
		Materials	*Labor*	*Overhead*
Cost accounted for as follows:				
Transferred out:				
Units from the beginning inventory:				
Cost in the beginning inventory	$ 16,800			
Cost to complete these units:				
Materials ($1.50 per EU)	—	—		
Labor ($2.00 per EU)	12,000		6,000	
Overhead ($0.50 per EU)	3,000			6,000
Total cost	31,800			
Units started and completed during the month: (57,000x $4.00)	228,000	57,000	57,000	57,000
Total cost transferred out	259,800			
Work in process, ending:				
Materials cost ($1.50 per EU)	7,500	5,000		
Labor cost ($2.00 per EU)	8,000		4,000	
Overhead cost ($0.50 per EU)	2,000			4,000
Total work in process, ending	17,500			
Total cost	$277,300			

Chapter 5

Systems Design: Activity-Based Costing and Quality Management

Chapter Study Suggestions

The chapter is divided into two parts. The first part covers activity-based costing, which is a more detailed version of the product costing described in Chapter 3. Exhibit 5-6 is the key to the activity-based costing material and you must understand it thoroughly in order to do homework problems.

The second part of the chapter is concerned with quality costs and reports. The four types of quality costs are listed in Exhibit 5-8, along with a number of examples. These four types of costs are used to structure a quality cost report as illustrated in Exhibit 5-10.

CHAPTER HIGHLIGHTS

A. Predetermined overhead rates can be computed at three levels in a company.

1. Level One is known as a plantwide overhead rate. A plantwide overhead rate encompasses all costs in a factory and it is typically based on direct labor-hours. Such an overhead rate results in distorted product costs when overhead costs aren't really caused by direct labor-hours.

2. Level Two uses a "two stage" allocation process that involves departmental overhead rates.

a. In the first stage, overhead costs are assigned to production departments.

b. In the second stage, costs are allocated from the production departments to individual jobs. These second stage allocations are made on various bases, but most often on the basis of direct labor-hours or machine-hours.

c. As a job moves along the production line, overhead is applied in each department according to the various overhead rates that have been set.

d. Departmental rates will not correctly assign overhead costs to products in situations where products differ in terms of lot size or complexity. Departmental rates assume that all products going through the department are similar.

3. Level Three, like Level Two, uses a "two stage" allocation process. Level Three is commonly called *activity-based costing*. Level Three is considered to be the most accurate overhead costing method.

a. An *activity* is any event or transaction that is a cost driver—that is, that causes the incurrence of cost. For example, the activity of setting up a machine causes setup costs, which are considered part of overhead. The key concept in activity-based costing is that activities are caused by products and services and that activities consume resources.

b. In the first stage of an activity-based costing system, overhead costs are assigned to cost pools that represent activities. For example, all the costs associated with machine setups will be assigned to the machine setup overhead cost pool.

c In the second stage, the costs in each overhead cost pool are assigned to jobs according to the number of these activities the jobs require.

B. Activity-based costing recognizes four general levels of activity centers, as follows:

a. *Unit-level activities*, which are performed each time a unit is produced. An example would be processing time on a milling machine.

b. *Batch-level activities*, which are performed each time a batch of goods is handled or processed. An example would be setup time on a particular machine.

c. *Product-level activities*, which are required to have a product at all. An example would be maintaining an up-to-date parts list and instruction manual for the product.

d. *Facility-level activities*, which simply sustain a facility's general manufacturing processes. An example would be grounds maintenance for the factory.

C. Carefully study the example of activity-based costing in Exhibit 5-6. You should see that activity-based costing is just like the methods for applying overhead to products as described in Chapter 3. The only difference is that there are many overhead cost pools and rates rather than just one.

1. For each activity center in turn:

a. Divide the estimated overhead for the activity center by its expected activity. For example, the "machine setups" activity center's estimated overhead cost is divided by the expected number of machine setups to determine the predetermined overhead rate per setup.

b. Multiply the predetermined overhead rate for the activity center by the expected activity for each product. This will determine each product's share of the activity center's overhead.

2. After all of the overhead has been allocated to products, add all of the overhead together for a product and then divide by the number of units of the product in order to determine the unit overhead cost.

D. *Quality of conformance* is the degree to which a product or service meets its design specifications and is free of defects or other problems that might affect appearance or performance. Defects and errors in products (i.e., poor quality of conformance) result in costs that may be classified as prevention costs, appraisal costs, internal failure costs, and external failure costs.

1. Internal failure costs and external failure costs result because of the existence of errors and defects in products.

a. *Internal failure costs* result from correcting defects in products before they are shipped to customers. Such costs include scrap, reworking of defective units, and downtime.

b. *External failure costs* result when a defective product is delivered to a customer. These costs include warranty repairs, exchanges, returns, and loss of future sales. These are the least desirable of all quality costs. A dissatisfied customer is less likely to buy from the company in the future and is likely to tell others of his or her dissatisfaction. If failure costs are going to occur, then it is generally better to identify them internally than to sell defective units to customers.

2. Prevention costs and appraisal costs are incurred in an effort to prevent defects and errors.

a. *Prevention costs* are incurred to reduce or eliminate defects. Defects can be prevented by something as simple as a metal shield that prevents a worker from drilling a hole in the wrong place. Preventive measures are often inexpensive.

b. *Appraisal costs* are incurred to identify defective products before the products are shipped to customers. These costs include wages of inspection workers and the costs of testing equipment.

3. Most companies would benefit from putting more effort into prevention. This reduces the need for appraisal and decreases the incidence of internal and external failures.

E. Quality costs are summarized for management on a *quality cost report* such as is illustrated in Exhibit 5-10.

1. Note the format of the report that classifies the costs into the four categories discussed above.

2. The report should summarize costs associated with defective products and services throughout the organization—all the way from research and development through customer service. The report should not be limited to describing just the costs associated with manufacturing.

3. Such a report helps managers see the financial significance of defects. It helps them identify the relative importance of the quality problems faced by the firm. And it aids managers in diagnosing whether their quality costs are poorly distributed (e.g., too much external failure cost relative to prevention cost).

Appendix 5A: Cost Flows in an Activity-Based System

A. The flow of costs through Raw Materials, Work In Process, and other accounts is basically the same under activity-based costing as we saw in Chapter 3. There is just more than one overhead rate under activity-based costing.

1. A separate predetermined overhead rate is computed for each activity center.

2. A separate calculation is made for each activity center of the amount of overhead applied. The predetermined overhead rate for the activity center is multiplied by the actual amount of the activity for the period.

3. The overhead overapplied or underapplied is determined for each activity center by comparing the applied overhead cost for the period to the actual overhead cost. If the applied overhead is greater than the actual overhead, the overhead is overapplied. If the applied overhead is less than the actual overhead, the overhead is underapplied.

B. See the numeric example in the appendix for an illustration of journal entries and T-accounts.

REVIEW AND SELF TEST
Questions and Exercises

True or False

For each of the following statements, enter a T or an F in the blank to indicate whether the statement is true or false.

___ 1. If direct labor is used as a base for overhead cost assignment and direct labor does not cause the overhead cost, the result will be distorted product costs.

___ 2. Where products differ in terms of lot size or complexity, departmental overhead rates will not correctly assign overhead costs to products.

___ 3. Activity-based costing involves a one-stage allocation process.

___ 4. The key concept underlying activity-based costing is that activities are caused by products and services and that activities consume resources.

___ 5. Process value analysis (PVA) involves choosing between a process costing system and a job-order costing system.

___ 6. Batch-level activities would include issuing purchase orders, issuing production orders, and performing machine setups.

___ 7. Maintaining parts inventories is a unit-level activity.

___ 8. A product containing defects has a poor quality of conformance.

___ 9. The best quality systems are those that put their emphasis on appraisal costs

___ 10. It is better to incur internal failure costs than to incur external failure costs.

___ 11. Quality cost reports focus on quality costs associated with just the manufacturing process.

___ 12. (Appendix 5A) A company will have only one predetermined overhead rate when activity-based costing is used, .

___ 13. (Appendix 5A) There will never be any under or overapplied overhead when activity-based costing is used.

Multiple Choice

Choose the best answer or response by placing the identifying letter in the space provided.

___ 1. Issuing a purchase order is a: a) unit-level activity; b) batch-level activity; c) product-level activity; d) facility-level activity.

___ 2. Plant occupancy is a: a) unit-level activity; b) batch-level activity; c) product-level activity; d) facility-level activity.

___ 3. Testing the prototype of a new product is a: a) unit-level activity; b) batch-level activity; c) product-level activity; d) facility-level activity.

___ 4. The cost of quality training is an example of: a) prevention cost; b) appraisal cost; c) internal failure cost; d) external failure cost.

___ 5. The cost of warranty repairs is an example of: a) prevention cost; b) appraisal cost; c) internal failure cost; d) external failure cost.

___ 6. The cost of rework labor is an example of: a) prevention cost; b) appraisal cost; c) internal failure cost; d) external failure cost.

___ 7. The cost of supplies used in testing and inspection is an example of: a) prevention cost; b) appraisal cost; c) internal failure cost; d) external failure cost.

___ 8. The cost of lost sales due to a reputation for poor quality is an example of: a) prevention cost; b) appraisal cost; c) internal failure cost; d) external failure cost.

Exercises

5-1. Listed below are activity centers that might be found in a company using activity-based costing. For each activity, place an X under the proper heading to indicate whether the activity center would be unit-level, batch-level, and so forth.

Activity Center	*Unit-Level Activity*	*Batch-Level Activity*	*Product-Level Activity*	*Facility Level Activity*
a. Parts inventory management	____	____	____	____
b. Labor-related	____	____	____	____
c. Plant occupancy	____	____	____	____
d. Purchase orders	____	____	____	____
e. Machine-related	____	____	____	____
f. General factory	____	____	____	____
g. Product prototype testing	____	____	____	____
h. Production orders	____	____	____	____
i. Product design	____	____	____	____
j. Machine setup	____	____	____	____
k. Personnel administration	____	____	____	____

5-2. Kozales Company uses activity-based costing to compute unit product costs for external financial reports. The company manufactures two products, the Regular Model and the Super Model. During the coming year the company expects to produce 20,000 units of the Regular Model and 5,000 units of the Super Model. Below are listed other selected data relating to the coming year. Compute the overhead cost per unit for each product by filling in the missing data in the schedules provided below.

Basic Data

Activity Center (and Cost Driver)	*Estimated Overhead Costs*	*Expected Activity*		
		Total	*Regular*	*Super*
Labor related (direct labor-hours)	$ 80,000	10,000	8,000	2,000
Machine setups (number of setups)	420,000	1,400	500	900
Product testing (number of tests)	600,000	8,000	6,400	1,600
General factory (machine-hours)	900,000	45,000	30,000	15,000
Total cost	$2,000,000			

Overhead Rates by Activity Center

Activity Center	*(a) Estimated Overhead Costs*	*(b) Expected Activity*	*(a) ÷ (b) Predetermined Overhead Rate*
Labor related	$ 80,000	10,000	$______ per ______
Machine setups	$420,000	1,400	$______ per ______
Product testing	$600,000	8,000	$______ per ______
General factory	$900,000	45,000	$______ per ______

Overhead Cost per Unit

	Regular Product		*Super Product*	
	Activity	*Amount*	*Activity*	*Amount*
Labor related, at ______	____	____	____	____
Machine setups, at ______	____	____	____	____
Product testing, at ______	____	____	____	____
General factory, at ______	____	____	____	____
Total overhead cost assigned (a)	____	____	____	____
Number of units produced (b)	____	____	____	____
Overhead cost per unit (a) ÷ (b)	____	____	____	____

5-3. (Appendix 5A) Lawson Company uses activity-based costing to compute product costs for external reports. The company has three activity centers and applies overhead using predetermined overhead rates for each activity center. Estimated costs and activities for the current year are presented below for the three activity centers:

Activity Center (and Cost Drivers)	*Estimated Overhead Cost*	*Expected Activity*
Batch setups (setups)	$ 52,900	2,300
Material handling (loads)	100,800	2,800
General factory (DLHs)	65,000	2,500
Total	$218,700	

Actual costs and activities for the current year were as follows:

Activity Center	*Actual Overhead Cost*	*Actual Activity*
Batch setups	$ 52,890	2,260
Material handling	98,990	2,770
General factory	64,980	2,440
Total	$216,860	

a. Determine how much total overhead was applied to products during the year by filling in the missing data in the schedules that have been provided below.

Activity Center	*Estimated Overhead Cost*	*Expected Activity*	*Predetermined Overhead Rate*
Batch setups	$ 52,900	2,300	______
Material handling	$100,800	2,800	______
General factory	$ 65,000	2,500	______

Activity Center	*Predetermined Overhead Rate*	*Actual Activity*	*Overhead Applied*
Batch setups	______	2,260	______
Material handling	______	2,770	______
General factory	______	2,440	______
Total overhead applied			______

b. Determine by how much was overhead overapplied or underapplied by filling in the missing data in the schedules provided below. (Be sure to clearly label whether the overhead was overapplied or underapplied.)

Activity Center	*Overhead Applied*	*Actual Overhead Cost*	*Overhead Overapplied (Underapplied)*
Batch setups	________	$ 52,890	________
Material handling	________	98,990	________
General factory	________	64,980	________
Total	________	$216,860	________

5-4. **Critical thought writing exercise:** Whitney Company manufactures 40,000 units of Product A and only 5,000 units of Product B each year. In prior years, the company has used direct labor-hours to apply overhead costs to its products, but the company has just switched to activity-based costing. The switch to activity-based costing has caused the per unit cost of the low volume product to increase dramatically. Explain the probable causes of the increase in per unit costs for the low volume product.

....

....

....

....

....

....

....

....

Answers to Questions and Exercises

True or False

1. T Distorted product costs will result because overhead will be assigned based on direct labor rather on the bases that actually cause the overhead.

2. T Departmental rates will not correctly assign overhead costs to products in situations where products differ in terms of lot size or complexity. Departmental rates assume that all products going through the department are similar.

3. F Activity-based costing involves a two-stage costing process.

4. T These are key assumptions underlying activity-based costing.

5. F Process value analysis is a systematic method of identifying value-added and non-value-added activities.

6. T These activities are batch-level since they are required every time a batch in initiated. See Exhibit 5-4.

7. F This a product-level activity. See Exhibit 5-4.

8. T Quality of conformance indicates how well a product meets its design specifications and is free of defects and other problems.

9. F The best quality systems are those that put their emphasis on prevention costs.

10. T Internal failure costs keep defective products from being shipped to customers, which can have a devastating effect on the company's reputation.

11. F Quality cost reports should focus on all quality costs throughout an organization from research and development through customer service.

12. F Under activity-based costing, a company will have a predetermined overhead rate for each activity center.

13. F There will usually be some under or overapplied overhead in each activity center.

Multiple Choice

1. b See Exhibit 5-4.
2. d See Exhibit 5-4.
3. c See Exhibit 5-4.
4. a See Exhibit 5-8.
5. d See Exhibit 5-8.
6. c See Exhibit 5-8.
7. b See Exhibit 5-8.
8. d See Exhibit 5-8.

Exercises

5-1.

	Activity Center	Unit-Level Activity	Batch-Level Activity	Product-Level Activity	Facility Level Activity
a.	Parts inventory management			X	
b.	Labor-related	X			
c.	Plant occupancy				X
d.	Purchase orders		X		
e.	Machine-related	X			
f.	General factory				X
g.	Product prototype testing			X	
h.	Production orders		X		
i.	Product design			X	
j.	Machine setup		X		
k.	Personnel administration				X

5-2.

Overhead Rates by Activity Center

Activity Center	*(a) Estimated Overhead Costs*	*(b) Expected Activity*	*(a) ÷ (b) Predetermined Overhead Rate*
Labor related	\$ 80,000	10,000	\$8.00 per direct labor hour
Machine setups	\$420,000	1,400	\$300.00 per setup
Product testing	\$600,000	8,000	\$75.00 per test
General factory	\$900,000	45,000	\$20.00 per machine hour

Overhead Cost per Unit

	Regular Product		*Super Product*	
	Activity	*Amount*	*Activity*	*Amount*
Labor related, at \$8 per DLH	8,000	\$ 64,000	2,000	\$ 16,000
Machine setups, at \$300 per setup	500	150,000	900	270,000
Product testing, at \$75 per test	6,400	480,000	1,600	120,000
General factory, at \$20 per MH	30,000	600,000	15,000	300,000
Total overhead cost assigned (a)		\$1,294,000		\$706,000
Number of units produced (b)		20,000		5,000
Overhead cost per unit (a) ÷ (b)		\$64.70		\$141.20

5-3. a. The first step is to compute the predetermined overhead rate for each activity center:

Activity Center	*Estimated Overhead Cost*	*Expected Activity*	*Predetermined Overhead Rate*
Batch setups	$ 52,900	2,300 setups	$23 per setup
Material handling	$100,800	2,800 loads	$36 per load
General factory	$ 65,000	2,500 DLHs	$26 per DLH

The amount of overhead applied to production is determined as follows:

Activity Center	*Predetermined Overhead Rate*	*Actual Activity*	*Overhead Applied*
Batch setups	$23 per setup	2,260 setups	$ 51,980
Material handling	$36 per load	2,770 loads	$ 99,720
General factory	$26 per DLH	2,440 DLHs	$ 63,440
Total overhead applied			$215,140

b. The overhead over or underapplied is computed as follows:

Activity Center	*Overhead Applied*	*Actual Overhead Cost*	*Overhead Overapplied (Underapplied)*
Batch setups	$ 51,980	$ 52,890	($ 910)
Material handling	99,720	98,990	730
General factory	63,440	64,980	(1,540)
Total	$215,140	$216,860	($1,720)

In total, overhead was underapplied by $1,720.

5-4. The increase in per unit costs for the low volume product is probably the result of two factors. First, rather than treating overhead cost as a lump amount and spreading it uniformly over both products, activity-based costing has traced the overhead costs to specific products. Since low volume products often require special equipment, special handling, and so forth, they typically are responsible for the incurrence of a disproportionately large amount of overhead cost. As this cost is traced to the low volume products, it drives their unit costs upward. Second, many overhead costs are incurred at the batch or product level. Since low volume products typically have fewer units processed per batch than high volume products, their average cost per unit is higher.

Chapter 6

Cost Behavior: Analysis and Use

Chapter Study Suggestions

Chapter 6 expands on the discussion of fixed and variable costs that was started in Chapter 2. In addition, the chapter introduces a new cost concept—mixed costs—and shows how mixed costs can be broken down into their basic fixed and variable elements. Focus the bulk of your study time on the section titled, "The Analysis of Mixed Costs," that is found midway through the chapter. Pay particular attention to how a *cost formula* is derived and how a cost formula is used to predict future costs at various levels.

Commit to memory the elements of the equation: $Y = a + bX$. An understanding of this equation is needed to complete most of the homework exercises and problems. At the end of the chapter, a new format to the income statement called the "contribution approach" is introduced. This format emphasizes cost behavior. Exhibit 6-12 illustrates the format of the contribution income statement. *This format should be memorized*—you will be using it throughout the rest of the book.

The appendix at the end of the chapter shows the computations required to analyze mixed costs using the least-squares regression method.

CHAPTER HIGHLIGHTS

A. A variable cost is a cost that varies, in total, in direct proportion to changes in the activity level. Variable costs are constant on a *per unit* basis.

1. A variable cost is shown graphically in Exhibit 6-1. Notice that the relationship between cost and activity is *linear* and the line goes right through zero on the graph.

2. Variable costs vary according to some activity base. The most common activity bases are hours worked, units produced, and units sold. Other examples of activity bases include miles driven by salespersons, the number of beds in a hospital, and the number of letters typed by a secretary.

3. Direct materials is a variable cost. Direct labor is also usually considered to be a variable cost. Overhead consists of both variable and fixed costs.

4. Variable costs may be either true variable or step variable.

a. A true variable cost is one that varies in direct proportion to changes in activity. Direct materials is an example of a true variable cost.

b. A step variable cost is one that is obtainable only in fairly large chunks and which increases or decreases only in response to fairly wide changes in the activity level. The wages of maintenance personnel is a step variable cost.

c. True variable and step variable costs are illustrated graphically in Exhibit 6-3.

5. The accountant ordinarily assumes a strictly linear relationship between cost and volume.

a. Many cost relationships are curvilinear, such as illustrated in Exhibit 6-4.

b. Curvilinear costs can be approximated by straight lines. The *relevant range* is the range of activity within which a particular straight line is a valid approximation to the curvilinear cost.

B. A fixed cost is a cost that remains constant in total. When expressed on a per unit basis, fixed costs vary inversely with changes in the activity level. As the activity level rises, fixed costs per unit fall.

1. Because fixed costs per unit change depending upon the level of activity, it is best to express fixed costs on a total cost basis when they are used for decision-making.

2. Fixed costs are growing relative to variable costs due to automation and trends toward more stable employment.

3. Fixed costs can generally be classified into two categories: committed and discretionary.

a. Committed fixed costs relate to the investment in facilities, equipment, and the basic organization of a firm. These costs are difficult to adjust.

b. Discretionary fixed costs result from annual decisions by management to spend in certain areas, such as advertising, research, and management development programs. These costs are easier to modify as circumstances change than committed fixed costs.

4. The concept of the relevant range also applies to fixed costs. If there is a big enough change in activity, even committed fixed costs may have to change. Exhibit 6-6 illustrates this idea.

C. A mixed cost is a cost that contains both variable and fixed cost elements. Mixed costs are sometimes called semivariable costs. Exhibit 6-7 shows the behavior of a mixed cost.

1. Examples of mixed costs include electricity, heat, repairs, costs of processing bills, costs of admitting patients to a hospital, and maintenance.

2. The fixed portion of a mixed cost represents the basic, minimum cost of having the service involved ready and available for use. The variable portion represents the cost incurred for actual consumption of the service.

3. Several methods are available for breaking a mixed cost down into its basic variable and fixed cost elements: the high-low method, the scattergraph method, and the least-squares regression method.

4. The fixed and variable cost elements of a mixed cost can be expressed in a *cost formula,* which can be used to predict costs at other levels of activity within the relevant range. This formula can be expressed as follows:

$Y = a + bX$

where:

Y = *dependent variable* (the total mixed cost)
a = vertical intercept (the total fixed cost)
b = slope of the line (the variable rate)
X = *independent variable* (the activity level)

5. Each of the methods discussed below can be used to estimate the variable cost per unit (b) and the total fixed cost (a). Then with the use of the cost formula, the expected amount of total cost (Y) can be computed for any expected activity level (X).

D. The *high-low method* bases its estimates of the variable and fixed elements of a mixed cost on data at the high and low levels of activity.

1. The difference in cost observed between the two extremes is divided by the change in activity to estimate the amount of variable cost. The formula is:

$$\frac{\text{Variable cost per}}{\text{unit of activity}} = \frac{\text{Change in cost}}{\text{Change in activity}}$$

2. Once the variable rate (i.e., variable cost per unit of activity) has been determined, it can be used to determine the amount of fixed cost as follows:

Total cost observed at the "high" activity level	$XXX
Less variable portion:	
Variable rate x "high" level of activity	XXX
Fixed portion of the mixed cost	$ XXX

3. The high-low method is the least accurate method of analyzing mixed costs because the high and low points may not be representative of costs throughout the entire relevant range. The high and low points tend to be unusual.

E. In the *scattergraph method* all the observed costs at various activity levels are plotted on a graph. A *regression line* is then fitted to the plotted points using a straightedge and judgment.

1. The slope of the regression line represents the variable cost per unit of activity. The point where the regression line cuts the vertical cost axis represents total fixed cost.

2. The scattergraph method is more accurate than the high-low method, since all the observed data points can be taken into account when the straight line is drawn. In contrast, the high-low method relies entirely on just two data points.

F. The *least-squares regression method* fits a regression line by means of statistical analysis. The method fits a straight line to the data to minimize the sum of the squared errors from the regression line. The computations involved are complex and are usually handled with a computer.

G. *Multiple regression* analysis should be used when more than one factor causes a cost to vary.

H. The *contribution approach* to preparation of an income statement emphasizes cost behavior.

1. The *traditional format* for income statements groups expenses into functional categories:

Sales	$XXX
Less: Cost of Goods Sold	XXX
Gross Margin	XXX
Less: Admin. and Selling Expense	XXX
Net Income	$XXX

2. The *contribution approach,* in contrast, groups expenses according to their cost behavior.

Sales	$XXX
Less: Variable Expenses	XXX
Contribution Margin	XXX
Less: Fixed Expenses	XXX
Net Income	$XXX

3. The *contribution margin* is determined by deducting variable expenses from sales. It contributes to covering fixed costs, and then to profits.

4. The contribution approach is very useful to managers for internal reports since it emphasizes the behavior of costs. However, it is not used in external reports where the traditional format must be used.

Appendix 6A: Least-Squares Regression

A. The formulas for computing the variable cost per unit (b) and total fixed cost(a) using the least-squares regression method are:

$$b = \frac{n(\sum XY) - (\sum X)(\sum Y)}{n(\sum X^2) - (\sum X)^2}$$

$$a = \frac{(\sum Y) - b(\sum X)}{n}$$

1. To use these formulas, you must first compute ΣY, ΣX, ΣXY, and ΣX^2. The "Σ" indicates that you take a sum. For example, to compute ΣXY, you must multiply X and Y for each observation and then sum the results. The term "n" in the above equation is the number of observations.

2. You must compute the variable cost per unit (b) before you compute the total fixed cost (a) because b is used in the formula for a.

REVIEW AND SELF TEST
Questions and Exercises

True or False

For each of the following statements, enter a T or an F in the blank to indicate whether the statement is true or false.

___ 1. Variable costs are costs that change, in total, in direct proportion to changes in the activity level.

___ 2. In cost analysis work, activity is known as the dependent variable.

___ 3. Within the relevant range, the higher the activity level, the lower the fixed costs will be when these costs are expressed on a per unit basis.

___ 4. Mixed costs are also known as semivariable costs.

___ 5. Contribution margin and gross margin are synonymous terms.

___ 6. Contribution margin is the difference between sales and variable expenses.

___ 7. Discretionary fixed costs arise from annual decisions by management to spend in certain program areas.

___ 8. Advertising would be an example of a committed fixed cost.

___ 9. Mixed costs can be defined as costs that contain both manufacturing and non-manufacturing cost elements.

___ 10. The accountant assumes the relationship between cost and activity is approximately a straight line within the relevant range.

___ 11. In order for a cost to be variable, it must vary with either units produced or units sold.

___ 12. There is a strong trend in industry today toward more fixed costs.

___ 13. A cost formula produced by the high-low method and a cost formula produced the scattergraph method would be the same within rounding error.

___ 14. The contribution approach to the income statement organizes costs according to behavior, rather than according to function.

___ 15. For decision-making purposes, fixed costs should be stated on a per unit basis.

Multiple Choice

Choose the best answer or response by placing the identifying letter in the space provided.

___ 1. A company's cost formula for maintenance is: Y = $4,000 + $3X, based on machine hours. During a period in which 2,000 machine hours were worked, the expected maintenance cost would be: a) $12,000; b) $6,000; c) $10,000; d) $4,000.

___ 2. The costs associated with a company's basic facilities, equipment, and organization are known as: a) committed fixed costs; b) discretionary fixed costs; c) mixed costs; d) variable costs.

___ 3. Last year, Barker Company's sales were $240,000, its fixed costs were $50,000, and its variable costs were $2 per unit. During the year, 80,000 units were sold. The contribution margin was: a) $200,000; b) $240,000; c) $30,000; d) $80,000.

___ 4. An example of a discretionary fixed cost would be: a) depreciation on equipment; b) rent on a factory building; c) salaries of top management; d) items a, b, and c are all discretionary fixed costs; e) none of the above.

___ 5. In March, Espresso Express had electrical costs of $225.00 when the total volume was 4,500 cups of coffee served. In April, electrical costs were $227.50 for 4,750 cups of coffee. Using the high-low method, what is the estimated fixed cost of electricity per month? a) $200; b) $180; c) $225; d) $150.

Chapter 6

Exercises

6-1. Data concerning the electrical costs at Doughboy Company follow:

	Machine hours	*Electrical cost*
Week 1	6,800 hrs.	$1,770
Week 2	6,000 hrs.	1,650
Week 3	5,400 hrs.	1,560
Week 4	7,900 hrs.	1,935

a. Using the high-low method of cost analysis, what is the variable rate per machine hour?

	Cost	*Machine Hours*
High activity level.	________	________
Low activity level.	________	________
Change	________	________

$$\frac{\text{Change in cost}}{\text{Change in activity}} = \frac{\_\_\_\_\_\_\_\_}{\_\_\_\_\_\_\_\_} = \$\_\_\_\_\_\_\_\_ \text{ per machine hour}$$

b. Using the high-low method of cost analysis, what is the total fixed cost?

Total cost at the "high" activity level .... ________
Less variable cost element:
________________ .... ________

Fixed cost element .... ________

c. Express the cost formula for electrical costs in terms of the equation for a straight line:

....

6-2. (Appendix 6A) Data on a week's activity in the shipping department of Osan, Inc. are given below:

	Units Shipped (X)	Shipping Cost (Y)	XY	X^2
Monday	12	$ 580	$ 6,960	144
Tuesday	17	655	11,135	289
Wednesday	10	550	5,500	100
Thursday	7	505	3,535	49
Friday	9	535	4,815	81
Saturday	5	475	2,375	25
	60	$3,300	$34,320	688

a. Using the least squares method, determine the variable cost per unit shipped:

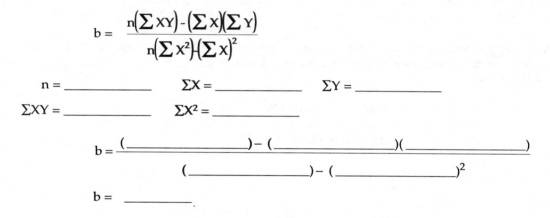

$$b = \frac{n(\Sigma XY) - (\Sigma X)(\Sigma Y)}{n(\Sigma X^2) - (\Sigma X)^2}$$

n = ____________ ΣX = ____________ ΣY = ____________

ΣXY = ____________ ΣX^2 = ____________

$$b = \frac{(\_\_\_\_\_\_) - (\_\_\_\_\_\_)(\_\_\_\_\_\_)}{(\_\_\_\_\_\_) - (\_\_\_\_\_\_)^2}$$

b = ________.

b. Determine the fixed cost per day:

$$a = \frac{(\Sigma Y) - b(\Sigma X)}{n}$$

Substitute the "b" term you solved for in part (a) in the above equation along with ΣY, ΣX, and n:

$$a = \frac{(\_\_\_\_\_\_) - (\_\_\_\_\_\_)(\_\_\_\_\_\_)}{(\_\_\_\_\_\_)}$$

a = ________

c. Express the cost formula for shipping costs in the form Y = a + bX: ____________________

6-3. During July, Simple Company (a merchandising firm) sold 500 units of product. The company's income statement for the month follows:

SIMPLE COMPANY
Income Statement
For the Month Ended July 31

Sales ($100/unit)		$50,000
Less cost of goods sold ($60/unit)		30,000
Gross margin		20,000
Less operating expenses:		
Commissions ($6/unit)	$3,000	
Salaries	8,000	
Advertising	6,000	
Shipping ($2/unit)	1,000	18,000
Net Income		$ 2,000

Redo the company's income statement for the month, by presenting it in the contribution format. Assume that cost of goods sold, commissions, and shipping expenses are variable costs and salaries and advertising expenses are fixed costs.

SIMPLE COMPANY
Income Statement
For the Month Ended July 31

Sales		$________
Less ____________:		
____________	$________	
____________	________	
____________	________	________
Contribution margin		________
Less ____________:		
____________	________	
____________	________	________
Net Income		$________

Answers to Questions and Exercises

True or False

1. T This is the definition of a variable cost.
2. F Activity is the independent variable.
3. T Fixed costs vary inversely with changes in activity when expressed on a per unit basis.
4. T A mixed cost contains both fixed and variable cost elements, and thus is sometimes called a semivariable cost.
5. F Contribution margin is sales less variable expenses; gross margin is sales less cost of goods sold.
6. T This is true by definition.
7. T Discretionary fixed costs are re-evaluated each year by management.
8. F Advertising is a discretionary fixed cost since the advertising program is typically re-evaluated on an annual basis.
9. F Mixed costs contain both variable and fixed cost elements.
10. T Accountants approximate complex cost relationships with straight lines that are valid within a relevant range.
11. F There can be many measures of activity besides units produced and units sold. Other measures include miles driven, number of occupied beds in a hospital, and number of flight hours.
12. T This trend toward more fixed costs is largely a result of automation
13. F The two methods are different and will produce the same results only if the regression line is drawn through the high and low points when the scattergraph method is used.
14. T The contribution approach groups variable costs together and fixed costs together; thus, the income statement is organized according to cost behavior.
15. F Fixed costs are most easily dealt with on a total basis since per unit fixed costs are not stable and therefore may be misleading or confusing to managers.

Multiple Choice

1. c The computation is:

Fixed cost	$ 4,000
Variable cost: $3 x 2,000 hours	6,000
Total cost	$10,000

2. a By definition, committed fixed costs relate to a company's basic facilities, equipment, and organization.

3. d The computation is:

Sales	$240,000
Less variable costs:	
$2 X 80,000 units	160,000
Contribution margin	$ 80,000

4. e All of the listed costs are generally considered to be committed fixed costs.

5. b The computations are:

	Cost	*Cups*
High activity level	$227.50	4,750
Low activity level	225.00	4,500
Change	$ 2.50	250

$$\frac{\text{Change in cost}}{\text{Change in activity}} = \frac{\$\,2.50}{250} = \$0.01$$

Total cost at the "high" activity level	$227.50
Less variable cost element:	
4,750 cups X $0.01 per cup	47.50
Fixed Cost Element	$180.00

Chapter 6

Exercises

6-1. a. Variable cost per machine-hour:

	Cost	*Machine Hours*
High activity level	$1,935	7,900
Low activity level	1,560	5,400
Change	$ 375	2,500

$$\frac{\text{Change in cost}}{\text{Change in activity}} = \frac{\$375}{2{,}500 \text{ hours}} = \$0.15 \text{ per machine hour variable cost}$$

b. Total fixed cost:

Total cost at the "high" activity level	$1,935
Less variable cost element:	
7,900 hours X $.15 per hour	1,185
Fixed Cost Element	$ 750

c. Cost formula for electrical costs: $750 per period, plus $.15 per machine hour, or

Y= $750 + $0.15X

6-2. a. Compute the variable cost per unit shipped as follows:

$$b = \frac{n(\Sigma XY) - (\Sigma X)(\Sigma Y)}{n(\Sigma X^2) - (\Sigma X)^2}$$

$n = 6$ $\Sigma X = 60$ $\Sigma Y = \$3{,}300$ $\Sigma XY = \$34{,}320$ $\Sigma X^2 = 688$

$$b = \frac{6(34{,}320) - (60)(3{,}300)}{6(688) - (60)^2}$$

b = $15 per unit shipped variable cost.

b. Compute the fixed cost per day as follows:

$$a = \frac{(\Sigma Y) - b(\Sigma X)}{n}$$

$$a = \frac{(3{,}300) - 15(60)}{6}$$

a = $400

c. Y = $400 + $15X

6-3.

SIMPLE COMPANY
Income Statement
For the Month Ended July 31,

Sales ($100/unit)		$50,000
Less variable expenses:		
Cost of goods sold ($60/unit)	$30,000	
Commissions ($6/unit)	3,000	
Shipping ($2/unit)	1,000	34,000
Contribution margin		16,000
Less fixed expenses:		
Salaries	8,000	
Advertising	6,000	14,000
Net Income		$ 2,000

Chapter 7

Cost-Volume-Profit Relationships

Chapter Study Suggestions

Chapter 7 is one of the key chapters in the book. Many of the chapters ahead will depend on concepts developed here. There are several sections in the chapter you should study with particular attention. The first of these is the section early in the chapter titled, "Contribution Margin." Note how changes in the contribution margin affect net income. The next section to be studied with particular care is the one titled "Contribution Margin Ratio." The contribution margin ratio is used in much of the analytical work in the chapter.

Another section to be given particular attention is the one titled "Some Applications of CVP Concepts." Much of the homework material is drawn from this section. The section titled "Break-Even Analysis" also forms the basis for much of the homework material. *You should memorize the break-even formulas in this section.* Finally, the latter part of the chapter contains a section titled "The Concept of Sales Mix" that shows how to use CVP analysis when there is more than one product. Notice particularly how the break-even point is computed if a company has more than one product line.

When studying the material in the chapter, try especially hard to understand the logic behind the solutions. Keep in mind that CVP analysis represents a *way of thinking,* rather than a mechanical set of procedures.

CHAPTER HIGHLIGHTS

A. The contribution margin is a key concept.

1. The essential definitions are:

$$\text{Unit contribution margin} = \text{Unit selling price} - \text{Unit variable cost}$$

$$\text{Contribution margin} = \text{Total sales} - \text{Total variable cost}$$

2. The contribution margin can be computed by multiplying the unit contribution margin by the number of units sold:

$$\text{Contribution margin} = \text{Unit contribution margin} \times \text{Total unit sales}$$

The term "total contribution margin" is also commonly used to refer to the contribution margin.

3. There is a definite relationship between the contribution margin and net income.

a. The contribution margin must first cover fixed expenses. If it doesn't then there is a loss.

b. The break-even point is reached when the total contribution margin generated on sales just equals the fixed costs.

c. Once the break-even point is reached, net income will increase by the amount of the unit contribution margin for each additional unit sold.

4. The relationship between contribution margin and net income provides a very powerful planning tool. It gives the manager the ability to predict what profits will be at various activity levels without the necessity of preparing detailed income statements.

B. The contribution margin ratio (CM ratio), which expresses the contribution margin as a percentage of sales, is another very powerful concept.

1. The contribution margin ratio can be computed in two ways:

$$\text{CM ratio} = \frac{\text{Contribution margin}}{\text{Sales}}$$

$$\text{CM ratio} = \frac{\text{Unit contribution margin}}{\text{Unit selling price}}$$

2. The contribution margin ratio can be used to predict the change in total contribution margin that would result from a given change in dollar sales:

$$\text{Change in dollar sales} \times \text{CM ratio} = \text{Change in contribution margin}$$

3. If fixed costs do not change, any increase (or decrease) in contribution margin will be reflected dollar-for-dollar in increased (or decreased) net income.

4. The CM ratio is often of more use to the manager than the unit contribution margin figure, particularly when a company has multiple products.

a. The CM ratio is expressed in terms of total dollar sales, which provides a useful common denominator when there is more than one product.

b. Generally, a company should concentrate its sales efforts on the products that have the highest CM ratio figures. A dollar of sales will have the greatest impact of net income if it comes from the product that has the highest CM ratio.

C. There are many applications of cost-volume-profit (CVP) concepts in day-to-day decisions. Study carefully the examples given under the heading "Some Applications of CVP Concepts" in the early part of the chapter.

1. Notice that each solution makes use of either the unit contribution margin or the CM ratio. This underscores the importance of these two concepts.

2. Also notice that several of the examples employ *incremental analysis*. An incremental analysis is based only on those items of cost or revenue that *differ* between alternatives.

D. Two particular examples of CVP analysis, called *break-even analysis* and *target net profit analysis*, are often used by managers. Break-even analysis is a special case of target net profit analysis, so target net profit analysis will be considered first.

1. Target net profit analysis is used when a manager would like to know how much the com-

pany would have to sell to attain a specific target net profit. The analysis is based on the following equation:

Profits = Sales - Variable expenses - Fixed expenses

2. There are two basic variations of target net profit analysis. In the first variation, the manager would like to know how many *units* would have to be sold. Then the following version of the above equation is used:

$$\text{Target net profit} = \text{Selling price} \times \text{Unit sales} - \text{Variable cost per unit} \times \text{Unit sales} - \text{Fixed expenses}$$

or

$$\text{Target net profit} = \left(\text{Selling price} - \text{Variable cost per unit}\right) \times \text{Unit sales} - \text{Fixed expenses}$$

or

$$\text{Target net profit} = \left(\text{Unit contribution margin}\right) \times \text{Unit sales} - \text{Fixed expenses}$$

This equation can be solved for unit sales, yielding the following formula:

$$\text{Unit sales to attain target net profit} = \frac{\text{Fixed expense + Target net profit}}{\text{Unit contribution margin}}$$

3. When the manager would like to know what total *sales dollars* would have to be in order to break-even, the following variation on the above formula is used:

$$\text{Dollar sales to attain target net profit} = \frac{\text{Fixed expense + Target net profit}}{\text{CM ratio}}$$

E. Break-even occurs when total sales equals total expenses, or, in other words, when profit is zero. Thus, break-even analysis is really just a special case of target net profit analysis in which the target net profit is zero. Therefore, the break-even formulas can be stated as follows:

$$\text{Unit sales to break even} = \frac{\text{Fixed expense}}{\text{Unit contribution margin}}$$

$$\text{Dollar sales to break even} = \frac{\text{Fixed expense}}{\text{CM ratio}}$$

F. CVP and break-even analysis can also be done graphically. Exhibits 7-1 through 7-5 show how the appropriate graphs are prepared.

1. Exhibits 7-1 and 7-2 show how the conventional CVP graph is prepared and interpreted. This graph is called a cost-volume-profit graph because it shows the relationships between sales, costs, and volume throughout wide ranges of activity.

2. Exhibit 7-3 shows an alternate format to the cost-volume-profit graph that is preferred by some managers. This format shows the fixed expenses on top of the variable expenses—the reverse of the conventional graph in Exhibit 7-2. Because of this reversal, the graph can also show the contribution margin.

3. Exhibits 7-4 and 7-5 illustrate a "profit-graph." It is preferred by some managers because it more directly shows how profits change with changes in the sales volume.

G. The "margin of safety" is the excess of budgeted (or actual) sales over the break-even volume of sales. It is the amount by which sales can drop before losses begin to be incurred in a company. The margin of safety can be stated in terms of either dollars or as a percentage of sales:

$$\text{Margin of safety in dollars} = \text{Total sales} - \text{Breakeven sales}$$

$$\text{Margin of safety percentage} = \frac{\text{Margin of safety in dollars}}{\text{Total sales}}$$

H. A company often has some latitude in trading off between fixed and variable costs.

1. A company with low fixed costs and high variable costs (a low CM ratio) will enjoy greater stability in net income, but will do so at the risk of losing substantial profits if sales trend sharply upward over time.

2. A company with high fixed costs and low variable costs (a high CM ratio) will experience wider movements in net income as sales fluctuate up and down, but will reap greater profits if sales trend sharply upward over time.

I. Operating leverage refers to the effect a given percentage increase in sales will have on net income.

1. The "degree of operating leverage" is defined as follows:

$$\text{Degree of operating leverage} = \frac{\text{Contribution margin}}{\text{Net income}}$$

2. A given *percentage* in sales is multiplied by the degree of operating leverage in order to estimate the resulting *percentage* change in sales.

$$\text{Degree of operating leverage} \times \text{Percentage change in total sales} = \text{Percentage change in net income}$$

3. *The degree of operating leverage is not constant.* It changes as sales increase or decrease. In general, *the degree of operating leverage decreases the further a company moves away from its break-even point.*

J. In most situations, commissions to salespersons should be based on the total contribution margin they are able to generate, rather than on total sales. This has the beneficial effect of encouraging the salespersons to focus their efforts on selling those products that will maximize total contribution margin and hence net income, rather than total sales.

K. When a company has more than one product, the *sales mix* can be crucial. The sales mix is the relative proportions in which the company's products are sold.

1. When CVP analysis involved more than one product, the analysis is normally based on the *overall* contribution margin ratio which is computed as follows:

$$\text{Overall CM ratio} = \frac{\text{Total contribution margin for all products}}{\text{Total sales for all products}}$$

2. When there is more than one product, the *overall* CM ratio is used in the target net profit and break-even formulas instead of the CM ratio.

3. As the mix of products being sold changes *the overall CM ratio will also change.* If the shift in mix is toward the less profitable products, then the overall CM ratio will fall; if the shift is toward the more profitable products, then the overall CM ratio will rise.

L. CVP analysis (particularly break-even and target net profit analysis) relies on a number of assumptions:

1. The selling price is constant. The price of a product or service will not change as the volume of unit sales changes.

2. Costs are linear. Costs can be accurately divided into variable and fixed elements. The variable cost per unit is constant and the total fixed cost is constant.

3. In multi-product situations, the sales mix is constant.

4. In manufacturing companies, the inventories do not change.

REVIEW AND SELF TEST
Questions and Exercises

True or False

For each of the following statements, enter a T or an F in the blank to indicate whether the statement is true or false.

___ 1. If product A has a higher unit contribution margin than product B, then product A will always have a higher CM ratio than product B.

___ 2. The break-even point occurs where the contribution margin is equal to total variable expenses.

___ 3. One of the assumptions of break-even analysis is that there is no change in inventories.

___ 4. The break-even point can be expressed either in terms of units sold or in terms of total sales dollars.

___ 5. If the product mix changes, the break-even point may change.

___ 6. For a given increase in sales dollars, a high CM ratio will result in a greater increase in profits than will a low CM ratio.

___ 7. If sales increase by 8 percent, and the degree of operating leverage is 4, then profits can be expected to increase by 12 percent.

___ 8. The degree of operating leverage for a given firm remains the same at all levels of sales activity.

___ 9. Once the break-even point has been reached, net income will increase by the unit contribution margin for each additional unit sold.

___ 10. A shift in sales mix toward less profitable products will cause the overall break-even point to fall.

___ 11. Incremental analysis focuses on the differences in costs and revenues between alternatives.

___ 12. If a company's cost structure shifts toward greater fixed costs and lower variable costs, one would expect the company's CM ratio to fall.

___ 13. One way to compute the break-even point is to divide total sales by the CM ratio.

___ 14. Basing sales commissions on contribution margin is generally less desirable from the company's standpoint than basing sales commissions on gross sales.

___ 15. A key assumption in break-even analysis when there is more than one product is that the sales mix will not change.

Multiple Choice

Choose the best answer or response by placing the identifying letter in the space provided.

___ 1. Lester Company has a single product. The selling price is $50 and the variable cost is $30 per unit. The company's fixed expenses are $200,000 per month. What is the company's unit contribution margin? a) $50; b) $30; c) $20; d) $80.

___ 2. Refer to the data for Lester Company in question 1 above. What is the company's contribution margin ratio? a) 0.60; b) 0.40; c) 1.67; d) 20.00.

___ 3. Refer to the data for Lester Company in question 1 above. What is the company's break-even in sales dollars? a) $500,000; b) $33,333; c) $200,000; d) $400,000.

___ 4. Refer to the data for Lester Company in question 1 above. How many units would the company have to sell to attain target profits of $50,000? a) 10,000; b) 12,500; c) 15,000; d) 13,333.

___ 5. The following figures are taken from Parker Company's income statement: Net income, $30,000; Fixed costs, $90,000; Sales, $200,000; and CM ratio, 60 percent. The company's margin of safety in dollars is: a) $150,000; b) $30,000; c) $50,000; d) $80,000.

___ 6. Refer to the data in question 5 above. The margin of safety in percentage form is: a) 60 percent; b) 75 percent; c) 40 percent; d) 25 percent.

___ 7. As a company's sales move further from its break-even point, one would expect the degree of operating leverage to: a) decrease; b) increase; c) remain unchanged; d) vary in direct proportion to changes in the activity level.

___ 8. If sales increase from $400,000 to $450,000, and if the degree of operating leverage is 6, one would expect net income to increase by: a) 12.5 percent; b) 75 percent; c) 67 percent; d) 50 percent.

___ 9. In multiple product firms, a shift in the sales mix from less profitable products to more profitable products will cause the company's break-even point to: a) increase; b) decrease; c) there will be no change in the break-even point; d) none of these.

___ 10. Herman Corp. has two products, A and B, with the following total sales and total variable costs:

	Product A	*Product B*
Total sales	$10,000	$30,000
Total variable costs	$4,000	$24,000

What is the overall contribution margin ratio? a) 70%; b) 50%; c) 30%; d) 40%.

Exercises

7-1. Hardee Company sells a single product. The selling price is $30 per unit and the variable expenses are $18 per unit. The company's most recent annual income statement is given below:

Sales (4,500 units)	$135,000
Less variable expenses	81,000
Contribution margin	54,000
Less fixed expenses	48,000
Net Income	$ 6,000

a. Compute the contribution margin per unit .... $________

b. Compute the CM ratio .... ________%

c. Compute the break-even point in sales dollars .... $________

d. Compute the break-even point in units sold .... ________ units

e. How many units must be sold next year to double the company's profits? .... __________ units

f. Compute the company's degree of operating leverage .... __________

g. Sales for next year (in units) are expected to increase by 5 percent. Using the operating leverage concept, net income should increase by .... __________%

h. Verify your answer to part g by preparing a contribution income statement showing a 5 percent increase in sales.

Sales (__________ units)	$__________
Less variable expenses (__________ units)	__________
Contribution margin	__________
Less fixed expenses	__________
Net income	$__________

7-2. Using the data below, construct a cost-volume-profit graph like the one in Exhibit 7-2 in the text:

Sales: 15,000 units at $10 each.
Variable expenses: $6 per unit.
Fixed expenses: $40,000 total.

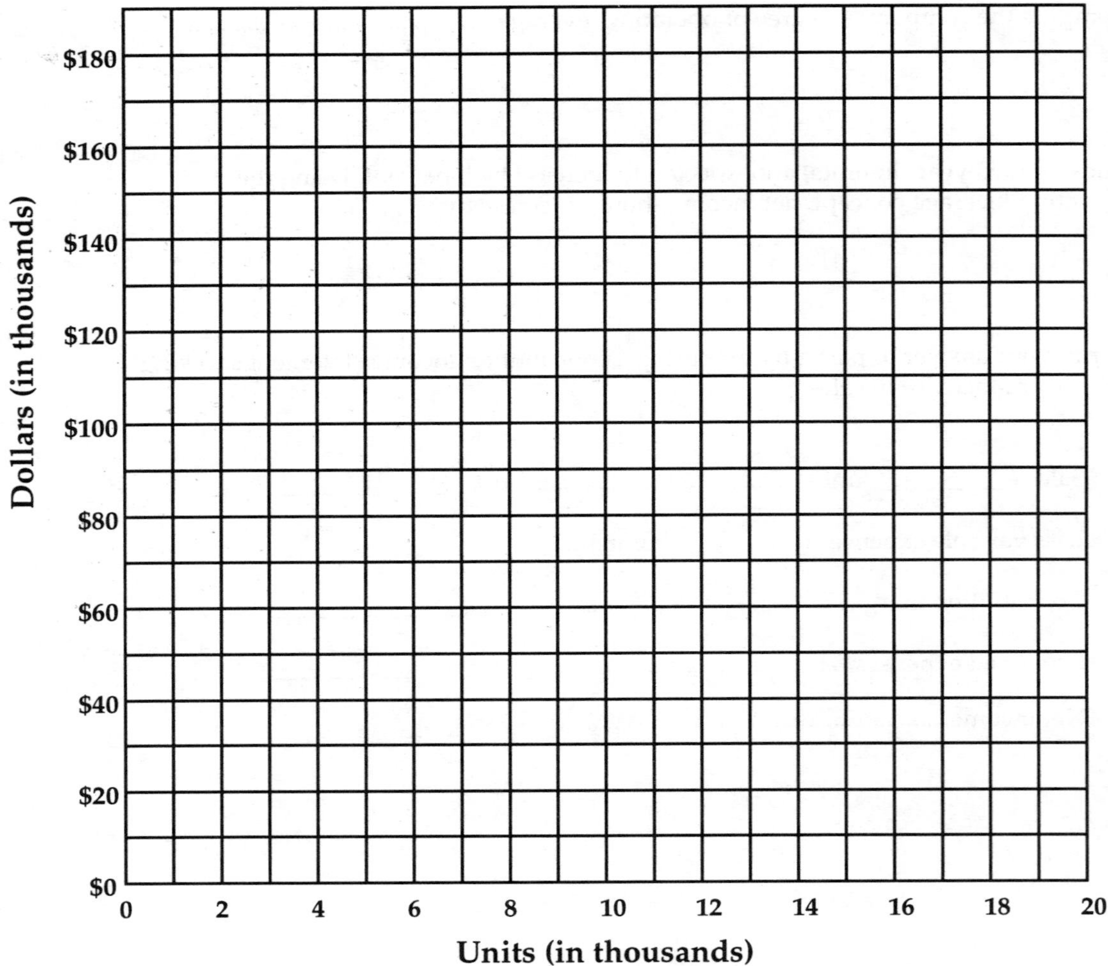

What is the break-even point in units? ______________________.

What is the break-even point in total sales dollars? ______________________

7-3. Seaver Company produces and sells two products, X and Y. Data concerning the products follow:

	Product X	*Product Y*
Selling price per unit	$10	$12
Variable expenses per unit	6	3
Contribution margin per unit	$ 4	$ 9

In the most recent month, the company sold 400 units of Product X and 600 units of Product Y. Fixed expenses are $5,000 per month.

a. Complete the following income statement for the most recent month (carry percentages to one decimal point):

	Product X		*Product Y*		*Total*	
	Amount	*%*	*Amount*	*%*	*Amount*	*%*
Sales	$______	___	$______	___	$______	___
Less variable expenses	______	___	______	___	______	___
Contribution margin	$______	___	$______	___	______	___
Less fixed expenses					______	
Net income (loss)					$______	

b. Compute the company's overall monthly break-even point in sales dollars $ ________

c. If the company continues to sell 1,000 units, in total, each month, but the sales mix shifts so that an equal number of units of each product is being sold, would you expect monthly net income to rise or fall? Explain.

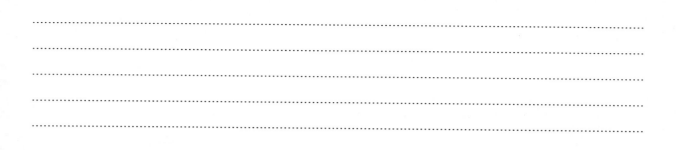

d. Refer to the data in part c above. If the sales mix shifts as explained, would you expect the company's monthly break-even point to rise or fall? Explain.

7.4. **Critical thought writing exercise:** Able Company and Baker Company are competing firms that sell a product at the same price. Both companies are operating above the break-even point. Able Company's costs are mostly variable, whereas Baker Company's costs are mostly fixed. In a time of increasing sales which company will tend to realize the most rapid increase in net income? Explain your answer.

Answers to Questions and Exercises

True or False

1. F The CM ratio depends on the relationship between selling price and contribution margin. One product might have a higher unit contribution than another, but its selling price may be so high that its CM ratio is lower.

2. F The break-even point occurs where the contribution margin is equal to fixed expenses.

3. T This is one of the basic assumptions of break-even analysis in a manufacturing company. (This point is considered further in Chapter 7.)

4. T The break-even point can be computed in terms of units sold or total sales dollars.

5. T A change in product mix usually means a change in the overall CM ratio. Exhibits 7-8 and 7-9 in the text illustrate the effect of such a change.

6. T The CM ratio measures how much of a sales dollar is translated into increased contribution margin and hence increased profit.

7. F Profits can be expected to increase by 32% = 4 X 8%.

8. F The degree of operating leverage decreases as a firm moves further and further from its break-even point.

9. T At the break-even point all fixed costs have been covered. All contribution margin generated from that point forward increases net income by the same amount.

10. F The reverse is true—the overall break-even point will rise since the average CM ratio will be lower as a result of selling less profitable products.

11. T By definition, an incremental analysis deals only with differences between alternatives.

12. F The reverse is true—one would expect the company's CM ratio to rise. The reason is that variable costs would be lower and hence the CM ratio would be higher.

13. F The break-even point is computed by dividing total *fixed costs* by the CM ratio.

14. F The opposite is true—basing sales commissions on contribution margin is usually more desirable. This is because using contribution margin as a base encourages the sales staff to focus their attention on maximizing total contribution margin rather than maximizing total sales.

15. T This is a key assumption since a change in the sales mix will change the break-even point.

Multiple Choice

1. c The computations are:

Selling price	$50
Variable expenses	30
Unit contribution margin	$20

2. b The unit contribution margin from the above is $20. The contribution margin ratio is determined by dividing this unit contribution margin by the selling price:

Unit contribution margin	$ 20
÷ Selling price	$ 50
Contribution margin ratio	0.40

3. a The formula approach can be used as follows:

$$\frac{\text{Fixed expenses}}{\text{CM ratio}} = \begin{array}{c}\text{Break-even point}\\ \text{in total sales dollars}\end{array}$$

$$\frac{\$200{,}000}{0.40} = \$500{,}000$$

4. b The formula approach can be used as follows:

$$\frac{\text{Fixed expenses} + \text{Target profit}}{\text{Unit contribution margin}} = \text{Units sold to attain target profit}$$

$$\frac{\$200{,}000 + \$50{,}000}{\$20} = 12{,}500$$

5. c The computations are:

$$\text{Break-even sales dollars} = \frac{\text{Fixed expense, } \$90{,}000}{\text{CM ratio, } 60\%} = \$150{,}000$$

Margin of safety = $200,000 - $150,000 = $50,000

6. d $50,000 ÷ $200,000 = 25%

7. a The degree of operating leverage decreases because the presence of fixed costs makes net income on a percentage basis less and less sensitive to changes in total sales as the total sales go up.

8. b The computations are:

$$\text{Percentage change in sales} = \frac{\$50{,}000}{\$400{,}000} = 12.5\%$$

6 x 12.5% = 75%

9. b A shift to more profitable products would result in an increase in the overall CM ratio. Thus, less sales would be needed to cover the fixed costs and the break-even point would therefore decrease.

10. c The computations are as follows:

	Product A	*Product B*	*Total*
Total sales	$10,000	$30,000	$40,000
Total variable costs	4,000	24,000	28,000
Total contribution margin	$ 6,000	$ 6,000	$12,000

Overall CM ratio = $12,000 ÷ $40,000 = 30%

Exercises

7-1. a.

	Per Unit	
Selling price	$30	100%
Less variable expenses	18	60
Unit contribution margin	$12	40%

b. $$\text{CM ratio} = \frac{\text{Contribution margin}}{\text{Sales}} = \frac{\$54{,}000}{\$135{,}000} = 40\%$$

c. Sales = Variable Expenses + Fixed Expenses + Profits
X = 0.60X + $48,000 + $0
0.40X = $ 48,000
X = $48,000 ÷ 0.40
X = $ 120,000

Alternate solution:

$$\text{Dollar sales to break even} = \frac{\text{Fixed expense}}{\text{CM ratio}} = \frac{\$48{,}000}{0.40} = \$120{,}000$$

d. Sales = Variable Expenses + Fixed Expenses + Profits
$30X = $18X + $48,000 + $0
$12X = $48,000
X = $48,000 ÷ $12
X = 4,000 units

Alternate solution:

$$\text{Unit sales to break even} = \frac{\text{Fixed expense}}{\text{Unit contribution margin}} = \frac{\$48{,}000}{\$12} = 4{,}000 \text{ units}$$

e. Sales = Variable Expenses + Fixed Expenses + Profits
$30X = $18X + $48,000 + $12,000
$12X = $60,000
X = $60,000 ÷ $12
X = 5,000 units

Alternate solution:

$$\text{Unit sales to attain target net profit} = \frac{\text{Fixed expense + Target net profit}}{\text{Unit contribution margin}} = \frac{\$48{,}000 + \$12{,}000}{\$12} = 6{,}000 \text{ units}$$

f. $$\text{Degree of operating leverage} = \frac{\text{Contribution margin}}{\text{Net income}} = \frac{\$54{,}000}{\$6{,}000} = 9$$

g. $$\text{Percentage change in net income} = \text{Degree of operating leverage} \times \text{Percentage change in total sales} = 9 \times 5\% = 45\%$$

h. New sales volume: 4,500 units x 105% = 4,725 units

Sales (4,725 units)	$141,750
Less variable expenses (4,725 units)	85,050
Contribution margin	56,700
Less fixed expenses	48,000
Net income	$ 8,700

Present net income	$ 6,000
Expected increase: $6,000 X 45%	2,700
Expected net income (as above)	$ 8,700

7-2. The completed CVP graph:

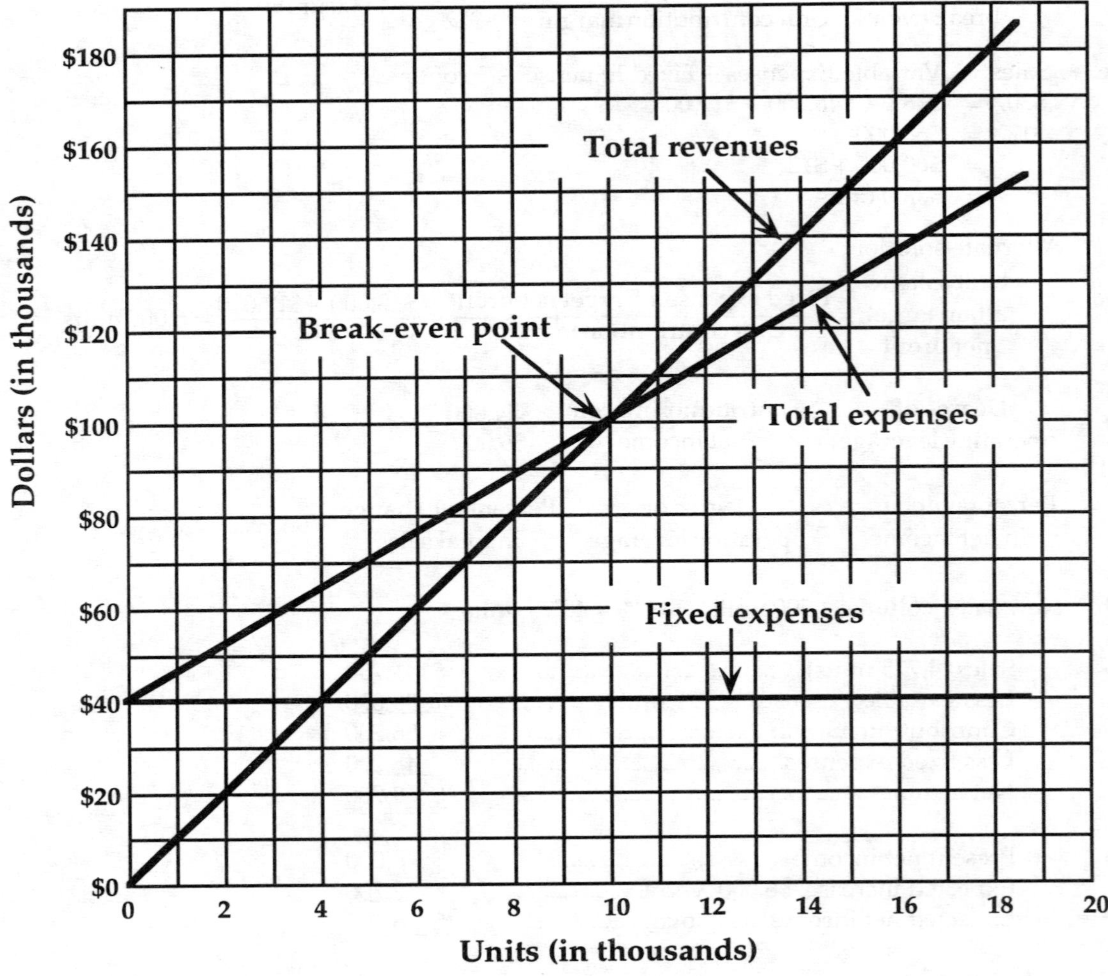

The break-even point in units is 10,000 units and in dollars is $100,000.

7-3. a. The completed income statement:

	Product X		*Product Y*		*Total*	
	Amount	*%*	*Amount*	*%*	*Amount*	*%*
Sales	$4,000	100	$7,200	100	$11,200	100.0
Less variable expenses	2,400	60	1,800	25	4,200	37.5
Contribution margin	$1,600	40	$5,400	75	7,000	62.5
Less fixed expenses					5,000	
Net income					$ 2,000	

b. $$\text{Dollar sales to break even} = \frac{\text{Fixed expense}}{\text{CM ratio}} = \frac{\$5{,}000}{0.625} = \$8{,}000$$

c. Monthly net income will fall. The shift in sales mix will mean that less of Product Y is being sold and more of Product X is being sold. Since Product Y has a higher contribution margin per unit than Product X, this means that less contribution margin in *total* will be available, and profits will therefore fall.

d. The monthly break-even point will rise. As explained above, the shift in sales mix will be toward the less profitable Product X, which has a CM ratio of only 40 percent as compared to 75 percent for Product Y. Thus, the company's *overall* CM ratio will fall, and the break-even point will rise since less contribution margin will be available per unit to cover the fixed costs.

7-4. Baker Company will realize the most rapid increase in net income. The reason is that Baker Company will have a higher contribution margin ratio (and contribution margin per unit) due to its lower variable costs. Thus, the company's contribution margin (and net income) will increase more rapidly than Able Company's as sales increase. The impact on net income can also be viewed in terms of operating leverage. At a given level of sales, Baker Company will have a higher degree of operating leverage than Able Company because of its higher fixed costs. Therefore, as sales increase, its net income will rise more rapidly than will Able Company's.

Chapter 8

Variable Costing: A Tool for Management

Chapter Study Suggestions

This chapter introduces a new method of determining product costs called variable costing. Throughout the chapter we compare variable costing with absorption costing, which was covered in Chapter 3.

In your study of Chapter 8, note that the difference between the two costing methods centers on the handling of the fixed portion of manufacturing overhead cost. This point is shown in graphic form in Exhibit 8-1. Exhibits 8-2 through 8-6 are the heart of the chapter, these exhibits show how to compute unit product costs under both variable and absorption costing, and they show the impact of the two methods on net income. Spend the bulk of your study time on these exhibits, and be sure you understand the computations they contain. You must understand these computations to complete the homework assignment material.

CHAPTER HIGHLIGHTS

A. Two different methods are used for determining product costs—*absorption costing* and *variable costing*.

1. Under absorption costing, all manufacturing costs, both variable and fixed, are included in product costs.

2. Under variable costing, only variable manufacturing costs—which consist of direct materials, direct labor, and variable manufacturing overhead—are included in product costs.

a. Variable costing focuses on cost behavior. One of the strengths of this costing method is that it harmonizes fully with both the contribution approach and the cost-volume-profit concepts discussed in the prior chapter.

b. Under the variable costing method, fixed manufacturing costs are treated as period costs and, like selling and administrative expenses, are charged against revenues in the period in which they are incurred.

c. Variable costing is sometimes referred to as *direct costing* or *marginal costing*.

B. The essential difference between the two costing methods is that under absorption costing fixed manufacturing overhead is treated as a product cost, whereas under variable costing it is treated as a period cost.

1. Advocates of variable costing argue that fixed manufacturing costs are incurred in order to have the *capacity* to produce output in a given period. These costs are incurred whether or not the capacity is actually used to make output. The costs have no *future service potential* since incurring them in the current period does not remove the necessity to incur them in future periods. Thus, fixed manufacturing overhead costs should be charged against the period and not included in product costs.

2. Advocates of absorption costing believe that all manufacturing costs—variable and fixed—are essential to the production process and should not be ignored when determining product costs.

C. Under absorption costing, a portion of the fixed manufacturing overhead costs of the current period can be deferred to future periods through the inventory account. That is, some of the fixed manufacturing overhead costs may wind up on the balance sheet as assets (i.e., inventory) rather than on the income statement as expenses.

1. The deferral occurs because units of product going into inventory carry a portion of the fixed manufacturing overhead costs of the period with them. This portion of the period's fixed manufacturing overhead costs is not charged against revenues of the current period, but rather is held (or deferred) in inventory until the units are sold in some future period.

2. Such a deferral is known as *fixed manufacturing overhead cost deferred in inventory*.

D. Exhibit 8-3 is a key exhibit illustrating the differences between variable and absorption costing. *Study this exhibit carefully before going on.*

E. Exhibit 8-4 is also a key exhibit that summarizes the relations between variable and absorption costing.

1. When production and sales (in units) are equal, the same net income will be reported under both variable and absorption costing.

2. When production exceeds sales (in units), greater net income will be reported under absorption costing than under variable costing.

a. When production exceeds sales, net income will be greater under absorption costing because some of the current period's fixed manufacturing overhead costs are deferred in inventory

b. The amount of fixed manufacturing overhead cost deferred is equal to the excess production times the fixed manufacturing overhead cost per unit.

3. When production is less than sales (in units), less net income will be reported under absorption costing than under variable costing.

a. When production is less than sales, net income will be less under absorption costing because fixed manufacturing overhead costs are released from inventory.

b. The amount of fixed manufacturing overhead cost released is equal to the excess units sold times the fixed manufacturing overhead cost per unit.

4. Over an extended period of time, the net income reported by the two costing methods will tend to be the same.

a. The reason is that over the long run sales can't exceed production, nor can production much exceed sales.

b. The shorter the period, the more the net income figures will tend to differ.

F. The following format, which is illustrated in Exhibit 8-5, can be used to reconcile the variable and absorption costing net income figures.

Variable costing net income	$XXX
Add: Fixed manufacturing overhead costs deferred in inventory under absorption costing	XXX
Deduct: Fixed manufacturing overhead costs released from inventory under absorption costing	(XXX)
Absorption costing net income	$XXX

G. Exhibit 8-6 shows the effect of changes in production on net income under both variable and absorption costing.

1. Net income under variable costing *is not* affected by changes in production.

2. Net income under absorption costing *is* affected by changes in production.

a. Net income will increase as production increases, and decrease as production decreases. This occurs because of changes in ending inventories. As inventories grow, fixed manufacturing overhead is deferred in inventories. As inventories shrink, fixed manufacturing overhead is released to the income statement.

b. These changes in net income are a major drawback of absorption costing, since a company can increase its reported net income by simply increasing production.

H. Several factors should be considered by a manager when choosing between the variable and absorption costing methods.

1. A weakness of the absorption costing method is its inability to dovetail well with CVP analysis. It is not possible, for example, to compute a break-even point under the absorption costing method unless an assumption is made that inventory levels will not change.

2. Advocates of variable costing argue that it provides more useful cost information for pricing decisions than does absorption costing.

3. Absorption costing is the generally accepted method for external reporting and for preparing income tax returns. Variable costing is usually limited to internal use in a company.

I. When companies employ JIT inventory methods, problems with net income under absorption costing are either eliminated or become insignificant.

1. The erratic movement of net income under absorption costing, and the differences in net income between absorption and variable costing, arise because of changing levels of inventory. Under JIT, goods are produced strictly to customers' orders, so inventories are largely eliminated.

2. Since inventories are largely eliminated, changes in inventories are insignificant. Thus, there is little opportunity for fixed manufacturing overhead costs to be shifted between periods under absorption costing. Thus, net income will be essentially the same whether variable and absorption costing is used, and the erratic movement in net income under absorption costing will be largely eliminated.

REVIEW AND SELF TEST
Questions and Exercises

True or False

For each of the following statements, enter a T or an F in the blank to indicate whether the statement is true or false.

___ 1. Variable costing focuses on cost behavior in computing unit product costs.

___ 2. Under variable costing, variable selling and administrative expenses are treated as product costs.

___ 3. Product costs under the absorption costing method consist of direct materials, direct labor, and both variable and fixed manufacturing overhead.

___ 4. Selling and administrative expenses are treated as period costs under both the variable costing and absorption costing methods.

___ 5. Fixed manufacturing overhead costs are treated the same way under both the variable costing and absorption costing methods.

___ 6. Advocates of variable costing argue that fixed manufacturing overhead costs are incurred in order to have the capacity to produce and are not part of the cost of producing any particular unit.

___ 7. Under absorption costing it is possible to defer some of the fixed manufacturing overhead costs of the current period to future periods.

___ 8. Advocates of variable costing argue that fixed manufacturing overhead costs should be expensed as incurred (i.e., treated as period costs) since fixed manufacturing overhead costs have no future service potential.

___ 9. Variable costing will always produce a higher net income figure than will absorption costing.

___ 10. When production and sales are equal, the same net income will be reported regardless of whether variable costing or absorption costing is being used.

___ 11. When production exceeds sales, the net income reported under absorption costing will generally be greater than the net income reported under variable costing.

___ 12. When production is less than sales, the net income reported under absorption costing will generally be less than the net income reported under variable costing.

___ 13. When production exceeds sales, fixed manufacturing overhead costs are released from inventory under absorption costing.

___ 14. When sales exceed production, fixed manufacturing overhead costs are released from inventory under absorption costing.

___ 15. Changes in the level of production do not affect net income under the variable costing method.

___ 16. When sales are constant but the level of production fluctuates, the absorption costing method will produce a more stable net income pattern than will the variable costing method.

___ 17. The variable costing method is not generally acceptable for external reporting or for income tax purposes.

___ 18. Absorption costing data are generally better suited for cost-volume-profit analysis than variable costing data.

Multiple Choice

Choose the best answer or response by placing the identifying letter in the space provided.

___ 1. White Company manufactures a single product and has the following cost structure:

Variable costs per unit:	
Direct materials	$3
Direct labor	4
Variable manufacturing overhead	1
Variable selling and admin. expense	2
Fixed costs per month:	
Fixed manufacturing overhead	$100,000
Fixed selling & admin.	60,000

The company normally produces 20,000 units each month. The unit product cost under absorption costing is: a) $10; b) $13; c) $15; d) $12.

___ 2. Refer to the data in question 1 above. The unit product cost under variable costing would be: a) $8; b) $10; c) $13; d) $11.

___ 3. Refer to the data in question 1 above. Assume there are no beginning inventories and 20,000 units are produced and 19,000 units are sold in a month. If the unit selling price is $20, what is the net income under absorption costing for the month? a) $30,000; b) $38,000; c) $35,000; d) $42,000.

___ 4. Refer to the data in question 1 above. Assume there are no beginning inventories and 20,000 units are produced and 19,000 units are sold in a month. If the unit selling price is $20, what is the net income under variable costing for the month? a) $30,000; b) $38,000; c) $35,000; d) $42,000.

___ 5. Which of the following costs are treated as period costs under the variable costing method? a) fixed manufacturing overhead and both variable and fixed selling and administrative expenses; b) both variable and fixed manufacturing overhead; c) only fixed manufacturing overhead and fixed selling and administrative expenses.

___ 6. When production exceeds sales, fixed manufacturing overhead costs: a) are released from inventory under absorption costing; b) are deferred in inventory under absorption costing; c) are released from inventory under variable costing; d) are deferred in inventory under variable costing.

___ 7. When sales are constant but production fluctuates: a) net income will be erratic under variable costing; b) absorption costing will always show a net loss; c) variable costing will always show a positive net income; d) net income will be erratic under absorption costing.

___ 8. Last year, Peck Company produced 10,000 units and sold 9,000 units. Fixed manufacturing overhead costs were $20,000, and variable manufacturing overhead costs were $3 per unit. For the year, one would expect net income under the absorption costing method to be: a) $2,000 more than net income under the variable costing method; b) $5,000 more than net income under the variable costing method; c) $2,000 less than net income under the variable costing method; d) $5,000 less than net income under the variable costing method.

Exercises

8-1. Selected data relating to the operations of Dole Company for last year are given below:

Units in beginning inventory	-0-
Units produced	40,000
Units sold	35,000
Variable costs per unit:	
Direct materials	$7
Direct labor	6
Manufacturing overhead	3
Selling and administration	2
Fixed costs:	
Manufacturing overhead	$160,000
Selling and administration	140,000

a. Assume that the company uses absorption costing.

Compute the unit product cost. .... $__________

Determine the value of the ending inventory. .... $__________

b. Assume that the company uses variable costing.

Compute the unit product cost. .... $__________

Determine the value of the ending inventory. .... $__________

c. Which method would show the highest net income, variable costing or absorption costing? By how much? .... $__________

8-2. The Hodex Company manufactures and sells a unique product that has been quickly accepted by consumers. The results of last month's operations are shown below (absorption costing basis):

Sales (10,000 units @ $20)	$200,000
Less cost of goods sold (10,000 units @ $14)	140,000
Gross margin	60,000
Less selling and administrative expenses	45,000
Net Income	$ 15,000

Variable selling and administrative expenses are $2 per unit. Variable manufacturing costs total $10 per unit, and fixed manufacturing overhead costs total $48,000 per month. There was no beginning inventory. The company produced 12,000 units during the month.

a. Redo the company's income statement in the contribution format, using variable costing.

Sales		$______
Less variable expenses:		
Variable cost of goods sold:		
Beginning inventory	$______	
Cost of goods manufactured	______	
Goods available for sale	______	
Less ending inventory	______	
Variable cost of goods sold	______	
Variable selling & admin.	______	______
Contribution margin		______
Less fixed expenses:		
Fixed manufacturing overhead	______	
Fixed selling and administrative	______	______
Net Income		$______

b. Reconcile the variable costing and absorption costing net income figures:

Variable costing net income	$______
____________________	
____________________	______
Absorption costing net income	$______

8-3. **Critical thought writing exercise:** Lake Company uses absorption costing in preparing statements for its annual report to stockholders. Last year, the company had $10,000,000 in sales and reported a $400,000 loss in its annual report. According to a CVP analysis prepared for management's use (using variable costing), $10,000,000 in sales is the break-even point for the company. Based on these data, was the company's ending inventory greater than, less than, or equal to its beginning inventory? Explain your answer.

Answers to Questions and Exercises

True or False

1. T Variable costing includes direct materials, direct labor, and variable manufacturing overhead as product costs.

2. F Both variable and fixed selling and administrative expenses are period costs under variable costing, the same as under absorption costing. The only difference between the two costing methods lies in their treatment of fixed manufacturing overhead.

3. T All manufacturing costs are included as product costs under absorption costing.

4. T Selling and administrative expenses are never treated as product costs under either costing method.

5. F Under variable costing, fixed manufacturing overhead costs are treated as period costs; under absorption costing, fixed manufacturing overhead costs are treated as product costs.

6. T Advocates of variable costing argue that fixed manufacturing overhead costs are incurred in order to have the capacity to produce and are not incurred in order to make any particular unit.

7. T Fixed manufacturing overhead costs will be deferred to the future under absorption costing whenever production exceeds sales.

8. T Fixed manufacturing overhead costs are viewed as having no future service potential since the incurrence of such costs in one year will not affect the incurrence of the same costs in a following year.

9. F Variable costing will produce a higher net income figure than absorption costing only when sales exceed production.

10. T The reason is that when sales and production are equal, there is no chance for fixed manufacturing overhead cost to be deferred in (or released from) inventory under absorption costing.

11. T When production exceeds sales, fixed manufacturing overhead cost is deferred in inventory under absorption costing, thus causing net income to be higher than under variable costing.

12. T When production is less than sales, fixed manufacturing overhead cost is released from inventory under absorption costing, thus causing net income to be lower than under variable costing.

13. F When production exceeds sales, fixed manufacturing overhead costs are deferred in inventory under absorption costing as units of product are added to the inventory account. This point is illustrated in Year 2 in Exhibit 8-3 (under the absorption costing part of the exhibit).

14. T When sales exceed production, units are taken out of inventory, thus releasing fixed manufacturing overhead costs that were previously deferred. This point is illustrated in Year 3 in Exhibit 8-3 (under the absorption costing part of the exhibit).

15. T Changes in the number of units sold—not produced—can affect net income under the variable costing method.

16. F If production fluctuates, the absorption costing method will produce an erratic net income pattern. The reason is that fixed manufacturing overhead cost will be shifted into and out of inventory as production goes up and down.

17. T Variable costing is used internally by managers for planning and decision making purposes.

18. F The reverse is true—variable costing data are better suited for CVP analysis than absorption costing data.

Chapter 8

Multiple Choice

1. b The computations are:

Variable manufacturing costs ($3+$4+$1)	$ 8
Fixed manufacturing costs ($100,000 ÷ 20,000 units)	5
Total unit product cost	$13

2. a Only the variable manufacturing costs are treated as product costs under the variable costing method. Thus, the unit product cost is $3 + $4 + $1 = $8.

3. c The absorption costing net income is computed as follows:

Sales	$380,000
Cost of goods sold:	
Beginning inventory	-0-
Cost of goods manufactured	260,000
Goods available for sale	260,000
Less ending inventory	13,000
Cost of goods sold	247,000
Gross margin	133,000
Less selling & admin. expenses:	
Variable selling & admin.	38,000
Fixed selling & admin.	60,000
Total selling & admin.	98,000
Net income	$ 35,000

4. a The variable costing net income is computed as follows:

Sales	$380,000
Less variable expenses:	
Variable cost of goods sold:	
Beginning inventory	-0-
Variable manuf. costs	160,000
Goods available for sale	160,000
Less ending inventory	8,000
Variable cost of goods sold	152,000
Variable selling & admin.	38,000
Total variable expenses	190,000
Contribution margin	190,000
Less fixed expenses:	
Fixed manuf. overhead	100,000
Fixed selling & admin.	60,000
Total fixed expenses	160,000
Net income	$ 30,000

5. a Fixed manufacturing overhead cost is expensed as incurred under variable costing. Also, both variable and fixed selling and administrative expenses are always treated as period costs under both variable or absorption costing.

6. b When production exceeds sales, units are added to inventory. Thus, fixed manufacturing overhead costs are deferred in inventory under absorption costing. See Year 2 in Exhibit 8-3.

7. d When production fluctuates, net income will be erratic under absorption costing since fixed manufacturing overhead costs will be shifted into and out of inventory as production goes up and down.

8. a Under the absorption costing method, fixed manufacturing overhead cost per unit will be: $20,000 ÷ 10,000 units produced = $2. If only 9,000 units are sold, then 1,000 units will go into inventory. Thus, under absorption costing, $2,000 in fixed manufacturing overhead cost will be deferred in inventory ($2 x 1,000 units = $2,000). Net income will therefore be $2,000 more under absorption costing than under variable costing.

Exercises

8-1. a.

Direct materials	$ 7
Direct labor	6
Variable manufacturing overhead	3
Fixed manufacturing overhead ($160,000 ÷ 40,000 units)	4
Unit product cost	$20
Ending inventory (5,000 units x $20)	$100,000

b.

Direct materials	$ 7
Direct labor	6
Variable manufacturing overhead	3
Unit product cost	$16
Ending inventory (5,000 units x $16)	$80,000

c. Absorption costing would show the highest net income, by $20,000. The reason is that the inventory has increased by 5,000 units, and each unit has taken $4 of fixed manufacturing overhead cost into inventory with it. This removes these costs from the income statement.

8-2. a.

Sales (10,000 units @ $20)		$200,000
Less variable expenses:		
Variable cost of goods sold:		
Beginning inventory	$ -0-	
Cost of goods manufactured @ $10	120,000	
Goods available for sale	120,000	
Less ending inventory	20,000	
Variable cost of goods sold @ $10	100,000	
Variable selling & admin. @ $2	20,000	120,000
Contribution margin		80,000
Less fixed expenses:		
Fixed manufacturing overhead	48,000	
Fixed selling and administrative	25,000*	73,000
Net Income		$ 7,000

*$45,000 - (10,000 units x $2) = $25,000

b.

Variable costing net income	$ 7,000
Add: fixed manufacturing overhead cost deferred in inventory under absorption costing: 2,000 units x $4*	8,000
Absorption costing net income	$ 15,000

*$48,000 ÷ 12,000 units produced = $4 per unit.

8-3. Since Lake Company reported a loss when its sales were at the break-even level, it must have had fixed manufacturing overhead costs released from inventory for the year under the absorption costing approach. (The break-even point is computed assuming either that variable costing is used or that there is no change in inventory.) Therefore, the company's inventory level for the year decreased. When inventory levels decrease, fixed manufacturing overhead costs are released from inventory under absorption costing. Thus, the fixed manufacturing overhead costs released from inventory would have resulted in a loss for the year, even though from a variable costing point of view the company should have broken even.

Chapter 9

Profit Planning

Chapter Study Suggestions

Before reading the chapter material, study the flow of budget data in Exhibit 9-2. This exhibit provides a good overview of the chapter and the budgeting process. Notice particularly how nearly all budgets eventually impact on the cash budget. As suggested by this exhibit, the cash budget is a key budget that serves to tie together much of the budget data in an organization. Schedule 8 in the text contains an example of a cash budget. It would be helpful to look over the contents of this schedule before reading the rest of the chapter.

Schedules 1 and 2, containing the sales and production budgets, are also very important and your homework assignments are very likely to concentrate on these two budgets. As you proceed through the chapter, you will see that all other budgets depend in some way on the sales budget in Schedule 1. Notice a Schedule of Expected Cash Collections accompanies the sales budget. Make sure you understand how the production budget is put together based on the sales budget and desired inventory levels.

CHAPTER HIGHLIGHTS

A. Profit planning is accomplished in most organizations with budgets. A *budget* is a detailed plan for the acquisition and use of financial and other resources over a specified time period.

1. The master budget is a financial summary of all phases of a company's plans and goals for the future. It sets specific targets for sales, production, and financing, activities and outlines how these targets are to be met.

2. There are two steps in the budgeting process — planning and control.

a. *Planning* involves developing objectives and formulating steps to achieve these objectives.

b. *Control* involves the steps taken by management to attempt to ensure that the objectives set down at the planning stage are attained.

3. There are a number of benefits from budgeting that include:

a The budget provides a vehicle for *communicating* management's plans throughout the entire organization.

b. The budgeting process forces managers to *think ahead* and to *formalize* their planning efforts.

c. The budgeting process provides a means of *allocating resources* to those parts of the organization where they can be used most effectively.

d. Budgeting uncovers potential *bottlenecks* before they occur.

e. The budget *coordinates* the activities of the entire organization by *integrating* the plans and objectives of the various parts.

f. The budget provides definite goals and objectives that serve as *benchmarks* for evaluating subsequent performance.

B. Most of this chapter and the next three chapters centers on the concept of *responsibility accounting*. The basic idea behind responsibility accounting is that each manager's performance should be judged by how well he or she manages those items—and only those items—under his or her control.

1. In the context of budgeting, each manager is assigned responsibility for those items of revenues and costs in the budget that the manager is able to control. The manager is then held responsible for deviations between budgeted goals and actual results.

2. Responsibility accounting personalizes accounting information by looking at costs from a *personal control* standpoint. This concept is central to any effective planning and control system.

3. A premise of responsibility accounting is that effective budget data can be generated as a basis for evaluating managerial performance. The purpose of this chapter is to illustrate the steps involved in budget preparation.

C. Budget preparation is a complex task requiring the cooperative effort of all levels of management.

1. One of the first steps is the choice of a budget period. Operating budgets (the budgets discussed in this chapter) are ordinarily set to cover a one-year period.

a. The budget year is generally divided into quarters, with the quarters subdivided into months.

b. Budgeting may follow a continuous or perpetual process. A *continuous budget* is a twelve-month budget that rolls forward one month as the current month is completed. This stabilizes the planning horizon by keeping the budget set a full twelve months ahead.

2. Capital budgets, involving the purchase of plant and equipment, have a longer planning horizon, extending many years into the future.

3. The most successful budget programs are those that fully involve managers in setting their own budgets.

a. When managers participate in preparing their own budgets, the budgets are said to be *self-imposed*. A manager is more likely to be committed to meeting the budget if he or she has played a central role in its development.

b. Notice from Exhibit 9-1 that the flow of budget data in an organization should be *upward*, rather than from top management downward.

4. A key element in a successful budgeting program is how top management *uses* budgeted data.

a. Employees will not be supportive of budgeting if it is used as a way of finding someone to blame for a problem.

b. The budget should be used as a positive instrument for aiding the company in setting objectives and in measuring results.

D. The *master budget* is a network consisting of many interdependent budgets. Exhibit 9-2 illustrates such a network. Study this exhibit carefully.

1. The *sales budget* is the beginning point in the budgeting process. It details the expected sales, in both units and dollars, for the budget period.

a. The sales budget is derived from the *sales forecast,* which contains general data about the economy, industry, market, competition and other factors likely to influence demand for the company's products and services.

b. The sales budget is supported by a "Schedule of Expected Cash Collections," which shows the anticipated cash inflow from sales and collections of accounts receivable for the budget period. Schedule 1 in the text illustrates such a schedule.

2. In a manufacturing firm, the sales budget is followed by the *production budget,* which shows what must be produced to meet both sales needs and inventory needs for the budget period. The format for the production budget is:

Expected sales in units	XXX
Add: Desired ending inventory in units	XXX
Total needs	XXX
Deduct: Beginning inventory in units	XXX
Required production in units	XXX

a. An example of a production budget appears in Schedule 2 in the text. Note that the production budget deals with finished goods rather than with raw materials. Study this schedule carefully.

b. Note that the "Year" column is not simply the sum of the figures for the Quarters in Schedule 2. The desired ending inventory for the year is the desired ending inventory for the 4th quarter. And the beginning inventory for the year is the beginning inventory for the 1st quarter. Warning: Students often overlook this important detail.

3. In a merchandising firm such as a clothing store, the sales budget is followed by a *merchandise purchases budget* instead of a production budget. This budget details the amount of goods that must be purchased from suppliers to meet customer demand and to maintain adequate stocks. The format for the merchandise purchases budget is (in units or dollars):

Budgeted cost of goods sold	XXX
Add: Desired ending inventory	XXX
Total needs	XXX
Deduct: Beginning inventory	XXX
Required purchases	XXX

4. In a manufacturing firm, the *direct materials budget* follows the production budget. It details the amount of raw materials that must be acquired to support production and to provide for adequate inventories. The format for the direct materials budget is:

Raw materials required for production	XXX
Add: Desired ending inventory	XXX
Total raw materials needs	XXX
Less: Beginning inventory	XXX
Raw materials to be purchased	XXX

a. The direct materials budget should be accompanied by a "Schedule of Expected Cash Disbursements" for raw materials.

b. An example of the direct materials budget appears in Schedule 3. As with the production budget, note that the "Year" column is not simply the sum of the figures for the Quarters.

5. In a manufacturing firm, a *direct labor budget* also follows the production budget. This budget details direct labor requirements for the budget period.

6. In a manufacturing firm, a *manufacturing overhead budget* also follows the production budget and details all of the production costs that will be required other than direct materials and direct labor.

7. In a manufacturing firm, the *ending finished goods inventory budget* provides computations of unit product costs and of the carrying value of the ending inventory.

8. In all types of companies, a *selling and administrative expense* budget is prepared that lists

expenses falling under the selling and administrative categories.

9. The *cash budget* summarizes all cash inflows and cash outflows appearing on the various budgets. The cash budget contains four major sections: cash receipts; cash disbursements; cash excess or deficiency; and financing.

a. The cash budget is one of the key budgets in the planning process and in many companies would be the single most important result of the budgeting process. Study the example in Schedule 8 with care, noting particularly how the financing section is handled.

b. As with the production budget and the direct materials budget, the "Year" column in Schedule 8 is not simply the sum of the figures for the Quarters. The beginning cash balance for the year is the beginning cash balance for the 1st quarter. And the ending cash balance for the year is the ending cash balance for the 4th quarter.

c. The cash budget is an extremely important document. It can provide critical advance warnings of potential cash problems. The cash budget allows managers to arrange beforehand for financing — which is often essential. Potential lenders are more likely to provide financing if managers appear to be in control and looking ahead rather than simply reacting to crises.

10. The budgeting process culminates with the preparation of a *budgeted income statement* and a *budgeted balance sheet*.

E. There is a distinction between JIT production and *JIT purchasing*.

1. JIT production can only be used by manufacturing companies, since it focuses on the processes used to manufacture goods.

2. JIT purchasing can be used by any organization with inventories — retail, wholesale, service, or manufacturing.

3. There are five key features of JIT purchasing.

a. Goods are delivered immediately before demand or use.

b. The number of suppliers is greatly reduced.

c. Long-term agreements are signed with suppliers, and these agreements stipulate the delivery schedule, the quality of the goods, and the price to be paid.

d. Incoming goods from suppliers are not inspected for defects.

e. Payments are not made for each shipment; rather, payments are periodically "batched" for each supplier.

4. Adopting JIT purchasing does not require that a company eliminate all inventories. But the amount of time that a good spends on the shelf or in a warehouse can be greatly reduced

F. In *zero-base budgeting* managers are required to start at zero budget levels every year and justify all costs as if the programs involved were being initiated for the first time. In traditional budgeting, only the changes in budgets from year to year are closely scrutinized.

1. The manager prepares "decision packages" that rank activities according to their importance and cost.

2. Opponents of the zero-base approach argue that a zero-base review every year is too costly and is likely to result in a less-than-thorough review.

Appendix 9A: Economic Order Quantity and the Reorder Point

A. There are three groups of costs associated with inventory: the costs of ordering inventory, the costs of carrying inventory, and the costs of not carrying sufficient inventory. In a broad, conceptual sense, the "right" inventory level is the level that minimizes the total of these three classes of costs.

B. Inventory cost minimization has two dimensions — how much to order and how often to do it. The "how much to order" is referred to as the economic order quantity, or EOQ.

1. Computing the economic order quantity is a matter of minimizing the first two classes of costs above — the costs of ordering inventory and the costs of carrying inventory.

2. If orders are placed more frequently for smaller amounts, the average number of units in inventory will fall. This will have the effect of *increasing* the total ordering costs (since more

orders are placed) and *decreasing* the total carrying costs.

3. The formula for finding the economic order quantity is:

$$E = \sqrt{\frac{2QP}{C}}$$

where: E = the economic order quantity; Q = the annual quantity used; P = the cost of placing one order; and C = the annual cost of carrying one unit in stock.

4. The EOQ formula can also be used to find the optimal production lot size. The problem with running small production lots is that each time a new lot is processed, setup costs are incurred to change over from one product to another. The economic production lot size can be found by inserting the set-up costs in place of the "cost of placing one order" in the above formula.

C. The "how often to place orders" dimension of inventory problem seeks to minimize the likelihood that the company will run out of inventory.

1. If the level of inventory is allowed to get too low, the inventory may be exhausted before a new shipment is received from suppliers. To prevent this, a *reorder point* is set that indicates the level of inventory at which an order should be initiated.

a. The lead time affects the reorder point. *Lead time* is the interval of time between when an order is placed and when it is finally received from the supplier. The larger the lead time, the more protective inventory the company requires and hence the higher the reorder point.

b. The *rate of usage* of the item also affects the reorder point. The higher the rate of usage, the more protective inventory the company will require.

c. If the rate of usage during the lead time is known with certainty, the reorder point is determined by the following formula:

Reorder point = Lead time X Average usage

2. If usage during the lead time is erratic, then a safety stock must be carried. The safety stock protects the company from stock-outs in the worst case scenario — when the rate of usage is at its maximum.

a. The safety stock is computed as follows when the lead time is measured in days:

Maximum expected usage ...	XX units per day
Less average usage	XX units per day
Excess	XX units per day
Lead time	x XX days
Safety stock	XX units

b. With safety stocks, the formula for the reorder point becomes:

$$\text{Reorder point} = \left(\text{Lead time} \times \text{Average usage}\right) + \text{Safety stock}$$

or, more simply,

Reorder point = Lead time X Maximum usage

c. The reorder point and the safety stock are both shown graphically in Exhibit 9A-3.

REVIEW AND SELF TEST
Questions and Exercises

True or False

For each of the following statements, enter a T or an F in the blank to indicate whether the statement is true or false.

___ 1. The usual starting point in budgeting is to make a forecast of sales.

___ 2. A self-imposed budget is one prepared by top management and imposed on other management levels as it is passed downward through an organization.

___ 3. Budgets are essentially planning devices, rather than control devices.

___ 4. The basic idea behind responsibility accounting is that each manager's performance should be judged by how well he or she manages those items directly under his or her control.

___ 5. Operating budgets generally have long time horizons and may extend many years into the future.

___ 6. A continuous or perpetual budget is one that maintains a constant twelve month planning horizon.

___ 7. Ending inventories occur because an organization is unable to sell all that it had planned to sell during a period.

___ 8. Only manufacturing companies use JIT purchasing.

___ 9. (Appendix 9A) The economic order quantity formula minimizes the sum of ordering costs and the costs of carrying inventory.

___ 10. (Appendix 9A) The lead time is a critical factor in computing the reorder point.

Multiple Choice

Choose the best answer or response by placing the identifying letter in the space provided.

___ 1. Most other budgets are dependent in some way on the: a) cash budget; b) income statement; c) direct materials budget; d) sales budget.

___ 2. If the beginning cash balance is $15,000, the required ending cash balance is $12,000, cash disbursements are $125,000, and cash collections from customers are $90,000, the company must: a) borrow $32,000; b) borrow $20,000; c) borrow $8,000; d) borrow $38,000.

___ 3. Archer Company has budgeted sales of 30,000 units in April, 40,000 units in May, and 60,000 units in June. The company has 6,000 units on hand on April 1. If the company requires an ending inventory equal to 20 percent of the following month's sales, production during May should equal: a) 32,000 units; b) 44,000 units; c) 36,000 units; d) 40,000 units.

___ 4. Refer to the data for Archer Company in question 3. Each unit requires 3 pounds of a material. A total of 24,000 pounds of the material were on hand on April 1, and the company requires materials on hand at the end of each month equal to 25 percent of the following month's production needs. For April, the company should purchase how many pounds of the material? a) 105,000; b) 19,000; c) 87,000; d) 6,000.

___ 5. Actual sales in Ward Company were $30,000 in June, $50,000 in July, and $70,000 in August. Sales in September are expected to be $60,000. If 30 percent of a month's sales are collected in the month of sale, 50 percent in the first month after sale, and 15 percent in the second month after sale, then cash receipts for September are budgeted to be: a) $60,500; b) $62,000; c) $57,000; d) $70,000.

___ 6. Beecher Inc. is planning to purchase inventory for resale costing $90,000 in October, $70,000 in November, and $40,000 in December. The company pays for 40% of its purchases in the month of purchase and 60% in the month following purchase. What would be the budgeted cash disbursements for purchases of inventory in December? a) $40,000; b) $70,000; c) $58,000; d) $200,000.

___ 7. (Appendix 9A) An item that costs $40 to purchase has an annual carrying cost of $2 per unit. The ordering cost is $16 per order and the annual usage of the item is 10,000 units. What is the economic order quantity for the item? a) 10,000 units; b) 250 units; c) 400 units; d) 500 units.

___ 8. (Appendix 9A) The average daily usage of an item is 10 units, the maximum daily usage is 15 units, and the lead time is 5 days for an order. What is the reorder point with safety stock for the item? a) 50 units; b) 75 units; c) 150 units; d) 100 units.

Chapter 9

Exercises

9-1. Billings Company produces and sells a single product. Expected sales for the next four months are given below:

	April	*May*	*June*	*July*
Sales in units	10,000	12,000	15,000	9,000

The company needs a production budget for the second quarter. Experience indicates that end-of-month inventories should equal 10 percent of the following month's sales in units. At the end of March, 1,000 units were on hand. Complete the following production budget for the quarter:

	April	*May*	*June*	*Quarter*
Budgeted sales	______	______	______	______
Add: Desired ending inventory	______	______	______	______
Total needs	______	______	______	______
Deduct: Beginning inventory	______	______	______	______
Units to be produced	______	______	______	______

9-2. Dodero Company's production budget for the next four months is given below:

	July	*August*	*September*	*October*
Production in units	15,000	18,000	20,000	16,000

Each unit of product uses five ounces of raw materials. At the end of June, 11,250 ounces of material were on hand. The company wants to maintain an inventory of materials equal to 15 percent of the following month's production needs.

Complete the following materials purchases budget for the third quarter:

	July	*August*	*September*	*Quarter*
Budgeted production in units	______	______	______	______
Raw material needs per unit	______	______	______	______
Production needs	______	______	______	______
Add: Desired ending inventory	______	______	______	______
Total needs	______	______	______	______
Deduct: Beginning inventory	______	______	______	______
Raw materials to be purchased	______	______	______	______

9-3. Whitefish Company budgets its cash two months at a time. Budgeted cash disbursements for March and April, respectively, follow: for inventory purchases, $90,000 and $82,000; for selling and administrative expenses (includes $5,000 depreciation each month), $75,000 and $70,000; for equipment purchases, $15,000 and $6,000; and for dividend payments, $5,000 and $-0-. Budgeted cash collections from customers are $150,000 and $185,000 for March and April, respectively. The company will begin March with a $10,000 cash balance on hand. There must be a minimum cash balance of $5,000 at the end of each month. If needed, the company can borrow money at 12 percent per year. All borrowings are at the beginning of a month, and all repayments are at the end of a month. Interest is paid only when principal is being repaid.

Complete the following cash budget for March and April:

	March	*April*	*Two Months*
Cash balance, beginning			
Add: Collections from customers			
Total cash available			
Less disbursements:			
______________________			
______________________			
______________________			
______________________			
Total disbursements			
Excess (deficiency) of cash available over disbursements			
Financing:			
Borrowings (at beginning)			
Repayments (at ending)			
Interest (12% per year)			
Total financing			
Cash balance, ending			

9-4. (Appendix 9A) Glidden Products produces a number of consumer items, including a microwave oven. A vital component part for the ovens is purchased from an outside supplier. In total, the company purchases 2,700 of the parts each year. It costs approximately $15 to place an order, and it costs $0.40 to carry one part in inventory for a year. The company works 50 weeks per year.

a. Compute the economic order quantity for the part, using the following formula:

$$E = \sqrt{\frac{2QP}{C}}$$

$$E = \sqrt{\frac{\qquad}{\qquad}}$$

E =

b. It takes about three weeks to receive an order of parts from the supplier. The company normally uses 54 parts each week in production; however, usage can be as much as 75 parts per week.

Compute the safety stock:

Maximum expected usage per week	________ parts
Average usage per week	________ parts
Excess	________ parts
Lead time..............	X ________
Safety stock	________ parts

c. Compute the reorder point:

Average weekly usage	________ parts
Lead time	X ________
Normal usage	________ parts
Safety stock	________ parts
Reorder point	________ parts

d. Referring to your answers above, explain when and in what quantity orders will be made:

....

....

....

9-5. **Critical thought writing exercise:** "The most important reason a company prepares a cash budget is to see how much cash it will have in the bank at the end of the year." Explain why you do or do not agree with this statement.

....

....

....

....

....

....

....

....

....

Answers to Questions and Exercises

True or False

1. T A forecast of sales is needed as a basis for establishing a company's sales budget. The sales budget, in turn, is the basis for most of the other documents in the master budget.

2. F A self-imposed budget is one in which a manager prepares his or her own budget estimates.

3. F Budgeting involves both planning and control. Once a budget is set, it then becomes a control device. It is the benchmark for assessing actual results.

4. T This is a clear, straightforward statement of the purpose of responsibility accounting.

5. F Operating budgets generally have planning horizons of one year or less.

6. T Under a continuous or perpetual budget, a new month is added on the end as the current month is completed; thus, a twelve month planning horizon is maintained.

7. F Ending inventories are carefully planned if a company is following good budget procedures.

8. F JIT purchasing is used by all types of organizations that have inventories.

9. T This point is illustrated in Exhibit 9A-2.

10. T The lead time is critical since there must be inventories on hand during the lead time to support production or sales. Exhibit 9A-3 illustrates this point.

Multiple Choice

1. d This point is illustrated in Exhibit 9-2.

2. a The computations are:

Beginning cash balance....	$ 15,000
Cash receipts....................	90,000
Cash available..................	105,000
Cash disbursements.........	125,000
Deficiency of cash.............	$(20,000)

Since the company desires an ending cash balance of $12,000, the company must borrow $32,000 to make up for the cash deficiency of $20,000.

3. b The computations are:

	April	*May*	*June*
Budgeted sales	30,000	40,000	60,000
Desired ending inventory	8,000	12,000	
Total needs	38,000	52,000	
Less beginning inventory	6,000	8,000	
Required production	32,000	44,000	

4. a The computations are:

	April	*May*
Required production..................	32,000	44,000
Material per unit.........................	X 3 lbs	X 3 lbs
Production needs........................	96,000	132,000
Desired ending inventory	33,000	
Total needs	129,000	
Less beginning inventory	24,000	
Required purchases	105,000	

5. a The computations are:

September sales, $60,000 X 30%	$18,000
August sales, $70,000 X 50%	35,000
July sales, $50,000 X 15%	7,500
Total cash receipts	$60,500

6. c The computations are:

November purchases \$70,000 X 60%.........	\$42,000
December purchases \$40,000 X 40%..........	16,000
Total cash disbursements............................	\$58,000

7. c The computations are:

$$E = \sqrt{\frac{2QP}{C}} = \sqrt{\frac{2(10{,}000)(\$16)}{\$2}} = 400 \text{ units}$$

8. b The computations are:

Average usage per day..............................	10 units
Lead time in days	X 5
Reorder point without safety stock	50 units

Maximum usage per day...........................	15 units
Average usage per day..............................	10 units
Excess	5 units
Lead time in days	X 5
Safety stock..	25 units

Reorder point with safety stock = 50 + 25
= 75 units

Exercises

9-1.

	April	*May*	*June*	*Second Quarter*
Budgeted sales	10,000	12,000	15,000	37,000
Add: Desired ending inventory	1,200	1,500	900	900
Total needs	11,200	13,500	15,900	37,900
Deduct: Beginning inventory	1,000	1,200	1,500	1,000
Units to be produced	10,200	12,300	14,400	36,900

9-2.

	July	*August*	*September*	*Third Quarter*
Budgeted production in units	15,000	18,000	20,000	53,000
Raw material needs per unit	X 5 oz	X 5 oz	X 5 oz	X 5 oz
Production needs in ounces	75,000	90,000	100,000	265,000
Add: Desired ending inventory	13,500	15,000	12,000*	12,000
Total needs in ounces	88,500	105,000	112,000	277,000
Deduct: Beginning inventory	11,250	13,500	15,000	11,250
Raw materials to be purchased	77,250	91,500	97,000	265,750

*16,000 units for October X 5 oz = 80,000 oz X 15%= 12,000 oz

9-3.

	March	*April*	*Two Months*
Cash balance, beginning	$ 10,000	$ 5,000	$ 10,000
Add: Collections from customers	150,000	185,000	335,000
Total cash available	160,000	190,000	345,000
Less Disbursements:			
For inventory purchases	90,000	82,000	172,000
For selling and administrative expenses	70,000	65,000	135,000
For equipment purchases	15,000	6,000	21,000
For dividends	5,000	—	5,000
Total disbursements	180,000	153,000	333,000
Excess (deficiency) of cash available over cash disbursements	(20,000)	37,000	12,000
Financing:			
Borrowings (at beginning)	25,000	—	25,000
Repayments (at ending)	—	(25,000)	(25,000)
Interest (12% per year)	—	(500)*	(500)
Total financing	25,000	(25,500)	(500)
Cash balance, ending	$ 5,000	$ 11,500	$11,500

* $25,000 X 12% X 2/12 = $500

9-4. a. $E = \sqrt{\frac{2QP}{C}} = \sqrt{\frac{2(2{,}700)(\$15)}{\$0.40}} = \sqrt{202{,}500} = 450$ parts

b.

Maximum expected usage per week	75	parts
Average usage per week	54	parts
Excess	21	parts
Lead time	X 3	weeks
Safety stock	63	parts

c.

Average weekly usage	54	parts
Lead time	X 3	weeks
Normal usage	162	parts
Safety stock	63	parts
Reorder point	225	parts

d. An order for 450 parts will be placed when the stock on hand drops to 225 parts.

9-5. This is not the most important reason a company prepares a cash budget, although it is one reason. The most important reason is to see the inflows and outflows of cash and additional cash needs *during* the year. By knowing cash needs during the year, a company will be able to foresee periods in which borrowing will be required, periods in which borrowing can be repaid, and any problems that may be developing regarding the company's uses of cash. Thus, bank loans and other sources of financing can be anticipated and arranged well in advance of the actual time of need, and problems can be anticipated and perhaps avoided.

Chapter 10

Standard Costs and Operating Performance Measures

Chapter Study Suggestions

The first part of the chapter deals with setting standard costs. This is important material, since it is easier to understand how standard costs are used if one first understands how they are derived. Exhibit 10-1 presents a standard cost card, which is the final product of the standard setting process. You will be using a standard cost card in the homework assignments in both this chapter and in Chapter 11, so be sure you understand what a standard cost card contains and how it is constructed.

The second part of the chapter deals with the use of standard costs in variance analysis. Exhibit 10-2 provides an overall perspective of variance analysis, and then Exhibits 10-3 through 10-6 give detailed examples of the analysis of materials, labor, and variable overhead. Notice that the figures used in the first part of the chapter to illustrate the setting of standards (see Exhibit 10-1) carry over into Exhibits 10-3, 10-4, and 10-5. As you study, follow the figures from Exhibit 10-l into the following exhibits. This will help you tie the various parts of the chapter together into one integrated whole. Also, pay particular attention to the definitions of terms.

The third part of the chapter discusses operating performance measures. Exhibit 10-9 summarizes these performance measures and is the key exhibit in this section. Spend the bulk of your study time on the delivery performance measures, which include computations of delivery cycle time, throughput, and manufacturing cycle efficiency.

The chapter concludes with a review problem that you should follow through step by step before attempting the homework material.

CHAPTER HIGHLIGHTS

A. A *standard* is a benchmark or "norm" for evaluating performance.

1. Fast food outlets set quantity standards on the amount of meat in a sandwich, and auto service centers set time standards on routine service work.

2. The broadest application of standards is found in manufacturing firms, where exacting standards relating to materials, labor, and overhead are developed for each product.

a. Standards are set for both the quantity and the price (cost) of inputs.

b. The standards are listed on a standard cost card, which indicates what the cost should be for a single unit of product.

c. Actual quantities and costs of inputs are compared to the standards shown on the standard cost card, with any differences brought to the attention of management. This is called *management by exception*.

B. Setting accurate quantity and cost standards is a vital step in the control process.

1. Many persons should be involved in setting standards: accountants, purchasing agents, industrial engineers, production supervisors, and line managers.

2. Standards tend to fall into two categories—either ideal or practical.

a. Ideal standards are those that can be attained only by working at top efficiency 100 percent of the time. They allow for no machine breakdowns or lost time.

b. Practical standards, by contrast, allow for breakdowns and normal lost time (such as for coffee breaks). Practical standards are standards that are "tight, but attainable."

c. Most managers feel that practical standards provide better motivation than ideal standards. The use of ideal standards can easily lead to frustration.

3. Direct material standards are set for both the price and quantity of inputs that go into units of product.

a. Price standards should reflect the final, delivered cost of materials. This price should include freight, handling, and other costs necessary to get the material into a condition ready to use. It should also reflect any cash discounts allowed.

b. Quantity standards should reflect the amount of material going into each finished product, as well as allowances for unavoidable waste, spoilage, and other normal inefficiencies.

4. Direct labor price and quantity standards are usually expressed in terms of labor rate and labor hours.

a. The standard direct labor rate per hour would include not only wages earned but also an allowance for fringe benefits, employment taxes, and other labor related costs.

b. The standard labor hours per unit should include allowances for coffee breaks, personal needs of employees, clean-up, and machine down time.

5. As with direct labor, the price and quantity standards for variable overhead are generally expressed in terms of a rate and hours. The rate represents the variable portion of the predetermined overhead rate. The quantity is usually expressed in terms of direct labor-hours.

6. The price and quantity standards for materials, labor, and overhead are summarized on a standard cost card.

a. Study the standard cost card in Exhibit 10-1 and trace the figures in it back through the examples on the preceding pages in the text.

b. Essentially, the standard cost per unit represents the budgeted variable production cost for a single unit of product.

C. A *variance* is the difference between standard prices and quantities on the one hand and actual prices and quantities on the other hand. The general model in Exhibit 10-2 is very helpful in variance analysis. Study this model with care.

1. Notice from the model that a price variance and a quantity variance can be computed for each of the three variable cost categories—materials, labor, and overhead.

2. Also notice from the model that variance analysis is a form of input/output analysis.

a. The inputs represent the actual cost or quantity of materials, labor, and overhead used in production; the output represents the good production of the period.

b. The *standard quantity allowed for the output* represents the amount of inputs that *should have been used* in completing the output of the period. This is a key term in the chapter!

3. Exhibit 10-3 shows the variance analysis of direct materials. As you study the exhibit, notice that the center column (Actual Quantity of Inputs, at Standard Price) plays a part in the computation of both the price and quantity variances. This is a key point in variance analysis.

a. The *materials price variance* can be expressed in formula form as:

(AQ X AP) — (AQ X SP) = Price variance
or
AQ (AP — SP) = Price variance

where:
AQ = Actual quantity of inputs purchased
AP = Actual price of inputs purchased
SP = Standard price of inputs

b. There are many possible causes of an unfavorable materials price variance including excessive freight costs, loss of quantity discounts, improper grade of materials purchased, and rush orders.

c. The *materials quantity variance* can be expressed in formula form as:

(AQ X SP) — (SQ X SP) = Quantity variance
or
SP (AQ — SQ) = Quantity variance

where:
AQ = Actual quantity of inputs used
SQ = Standard quantity of input allowed for the actual output
SP = Standard price of inputs

d. There are many possible causes of an unfavorable materials quantity variance including untrained workers, faulty machines, and low quality materials.

e. The materials price variance is generally computed when materials are purchased, whereas the quantity variance is computed when materials are used in production.

4. Exhibit 10-5 shows the variance analysis of direct labor. Notice that the format is the same as for direct materials, but the terms "rate" and "hours" are used in place of the terms "price" and "quantity".

a. The price variance for labor is called the *labor rate variance*. The formula is:

(AH x AR) — (AH X SR) = Rate variance
or
AH (AR - SR) = Rate variance

where:
AH = Actual labor hours
AR = Actual labor wage rate
SR = Standard labor wage rate

b. There are many possible causes of an unfavorable labor rate variance. The possible causes include poor assignment of workers to jobs, unplanned overtime, and pay increases.

c. The quantity variance for labor is called the *labor efficiency variance*. The formula is:

(AH X SR) — (SH X SR) = Efficiency variance
or
SR (AH - SH) = Efficiency variance

where:
AH = Actual labor hours
SH = Standard labor hours allowed for the actual output
SR = Standard labor wage rate

d. There are many possible causes of an unfavorable labor efficiency variance including poorly trained workers, poor quality materials, faulty equipment, poor supervision, and insufficient orders to keep the work force busy.

5. Exhibit 10-6 shows the variance analysis of variable manufacturing overhead. Notice that the format is the same as for direct labor.

a. The price or rate variance for variable manufacturing overhead is called the *variable overhead spending variance*. The formula for this variance is:

(AH x AR) — (AH X SR) = Spending variance
or
AH (AR - SR) = Spending variance

where:

AH = Actual hours (usually labor hours)
AR = Actual variable manufacturing overhead rate
SR = Standard variable manufacturing overhead rate

b. The quantity or efficiency variance for variable manufacturing overhead is called the *variable overhead efficiency variance*, The formula for this variance is:

(AH X SR) — (SH X SR) = Efficiency variance
or
SR (AH - SH) = Efficiency variance

where:
AH = Actual hours (usually labor hours)
SH = Standard hours allowed for the actual output
SR = Standard variable manufacturing overhead rate

D. There are advantages and disadvantages associated with the use of standard costs.

1. Standard costs facilitate the use of "management by exception." Standard costs also aid in planning. And they can be used to simplify the bookkeeping process.

2. The use of standard costs can cause a number of behavioral problems in an organization. When the focus is always on unfavorable variances, employees may feel that they are always being criticized and never congratulated for a job well done. In addition, when labor is fixed, the only way to generate more favorable labor efficiency variances is to create more output. This creates pressures to build unnecessary work in process inventory.

E. Performance in a standard cost system is communicated to management through a pyramiding system of reports.

1. Performance reports build upward, with each manager receiving information on his or her own performance, as well as on the performance of each subordinate.

2. Each manager is charged *only* with those costs over which he or she has control. Exhibit 10-7 shows how reports are structured in a standard costing system.

3. Through a system of performance reports such as shown in Exhibit 10-7, managers at each level of responsibility can see where their time and their subordinates' time can best be spent in order to control costs and achieve the company's goals.

F. Not all differences between standard costs and quantities and actual costs and quantities warrant management attention. The manager should be interested only in the differences that are significant.

1. Statistical analysis may be used to determine whether variances are significant exceptions that require further investigation. Statistical control charts, such as is illustrated in Exhibit 10-8, can be used to identify the variances that are worth investigating.

G. Traditional standards as discussed above are being supplemented, and even replaced, in some companies, by operating performance measures.

1. For companies that have heavily invested in automation, labor is less significant and tends to be more fixed. Thus, the traditional labor variances are of little use to management, and a focus on items such as the labor efficiency variance may even result in production of needless inventories that create operational problems.

2. A key objective in the new manufacturing environment is to increase quality rather than to just minimize cost. A preoccupation with items such as the materials price variance can, for example, result in the purchase of low quality materials.

3. Companies involved in TQM, TOC, JIT, and similar management approaches that stress continual improvement argue that just meeting standards is not enough.

H. Operating performance measures can be classified into five general groupings, as shown in Exhibit 10-9. Study this exhibit carefully. Make sure you understand what each of the performance measures means and whether an increase or a decrease in the performance measure is desired. The computation and use of these performance measures differs in several ways from standard costs.

1. First, the operating performance measures are often computed on an on-line basis so that management is able to monitor activities continually. On-line access to data allows problems to be identified and corrected immediately.

2. Second, many of the performance measures are computed at the plant level, rather than at a

department level in order to emphasize the importance of the plant as a system.

3. Third, managers focus on trends over time. The key objectives are progress and improvement, rather than meeting specific standards.

I. Delivery performance, is often one of the keys to success. Several key definitions relate to delivery performance in a company.

1. The *delivery cycle time* represents the amount of time required from receipt of an order from a customer to shipment of the completed goods. It consists of wait time plus throughput time, as shown in Exhibit 10-10. Study this exhibit carefully in order to understand the definitions of *Delivery Cycle Time, Throughput Time, Wait Time, Process Time, Inspection Time, Move Time,* and *Queue Time.*

2. *Throughput time* measures the amount of time required to turn raw materials into completed products. It is also known as the manufacturing cycle time.

3. The *manufacturing cycle efficiency (MCE)* is a measure of the efficiency of the production process. It is computed by the following formula:

$$\text{MCE} = \frac{\text{Value-Added (Process) Time}}{\text{Throughput (Manufacturing Cycle) Time}}$$

a. If the MCE is less than 1, non-value-added time is present in the production process. An MCE of 0.25 for example, would mean that 75% of the total production time consisted of the non-value-added activities Inspection Time, Move Time, and Queue Time.

b. By monitoring the MCE, companies aim to pare away non-value-added activities and thus get products into the hands of customers more quickly.

J. With the introduction of operating performance measures, important changes have taken place in the way standard costs are used in some companies:

1. Standard costs are used less frequently to measure performance. Instead, they are used to value inventory and determine cost of goods sold.

2. Engineered standard are often replaced either by a rolling average of actual costs or by target costs.

3. Variances are computed on a more frequent basis, and the focus is on the *trend* of the variances rather on their magnitude.

4. Standard costs are generally used only for materials and overhead, since labor often is not accounted for as a separate element of cost.

Appendix 10A: General Ledger Entries to Record Variances

A. Most companies that use standard costs prefer to make general ledger entries to record variances in the books of account. There are two reasons why this is so:

1. Entry into the accounting records gives variances a greater emphasis than is possible through informal, out-of-records computations.

2. Entry into the accounting records simplifies the bookkeeping process, by allowing companies to carry inventories at standard cost.

B. Favorable variances are recorded by credits, and unfavorable variances are recorded by debits in the accounting records. Examples follow below:

1. An entry to record an unfavorable material price variance would be:

Raw Materials	XXX	
Materials Price Variance (U)	XXX	
Accounts Payable		XXX

2. An entry to record a favorable material quantity variance would be:

Work in Process	XXX	
Materials Quantity Variance (F)		XXX
Raw Materials		XXX

3. An entry to record an unfavorable labor efficiency variance and a favorable labor rate variance be:

Work in Process	XXX	
Labor Efficiency Variance (U)	XXX	
Labor Rate Variance (F)		XXX
Wages Payable		XXX

4. Variable overhead variances generally aren't recorded in the accounts separately; rather, they are determined as part of the general analysis of overhead as illustrated in Chapter 11.

REVIEW AND SELF TEST
Questions and Exercises

True or False

For each of the following statements, enter a T or an F in the blank to indicate whether the statement is true or false.

___ 1. Practical standards are generally viewed as having better motivational characteristics than ideal standards.

___ 2. Ideal standards allow for machine breakdown time and other normal inefficiencies.

___ 3. In determining a material price standard, the invoice cost should be included, but any freight or handling costs should be excluded.

___ 4. The material used in rejected or spoiled units of product should be added to good units in computing the standard quantity of material allowed per unit.

___ 5. The standard rate for variable overhead consists of the variable portion of the predetermined overhead rate.

___ 6. Raw materials price variances are best isolated when materials are placed into production.

___ 7. Price- and quantity-type variances can be computed for materials, labor, and overhead.

___ 8. Waste on the production line will result in a materials price variance.

___ 9. If the actual price or quantity exceeds the standard price or quantity, the variance is unfavorable.

___ 10. Raw materials are generally carried in inventory at standard cost.

___ 11. Labor rate variances are largely out of the control of management.

___ 12. All differences (variances) between standard cost and actual cost should be given attention by management.

___ 13. In a company with fixed labor costs, a focus on the labor efficiency variance may result in the production of needless inventories.

___ 14. Managers who use operating performance measures tend to focus more on trends over time than on meeting any specific standards.

___ 15. A decreasing turnover of inventory would be a positive sign.

___ 16. A desirable goal is to keep all non-bottleneck machines in use 100% of the time.

___ 17. If the MCE is less than 1, then non-value-added time is present in the production process.

___ 18. (Appendix 10A) The use of standard costs simplifies bookkeeping.

___ 19. (Appendix 10A) An unfavorable variance would be recorded as a debit in the general ledger.

Multiple Choice

Choose the best answer or response by placing the identifying letter in the space provided.

___ 1. The labor rate variance is determined by multiplying the difference between the actual labor rate and the standard labor rate by: a) the standard hours allowed; b) the actual hours worked; c) the budgeted hours allowed; d) none of these.

___ 2. If inferior-grade materials are purchased, the result may be: a) an unfavorable materials price variance; b) a favorable materials price variance; c) an unfavorable labor efficiency variance; d) a favorable labor efficiency variance; e) responses b and c are both correct; f) responses a and d are both correct.

___ 3. During June, Bradley Company produced 4,000 units of product. The standard cost card indicates the following for labor costs per unit of output: 3.5 hours @ $6 per hour = $21. During the month, the company worked 15,000 hours. The standard hours allowed for the month were: a) 14,000 hours; b) 15,000 hours; c) 24,000 hours; d) 18,000 hours.

___ 4. Refer to the data in question 3 above. What is the labor efficiency variance for June? (F indicates a Favorable variance and U indicates an Unfavorable variance.) a) $1,000 F; b) $1,000 U; c) $6,000 F; d) $6,000 U.

___ 5. Refer to the data in question 3 above. The total labor cost during June was $88,000 for the 15,000 hours that were worked. What is the labor rate variance for June? a) $6,000 F; b) $6,000 U; c) $2,000 F; d) $2,000 U.

___ 6. During July, Bradley Company produced 3,000 units of product. The standard cost card indicates the following for materials costs per unit of output: 2 pounds @ $0.50 = $1. During July, 8,000 pounds of material were purchased at a cost of $3,900. The materials price variance for July is: a) $100 F; b) $100 U; c) $4,100 F; d) $4,100 U.

___ 7. Refer to the data in question 6 above. 6,100 pounds of material were used in July to produce the output of 3,000 units. The materials quantity variance for July is: a) $1,550 F; b) $1,550 U; c) $50 F; d) $50 U.

___ 8. During August, Bradley Company produced 3,500 units of product using 12,750 labor hours. The standard cost card indicates the following variable manufacturing overhead costs per unit of output: 3.5 labor hours @ $2 per labor hour = $7. During the month, the actual variable manufacturing overhead cost incurred was $25,000. The variable overhead spending variance was: a) $500 U; b) $500 F; c) $24,500 U; d) $24,500 F.

___ 9. Refer to the data in question 8 above. The variable overhead efficiency variance was: a) $7,000 F; b) $7,000 U; c) $1,000 F; d) $1,000 U.

___ 10. The "price" variance for variable overhead is called a: a) rate variance; b) spending variance; c) budget variance; d) none of these.

___ 11. The delivery cycle time consists of: a) the time required to get a product to a customer after production is complete; b) the time required to get delivery of raw materials; c) the velocity of production plus the throughput time; d) the time required from receipt of an order from a customer to shipment of the completed goods.

___ 12. Given the following data:

Wait time to start production	15.0 days
Inspection time	0.6 days
Process time	3.0 days
Move time	1.4 days
Queue time	7.0 days

The throughput time would be: a) 12.0 days; b) 7.0 days; c) 5.0 days; d) 20.0 days.

___ 13. Refer to the data in question 12 above. The MCE would be: a) 75%; b) 30%; c) 25%; d) 42%.

___ 14. Refer again to the data in question 12 above. What percentage of the throughput time is spent in non-value-added activities: a) 25%; b) 70%; c) 75%; d) 58%.

Chapter 10

Exercises

10-1. Selected data relating to Miller Company's operations for April, are given below:

Number of units produced	500 units
Number of actual direct labor hours worked..................	1,400 hours
Total actual direct labor cost..	$10,850

The standard cost card indicates that 2.5 hours of direct labor time is allowed per unit, at a rate of $8 per hour.

a. Complete the following analysis of direct labor cost for the month:

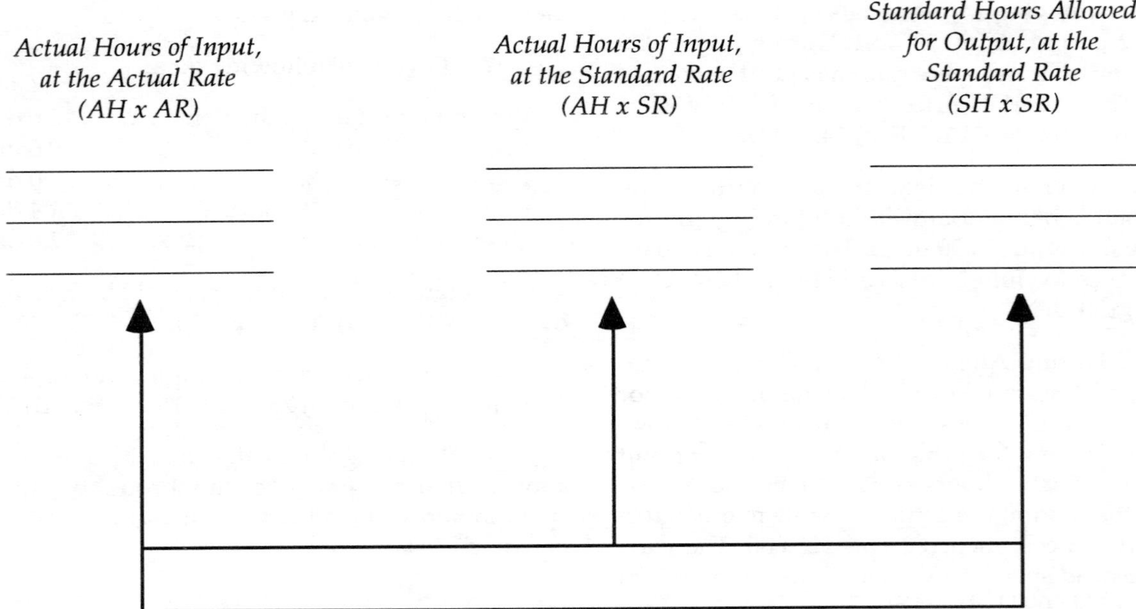

b. Redo the above analysis of direct labor cost for the month, using the following "short-cut" formulas:

Labor Rate Variance = AH (AR— SR)

Labor Efficiency Variance = SR (AH— SH)

10-2. The following activity took place in Solo Company during May:

Number of units produced	450 units
Material purchased	1,500 feet
Material used in production	720 feet
Cost per foot for material purchased	$3

The standard cost card indicates that 1.5 feet of materials are allowed for each unit of product. The standard cost of the materials is $4 per foot.

a. Complete the following analysis of direct materials cost for the month:

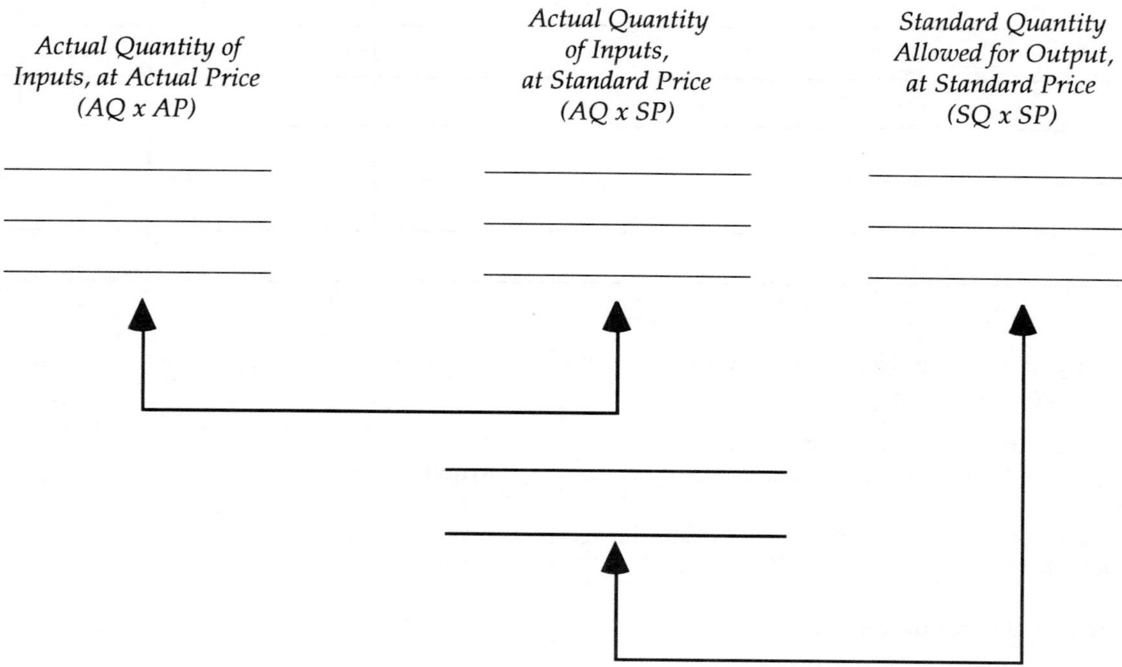

(A total variance can't be computed in this situation, since the amount of materials purchased differs from the amount of materials used in production.)

b. Redo the above analysis of direct materials cost for the month, using the following "shortcut" formulas:

Materials Price Variance = AQ (AP— SP)

Materials Quantity Variance = SP (AQ— SQ)

10-3. (Appendix 10A) Refer to the data for Solo Company in exercise 10-2 on the previous page. Prepare journal entries to record all activity relating to direct materials for the month:

	Debit	*Credit*

10-4. During the last quarter, Scott Company recorded the following average times for each order received and processed:

Wait time to start production	9.0 days
Inspection time	0.8 days
Process time	3.0 days
Move time	0.2 days
Queue time	6.0 days

a. Compute the throughput time.

Throughput time = Process time + Inspection time + Move time + Queue time

Throughput time =

b. Compute the manufacturing cycle efficiency (MCE).

$$\text{MCE} = \frac{\text{Value} - \text{Added (Process) Time}}{\text{Throughput (Manufacturing Cycle) Time}}$$

MCE =

c. What percentage of the production time is spent in non-value-added activities?

d. Compute the delivery cycle time.

Delivery Cycle Time = Wait time + Throughput time

Delivery Cycle Time =

10-5. **Critical thought writing exercise:** What information, if any, does the variable overhead efficiency variance convey concerning the efficiency with which variable overhead resources were used?

Answers to Questions and Exercises

True or False

1. T Practical standards have better motivational characteristics because they are attainable by workers.

2. F Ideal standards do not allow for either machine breakdown time or other normal inefficiencies.

3. F Freight and handling costs should be included in the material price standard, along with the invoice cost of the material.

4. T By including the material used in rejected or spoiled units, the standard becomes a practical standard that is usable to control abnormal variances.

5. T This statement is true by definition.

6. F Raw materials price variances are best isolated when materials are purchased.

7. T This point is illustrated in Exhibit 10-2.

8. F Waste will result in a materials quantity variance.

9. T This statement is true by definition.

10. T This simplifies the bookkeeping for raw materials. Any variance is broken out at time of purchase.

11. F Labor rate variances can arise from how labor is used, and the use of labor is within the control of management.

12. F Only the significant variances should be given attention by management.

13. T When labor is fixed, the only way to generate a more favorable labor efficiency variance is to create more output.

14. T Managers who use operating performance measures tend to set goals in terns of progress and improvement rather than in terms of meeting specific standards.

15. F Since companies usually want to decrease inventories, an increasing inventory turnover would be a positive sign.

16. F Only machines in bottleneck operations should be in use 100% of the time. If other machines are used 100% of the time, the result will be a build-up of work in process inventories with no increase in overall output of finished goods.

17. T Since the MCE is measured by value-added time divided by throughput time, an MCE of less than 1 means that the throughput time contains some amount of non-value-added time.

18. T The use of standard costs simplifies the bookkeeping process since standards permit all units to be carried at the same cost.

19. T Unfavorable variances have the effect of decreasing income. Therefore, they are debit entries just as an expense is a debit entry.

Multiple Choice

1. b This point is illustrated in Exhibit 10-5.

2. e The materials price variance will probably be favorable, since the inferior grade materials probably will cost less; the labor efficiency variance probably will be unfavorable, since the inferior grade materials probably will require more work time on the assembly line.

3. a The computation is: 4,000 units x 3.5 hours = 14,000 standard hours.

4. d Efficiency variance = SR (AH - SH)
= $6 (15,000 - 14,000)
= $6,000 U

5. c Rate variance = (AH x AR) - (AH x SR)
= ($88,000) - (15,000 x $6)
= $2,000 F

6. a Price variance = (AQ x AP) - (AQ x SP)
= ($3,900) - (8,000 x $0.50)
= $100 F

7. d Quantity variance = SP (AQ - SQ)
= \$0.50 (6,100 - 2x3,000)
= \$50 U

8. b Spending variance = (AH x AR) - (AH x SR)
= (\$25,000) - (12,750 x \$2)
= \$500 F

9. d Efficiency variance = SR (AH - SH)
= \$2 (12,750 - 3.5x 3,500)
= \$1,000 U

10. b This point is illustrated in Exhibit 10-2.

11. d This point is illustrated in Exhibit 10-10.

12. a Throughput time
= Process time + Inspection time + Move time + Queue time
= 3.0 days + 0.6 days + 1.4 days + 7.0 days
= 12.0 days

13. c MCE = $\frac{\text{Value-added time}}{\text{Throughput time}}$
= $\frac{\text{3.0 days}}{\text{12.0 days}}$ = 25%

14. c If the MCE is less than one, then it means that non-value-added time is present in the production process. In this case, since the MCE is 25%, 75% of the time is spent in non-value-added activities (1.00- 0.25 = 0.75 or 75%)

Exercises

10-1. a.

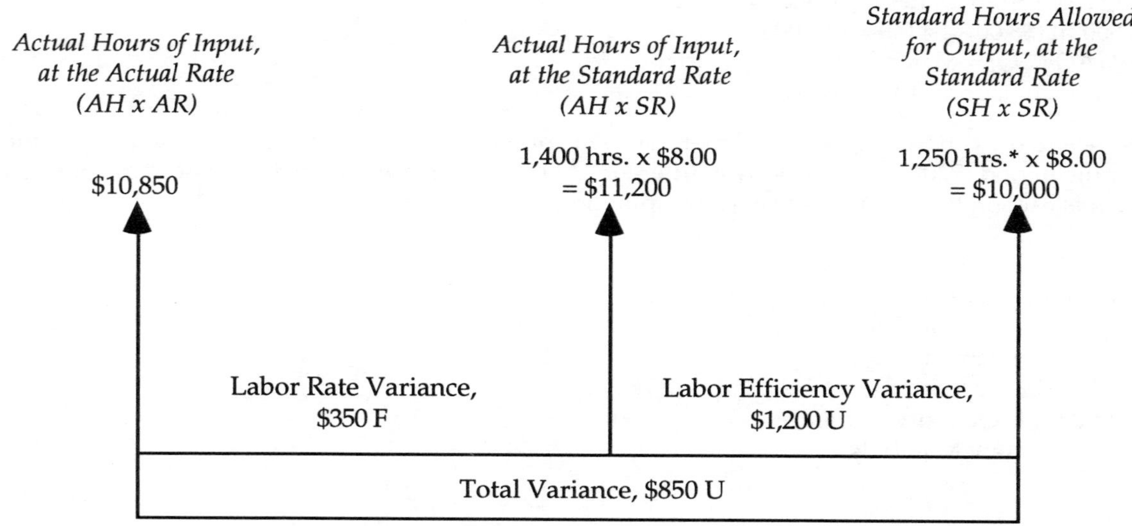

*500 units X 2.5 hrs. = 1,250 hrs.

b. AR = \$10,850 ÷ 1,400 hrs. = \$7.75 per hr.
AH (AR - SR) = Labor Rate Variance
1,400 hrs. (\$7.75 - \$8.00) = \$350 F

SR (AH - SH) = Labor Efficiency Variance
\$8.00 (1,400 hrs. - 1,250 hrs.) = \$1,200 U

10-2. a.

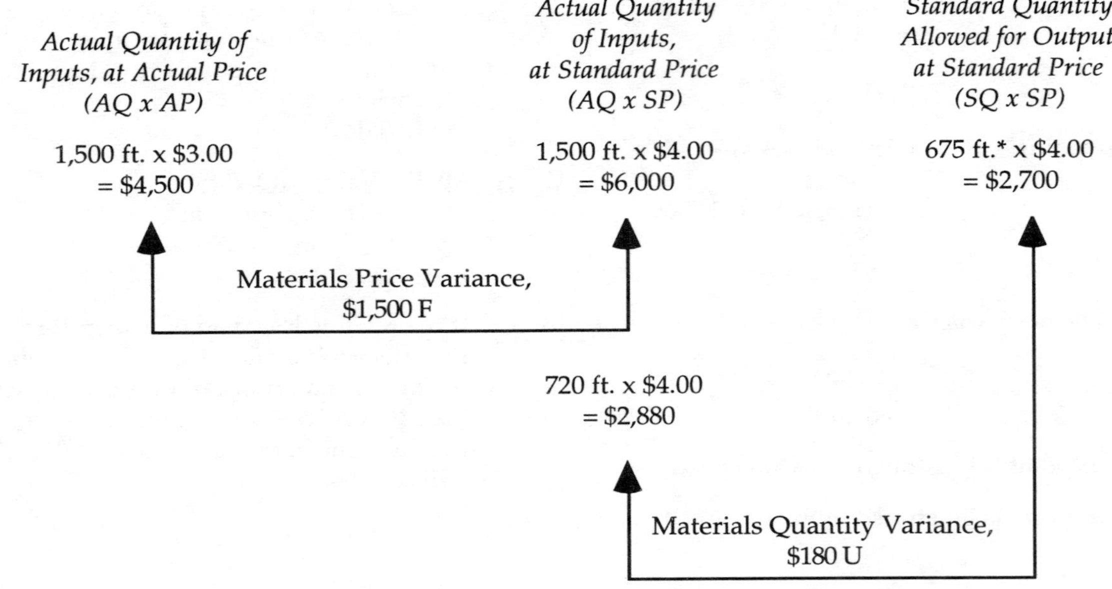

*450 units X 1.5 ft. = 675 ft.

b. AQ (AP - SP) = Materials Price Variance
1,500 ft. ($3.00 - $4.00) = $1,500 F
SP (AQ - SQ) = Materials Quantity Variance
$4.00 (720 ft. - 675 ft.) = $180 U

Notice that a different quantity of materials was purchased (1,500 ft.) than was used in production for the period (720 ft.). This is why a different "AQ" figure is used in the price variance computation than is used in the quantity variance computation.

10-3.

Raw Materials	6,000	
Materials Price Variance		1,500
Accounts Payable		4,500
Work in Process	2,700	
Materials Quantity Variance	180	
Raw Materials		2,880

10-4. a. Throughput time = Process time + Inspection time + Move time + Queue time
= 3.0 days + 0.8 days + 0.2 days + 6.0 days
= 10.0 days

b. $\text{MCE} = \frac{\text{Value-added-time, 3.0 days}}{\text{Throughput time, 10.0 days}} = 30\%$

c. Since the MCE is 30,% the complement of this figure, or 70% of the total production time, is spent in non-value-added activities.

d. Delivery cycle time = Wait time + Throughput time
= 9.0 days + 10.0 days
= 19.0 days

10-5. The variable overhead efficiency variance is computed as follows: SR (AH - SH). The variance is unfavorable if the actual hours exceeds the standard hours allowed for the actual output and is favorable otherwise. The hours refers to the basis on which variable manufacturing overhead is applied to products, which is usually direct labor-hours. Consequently, the variable overhead efficiency variance is unfavorable if "too many" direct labor-hours were used to make the actual output of the period. While this may tell us something about the efficiency of direct labor, it is not clear that it tells us anything about the efficiency with which variable manufacturing overhead resources were used. In other words, too many direct labor hours may have been used during a period, but managers and workers may have done a good job of using only as much of the variable overhead resources such as miscellaneous supplies as was absolutely necessary.

Chapter 11

Flexible Budgets and Overhead Analysis

Chapter Study Suggestions

The chapter is divided into three parts. The first part covers flexible budgets, with Exhibit 11-8 providing a comprehensive example of how a flexible budget is prepared. As you study the material in this part, pay close attention to the differences between a flexible budget and a static budget. These differences are subtle but important.

The middle part of the chapter expands on the variance analysis of variable overhead that was introduced in Chapter 10. Exhibits 11-5, 11-6, and 11-7 are the key exhibits here. Notice particularly how the flexible budget data from Exhibit 11-5 ties into the performance reports in Exhibits 11-6 and 11-7.

The last part of the chapter covers fixed overhead analysis. Three things in this part deserve special attention. First, be sure you understand fully what the "denominator activity" is, and how it is used. Second, be sure you understand the difference between a "normal-cost system" and a "standard-cost system," as illustrated in Exhibit 11-10. Third, be sure you understand the variance analysis of fixed overhead illustrated in Exhibit 11-11.

The chapter concludes with a detailed example of flexible budgets and fixed overhead analysis. Follow the example through step by step before attempting the homework material.

CHAPTER HIGHLIGHTS

A. The sales budgets, production budgets, and cash budgets in Chapter 8 are *static budgets*. They are static in the sense that they are geared toward a single level of activity.

1. The main deficiency of a static budget is that it fails to distinguish between the production control and cost control dimensions of a manager's responsibilities.

a. Production control basically means meeting production output goals.

b. Cost control means producing the output of a period at the least possible cost, consistent with quality standards.

2. Of these two responsibilities, the static budget does a good job of measuring only how well production goals are being met. The static budget can't be used to measure cost control, since actual activity will rarely coincide with the original activity level assumed in the static budget.

B. A *flexible budget* is geared to a range of activity, rather than to a single level. This can be seen from the flexible budget presented in Exhibit 11-3. Notice especially how a "cost formula" is used in the flexible budget.

1. There are four basic steps involved in preparing a flexible budget:

a. Determine the relevant range of activity.

b. Separate costs by their cost behavior patterns (variable, fixed, mixed).

c. Analyze the mixed costs, as discussed in Chapter 6, by determining their fixed and variable elements.

d. Using the cost formulas developed in "b" and "c" above, prepare a budget showing what costs will be incurred at various points throughout the relevant range.

2. The flexible budget is a dynamic tool. Using the flexible budget, budgeted costs can be developed to correspond to any actual level of activity within the relevant range.

3. The activity base underlying the flexible budget must be carefully chosen. Generally, this will be the same base as used in computing predetermined overhead rates (direct labor hours, machine hours, etc.). Three general criteria are used in selecting an activity base:

a. Variations in the activity base should actually cause variations in the costs in the flexible budget. The flexible budget assumes that the variable costs change in proportion to changes in the activity base.

b. The activity base should not be expressed in dollars. For example, direct labor cost should not be used as an activity base since changes in labor wage rates may have little affect on the costs in the flexible budget.

c. The activity base should be simple and easy to understand.

4. Although the term "flexible budget" implies only variable costs, fixed costs are often included as well. Exhibit 11-8 illustrates this approach.

a. One reason for including fixed costs is that the manager may have control over the fixed costs; if so, they should be used in the evaluation of his or her performance.

b. A second reason for including fixed costs is that the flexible budget is often used as a basis for computing predetermined overhead rates.

C. A *performance report for variable overhead* can be constructed to show just a spending variance or both a spending and an efficiency variance.

1. Just a spending variance will be shown on the performance report if budget allowances are based on the actual number of hours worked during the period.

a. In preparing a performance report under this approach, the cost formulas in the flexible budget are applied to the actual number of hours worked for the period.

b. The budget allowances computed in "a" above are then compared to actual costs of the period and a spending variance results. Exhibit 11-6 illustrates this procedure.

2. The overhead spending variance consists of two things: price variations and waste or excessive usage of overhead items.

3. Both a spending and an efficiency variance will be shown on the performance report if budget allowances are based on both the actual number of hours worked and the standard hours allowed for the output of the period.

a. Exhibit 11-7 contains a performance report using this approach. Study the column headings in this exhibit carefully.

b. The term "overhead efficiency variance" is a misnomer. The inefficiency is really in the base underlying the application of overhead.

D. The flexible budget often serves as the basis for computing predetermined overhead rates for product costing purposes. The formula is:

$$\frac{\text{Estimated manufacturing overhead costs}}{\text{Estimated total units in the base (MH, DLH, etc.) (denominator activity)}} = \text{Predetermined overhead rate}$$

1. Notice that the estimated activity part of the formula is termed the *denominator activity*.

2. The predetermined overhead rate can be divided into two parts, one for the variable overhead costs and the other for the fixed overhead costs. The fixed portion of the predetermined overhead rate depends upon the level of the denominator activity that is chosen. The larger the denominator activity, the lower the rate will be. Most managers want stable unit costs, so the denominator activity is usually changed no more frequently than once a year.

E. Exhibit 11-10 is an extremely important exhibit. It shows that overhead is applied to work in process differently under a *standard cost system* than it is under a *normal cost system.*

1. We studied normal cost systems in Chapter 3. There we learned that overhead is applied by multiplying the predetermined overhead rate by the actual hours of activity for a period.

2. In contrast, under a standard cost system overhead is applied to work in process by multiplying the predetermined overhead rate by the standard hours allowed for the output of the period. As in Chapter 10, the standard hours allowed for the output is computed by multiplying the standard hours per unit of output by the actual output of the period.

F. Two variances can be computed for fixed overhead—a budget variance and a volume variance.

1. The *fixed overhead budget variance,* or simply "budget variance," represents the difference between actual fixed overhead costs and budgeted fixed overhead costs. The formula for the variance is

$$\text{Actual fixed overhead cost} - \text{Flexible budget fixed overhead cost} = \text{Budget variance}$$

a. The fixed overhead budget variance is similar to the variable overhead spending variance.

b. Some fixed costs, such as rent, may be beyond immediate managerial control. When this is true, the budget variance will be largely informational in nature rather than a measure of managerial performance.

2. The *fixed overhead volume variance,* or simply "volume variance," is a measure of utilization of plant facilities. The formula is:

$$\text{Fixed rate} \times \left(\text{Denom. hours} - \text{Std. hours allowed for output}\right) = \text{Volume variance}$$

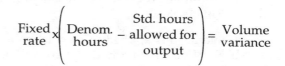

where the "fixed rate" is the fixed portion of the predetermined overhead rate.

a. The volume variance does not measure how well spending was controlled. It only measures plant utilization.

b. If the denominator activity is greater than the standard hours allowed for the output of the period, then there is an unfavorable volume variance.

c. If the denominator activity is less than the standard hours allowed for the output of the period, then the volume variance is favorable.

REVIEW AND SELF TEST
Questions and Exercises

True or False

For each of the following statements, enter a T or an F in the blank to indicate whether the statement is true or false.

___ 1. A budget prepared for a single level of activity is called a static budget.

___ 2. The difference between a flexible budget and a static budget is that a flexible budget never contains fixed costs.

___ 3. Although a static budget is effective in measuring production control, it is not effective in measuring cost control.

___ 4. Direct labor cost would generally be a better base to use in preparing a flexible budget than direct labor hours.

___ 5. A variable overhead spending variance is affected by waste and excessive usage as well as price differentials.

___ 6. The term "overhead efficiency variance" is really a misnomer since this variance has nothing to do with efficiency in the use of overhead.

___ 7. If overhead is applied to production on a basis of direct labor hours, there will be a close relationship between the labor efficiency variance and the overhead efficiency variance.

___ 8. Fixed costs should never be included in the flexible budget.

___ 9. The fixed overhead volume variance measures how well fixed overhead spending was controlled.

___ 10. If the denominator activity level exceeds the standard hours allowed for the output, the volume variance will be favorable.

Multiple Choice

Choose the best answer or response by placing the identifying letter in the space provided.

___ 1. In a standard cost system, overhead is applied to production on a basis of: a) the actual hours required to complete the output of the period; b) the standard hours allowed to complete the output of the period; c) the denominator hours chosen for the period; d) none of these.

___ 2. A flexible budget: a) is geared to a range of activity; b) excludes fixed costs; c) is conceptually inferior to a static budget; d) none of these.

___ 3. If the standard hours allowed for the output of a period exceed the denominator hours used in setting overhead rates, there will be: a) a favorable budget variance; b) an unfavorable budget variance; c) a favorable volume variance; d) an unfavorable volume variance.

___ 4. If a company has a large unfavorable volume variance and a small budget variance, one would expect the Manufacturing Overhead account to show: a) underapplied overhead; b) overapplied overhead; c) the volume variance would have no effect on the manufacturing overhead account; d) none of these.

___ 5. Baxter Company uses a standard cost system in which manufacturing overhead is applied to units of product on the basis of direct labor hours. The variable portion of the company's predetermined overhead rate is $3 per direct labor hour. The standards call for 2 direct labor hours per unit of output. In March, the company produced 2,000 units using 4,100 direct labor hours and the actual variable overhead cost incurred was $12,050. What was the variable overhead spending variance? a) $250 U; b) $250 F; c) $6,050 U; d) $6,050 F.

___ 6. Refer to the data in part (5) above concerning Baxter Company. What was the variable overhead efficiency variance for March? a) $6,300 F; b) $6,300 U; c) $300 F; d) $300 U.

___ 7. Baxter Company's flexible budget for manufacturing overhead indicates that the fixed overhead should be $30,000 at the denominator level of 3,000 standard direct labor hours. In March, the actual fixed overhead cost incurred was $33,000. Recall from the above data concerning Baxter Company that the standards call for 2 direct labor hours per unit of output and that in March, the company produced 2,000 units using 4,100 direct labor hours (DLHs). What is the fixed portion of the predetermined overhead rate? a) $10 per DLH; b) $11 per DLH; c) $30 per DLH; d) $2 per DLH.

___ 8. Refer to the data in parts (5) and (7) above concerning Baxter Company. How much overhead (both variable and fixed) was applied to units of product during March? a) $12,000; b) $30,000; c) $52,000; d) $42,000.

___ 9. Refer to the data in part (7) above concerning Baxter Company. What was the fixed overhead budget variance for March? a) $10,000 F; b) $10,000 U; c) $3,000 U; d) $3,000 F.

___ 10. Refer to the data in part (7) above concerning Baxter Company. What was the fixed overhead volume variance for March? a) $10,000 F; b) $10,000 U; c) $3,000 U; d) $3,000 F.

Exercises

11-1. Herbold Corporation uses the following cost formulas in its flexible budget for manufacturing overhead:

Item	*Cost Formula*
Utilities..	$ 6,000 per year, plus $0.30 per machine hour (MH)
Supplies	$10,000 per year, plus $0.80 per machine hour
Depreciation..	$25,000 per year
Indirect labor..	$21,000 per year, plus $0.40 per machine hour

Using these cost formulas, complete the following flexible budget:

	Cost Formula		Machine Hours	
Overhead Costs	*(per MH)*	*8,000*	*10,000*	*12,000*
Variable overhead costs:				
______________	________	________	________	________
______________	________	________	________	________
______________	________	________	________	________
Total variable costs	========	________	________	________
Fixed overhead costs:				
______________		________	________	________
______________		________	________	________
______________		________	________	________
______________		________	________	________
Total fixed costs		________	________	________
Total overhead Costs		========	========	========

11-2. Refer to the flexible budget data in Exercise 11-1. The standard time to complete one unit of product is 1.6 machine hours. Last year the company budgeted to operate at the 10,000 machine-hour level of activity. During the year the following actual activity took place:

Number of units produced	5,000 units
Actual machine hours worked	8,500 hours
Actual overhead costs:	
Utilities ($6,000 fixed)	$ 8,500
Supplies ($10,000 fixed)	17,000
Indirect labor ($21,000 fixed)	25,000
Depreciation	25,000

Prepare a performance report for the year using the format that appears below. Do not compute efficiency variances for variable overhead items.

Performance Report
Herbold Corporation

Budgeted machine hours	________
Actual machine hours	________
Standard machine hours	________

	Cost Formula (per MH)	*Actual Costs 8,500 MHs*	*Budget Based on ____ MHs*	*Spending or Budget Variance*
Variable overhead costs:				
________	________	________	________	________
________	________	________	________	________
________	________	________	________	________
Total variable costs	========	________	________	________
Fixed overhead costs:				
________		________	________	________
________		________	________	________
________		________	________	________
________		________	________	________
Total fixed costs		________	________	________
Total overhead Costs		========	========	========

11-3. The flexible budget for manufacturing overhead for Marina Company is given below:

MARINA COMPANY
Flexible Budget

Overhead Costs	*Cost Formula (per DLH)*	*Direct Labor Hours* 10,000	12,000	14,000
Variable costs:				
Electricity	$0.15	$ 1,500	$ 1,800	$ 2,100
Indirect materials	0.50	5,000	6,000	7,000
Indirect labor	0.25	2,500	3,000	3,500
Total variable costs	$0.90	9,000	10,800	12,600
Fixed costs:				
Depreciation		11,500	11,500	11,500
Property taxes.		8,500	8,500	8,500
Insurance		4,000	4,000	4,000
Total fixed costs		24,000	24,000	24,000
Total Overhead Costs		$33,000	$34,800	$36,600

Marina Company uses a standard cost system in which manufacturing overhead is applied to units of product on the basis of direct labor hours (DLHs). A denominator activity level of 12,000 direct labor hours is used in setting predetermined overhead rates. The standard time to complete one unit of product is 1.5 direct labor hours.

For the company's most recent year, the following actual operating data are available:

Units produced	9,000 units
Actual direct labor hours worked	14,000 hours
Actual variable overhead cost	$12,880
Actual fixed overhead cost	$23,750

a. Compute the predetermined overhead rate that would be used by the company, and break it down into variable and fixed cost elements:

Predetermined overhead rate .... ________

Variable cost element .... ________

Fixed cost element .... ________

b. How much overhead would have been applied to work in process during the year? ________

c. Complete the following variance analysis of variable overhead cost for the company's most recent year (see Chapter 10):

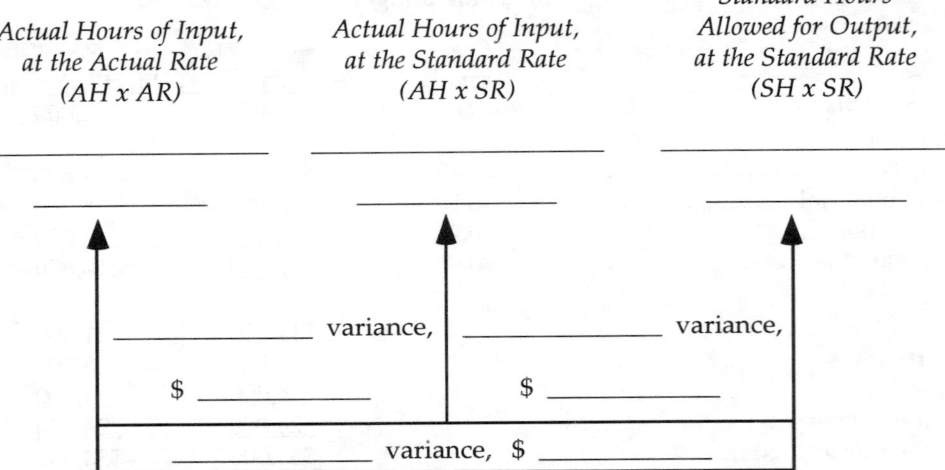

d. Complete the following variance analysis of fixed overhead cost for the company's most recent year:

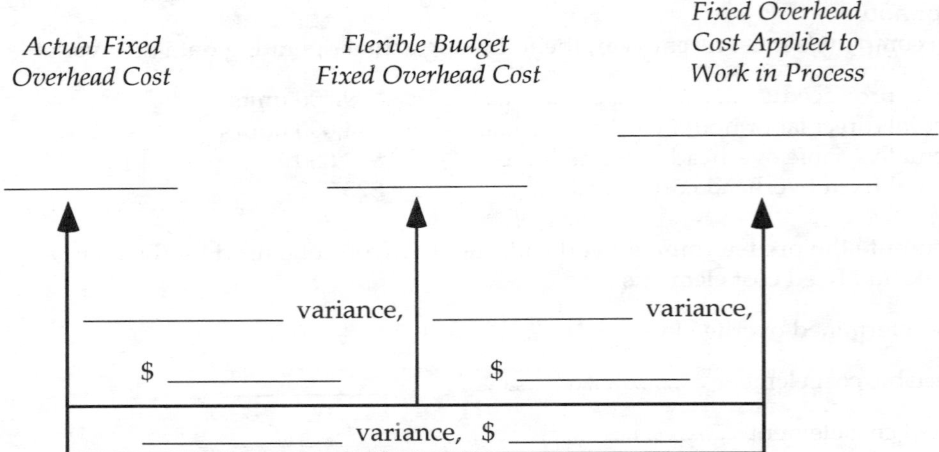

11-4. **Critical thought writing exercise:** Taylor Company's manufacturing overhead cost was overapplied last year. Would you expect the total of the company's overhead variances for the year to be favorable or unfavorable? Why?

Answers to Questions and Exercises

True or False

1. T A static budget is prepared for only one level of activity.

2. F The difference between a flexible budget and a static budget is that a flexible budget is geared to a range of activity whereas a static budget is geared toward only a single level of activity.

3. T The major problem with the static budget approach is that it is not effective in measuring cost control.

4. F It is generally best to avoid using dollars in the activity base.

5. T The inclusion of waste elements in the spending variance is what makes it different from the materials price variance and the labor rate variance.

6. T The overhead efficiency variance really measures efficiency in the base underlying the application of overhead.

7. T The reason for the close relationship is that both variances are based on the difference between the actual direct labor hours and the standard direct labor hours allowed for the actual output.

8. F Fixed costs should always be included in the flexible budget (1) if the manager has control over the costs or (2) if the flexible budget is to be used as a basis for preparing predetermined overhead rates.

9. F The fixed overhead volume variance is a measure of capacity utilization—not a measure of spending.

10. F The reverse is true—one would expect the volume variance to be unfavorable.

Multiple Choice

1. b This point is illustrated in Exhibit 11-10.

2. a A flexible budget is geared to all levels of activity within the relevant range.

3. c The volume variance will be favorable because more of the capacity of the plant was utilized than had been assumed with the choice of the denominator activity level.

4. a An unfavorable volume variance would mean that less overhead cost was applied to production than planned; therefore, the Manufacturing Overhead account would show underapplied overhead cost.

5. b The computations are:

   Spending var. = (AH x AR) - (AH x SR)
   = ($12,050*) - (4,100 x $3)
   = $250 F

   * AH x AR is equal to the total variable overhead cost for the month.

6. d The computations are:

   Efficiency var. = (AH x SR) - (SH x SR)
   = (4,100 x $3) - (4,000* x $3)
   = $300 U

   * 2,000 units x 2 DLHs/unit = 4,000 DLHs

7. a The computations are:

$$\text{Fixed portion of the predetermined overhead rate} = \frac{\text{Estimated fixed manufacturing overhead cost}}{\text{Denominator activity}}$$

$$= \frac{\$30{,}000}{3{,}000 \text{ DLHs}}$$

$$= \$10 \text{ per DLH}$$

8. c The computations are:

$$\text{Predetermined overhead rate} = \$3 + \$10 = \$13 \text{ per DLH}$$

$$\text{Standard hours allowed for the output} = \text{2,000 units} \times \text{2 DLH per unit} = \text{4,000 DLHs}$$

$$\text{Overhead applied} = \$13 \times 4{,}000 = \$52{,}000$$

9. c The computations are:

$$\text{Budget variance} = \text{Actual fixed overhead cost} \times \text{Flexible budget overhead cost}$$

$$= \$33{,}000 - \$30{,}000$$
$$= \$3{,}000 \text{ U}$$

10. a The computations are:

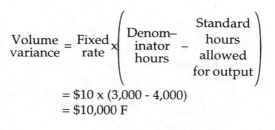

$$\text{Volume variance} = \text{Fixed rate} \times \left(\text{Denom–inator hours} - \text{Standard hours allowed for output}\right)$$

$$= \$10 \times (3{,}000 - 4{,}000)$$
$$= \$10{,}000 \text{ F}$$

Chapter 11

Exercises

11-1.

Overhead Costs	Cost Formula (per MH)	Machine Hours 8,000	10,000	12,000
Variable overhead costs:				
Utilities	$0.30	$ 2,400	$ 3,000	$ 3,600
Supplies	0.80	6,400	8,000	9,600
Indirect labor	0.40	3,200	4,000	4,800
Total variable costs	$1.50	12,000	15,000	18,000
Fixed overhead costs:				
Utilities.		6,000	6,000	6,000
Supplies		10,000	10,000	10,000
Depreciation		25,000	25,000	25,000
Indirect labor		21,000	21,000	21,000
Total fixed costs		62,000	62,000	62,000
Total overhead Costs		$74,000	$77,000	$80,000

11-2. Performance Report

Budgeted machine hours	10,000
Actual machine hours	8,500
Standard machine hours	8,000

	Cost Formula (per MH)	Actual Costs 8,500 MHs	Budget Based on 8,500 MHs	Spending or Budget Variance
Variable overhead costs:				
Utilities	$0.30	$ 2,500*	$ 2,550	$ (50)
Supplies	0.80	7,000	6,800	200
Indirect labor	0.40	4,000	3,400	600
Total variable costs	$1.50	13,500	12,750	750
Fixed overhead costs:				
Utilities		6,000	6,000	--
Supplies		10,000	10,000	--
Depreciation		25,000	25,000	--
Indirect labor		21,000	21,000	--
Total fixed costs		62,000	62,000	--
Total overhead Costs		$75,500	$74,750	$750

*$8,500 - $6,000 = $2,500

11-3. a. Predetermined overhead rate ($34,800 ÷ 12,000 DLH) $2.90 per DLH
Variable element ($10,800 ÷ 12,000 DLH) $0.90 per DLH
Fixed element: ($24,000 ÷ 12,000 DLH) $2.00 per DLH

b. Overhead applied:
9,000 units x 1.5 DLHs per unit = 13,500 DLHs allowed
13,500 DLHs x $2.90 per DLH = $39,150 overhead applied

c. Variable overhead variance analysis:

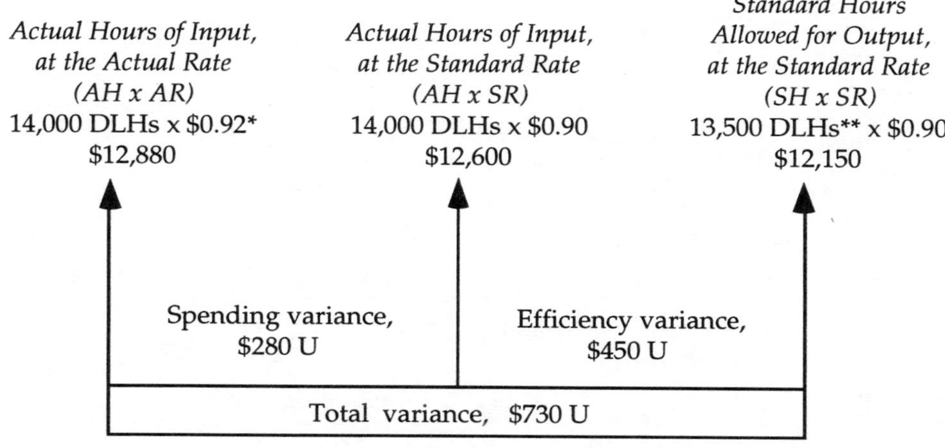

* $12,880 ÷ 14,000 DLHs = $0.92 per DLH
** 9,000 units x 1.5 DLHs per unit = 13,500 DLHs

d. Fixed overhead variance analysis:

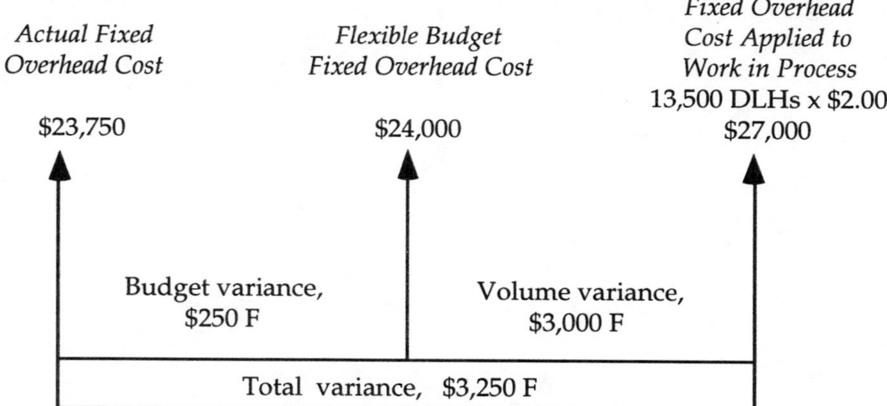

11-4. As indicated in the chapter, the total of all the variances is equal to the over- or underapplied overhead for the period. If manufacturing overhead cost is overapplied for the year, then the total of the variances must be favorable since more overhead cost was applied to units of product, using the standard hours allowed, than was actually incurred during the period.

Chapter 12

Segment Reporting, Profitability Analysis, and Decentralization

Chapter Study Suggestions

The first part of the chapter covers segment reporting. Before you start reading this part of the chapter, study Exhibits 12-2, and 12-3. These exhibits illustrate what is meant by the term segment reporting. Notice particularly that on a segmented report the total company is divided into smaller parts, so that the manager can look at various pieces of the company rather than just at the whole. In studying the text material, spend the time necessary to fully understand the difference between direct and common costs, and the difference between segment margin and contribution margin. You should memorize the format for a segment report.

The second part of the chapter covers responsibility accounting, along with return on investment (ROI) and residual income computations. Memorize the formulas for ROI and residual income since they are used extensively in the homework material.

The appendix to the chapter deals with transfer pricing. The key ideas in this appendix are the lower limits and the upper limits on the transfer price. Make sure you understand how to compute these limits.

CHAPTER HIGHLIGHTS

A. To operate effectively, the manager needs much more information than that provided by a single income statement. He or she needs information that focuses on the segments of the organization.

1. A *segment* is any part or activity of an organization about which the manager seeks cost data. Examples of segments would include sales territories, manufacturing divisions, producing departments, and groups or lines of products.

2. Internally, segmented reports should be prepared in the contribution format with which you are already largely familiar.

3. Exhibit 12-2 contains an illustration of a series of segmented reports. Notice that as we go from one segmented report to another in the exhibit, we are looking at smaller and smaller pieces of the company.

4. By preparing segmented reports such as those illustrated in Exhibit 12-2, the manager may uncover problems and opportunities that otherwise would have remained hidden from view. For example, some product lines may be unprofitable; some sales territories may have a poor sales mix; other sales territories may be using ineffective promotional strategies, etc. Such problems can be highlighted with segmented reports.

B. Two general guidelines should be used in assigning costs to the various segments when the contribution approach is used.

1. First, costs are assigned according to cost behavior patterns; that is, according to whether they are variable or fixed.

2. Second, costs are assigned according to whether they are traceable or common to the various segments.

a. Only *traceable costs* should be charged to the segments. The traceable costs of a segment consist of those costs, including fixed costs, that arise because of the existence of the segment. The general rule is to treat as traceable costs only those costs that would disappear over time if the segment itself disappeared.

b. *Common costs* should not be charged to the segments. Common costs are costs that relate to overall operating activities. They would not disappear over time if a segment were eliminated and therefore they should not be allocated to segments.

C. The format of a segmented income statement is very important and should be memorized. The format is:

	Total	*Segment A*	*Segment B*
Sales	$XXX	$XXX	$XXX
Less variable expenses	XXX	XXX	XXX
Contribution margin	XXX	XXX	XXX
Less traceable fixed expenses	XXX	XXX	XXX
Segment margin	XXX	$XXX	$ XXX
Less common fixed expenses	XXX		
Net Income.	$ XXX		

1. The segmented income statement emphasizes the distinctions between variable and fixed costs and between traceable and common costs.

2. As an organization is segmented into smaller and smaller pieces, some costs that were previously traceable will become common to the smaller segments. There are limits to how finely a cost can be divided.

3. The *segment margin* shows the profitability of a segment after it has covered all of the costs which can be traced directly to it.

a. The segment margin is used by the manager in decision situations relating to long-run needs and—performance, such as capacity changes, long-run pricing policy, and segment return on investment.

b. By contrast, the contribution margin is most useful in those situations involving short-run decisions, such as pricing of special orders and special promotional campaigns.

4. Common costs should not be allocated to segments, since such an allocation would destroy the usefulness of the segment margin as a tool for assessing segment performance.

D. A *responsibility accounting* system functions best in a decentralized organization. A *decentralized organization* is one in which decision making is spread throughout the organization, with managers at all levels making decisions relating to their sphere of responsibility. In a decentralized organization the responsibility accounting system is structured around cost centers, profit centers, and investment centers, each of which defines an area of responsibility in the organization.

1. A *cost center* is any responsibility center where a manager has control over the incurrence of cost but not over revenues or investments. A cost center manager is usually held responsible for minimizing cost while fulfilling all obligations to provide quality goods and services as requested.

2. The manager of a *profit center* has control over both cost and revenue. A profit center manager is usually held responsible for maximizing profit.

3. The manager of an *investment center* has control over cost and revenue, and also has control over investment in plant and equipment, receivables, inventory, and other assets.

E. Performance in an investment center is often measured by *return on investment (ROI)*. The ROI formula is:

ROI = Margin x Turnover where:

$$\text{Margin} = \frac{\text{Net operating income}}{\text{Sales}}$$

$$\text{Turnover} = \frac{\text{Sales}}{\text{Average operating assets}}$$

Therefore, the ROI formula becomes:

$$\text{ROI} = \frac{\text{Net operating income}}{\text{Sales}} \times \frac{\text{Sales}}{\text{Average operating assets}}$$

The formula can be simplified by eliminating Sales as follows:

$$\text{ROI} = \frac{\text{Net operating income}}{\text{Average operating assets}}$$

1. *Net operating income* is income before interest and taxes.

2. *Operating assets* include cash, accounts receivable, inventory, and all other assets held for productive use in an organization. Operating assets do *not* include, for example, investments in other companies and investments in undeveloped land. Assets common to all divisions (such as assets associated with corporate headquarters) should not be allocated to the divisions when making ROI computations.

3. A company's return on investment can be improved if the manager can either (1) increase sales, (2) reduce expenses, or (3) reduce assets, holding all other things constant.

4. ROI is criticized for several reasons. One of the most important criticisms is that a manager who is evaluated based on ROI will tend to reject projects whose ROIs are less than the manager's current ROI but greater than the company's minimum rate of return. This would not be in the best interests of the overall organization since a project whose rate of return exceeds the minimum rate of return should ordinarily be accepted.

F. Another approach to measuring performance in an investment center is known as residual income. *Residual income* is the net operating income that an investment center is able to earn above some minimum rate of return on operating assets. *Economic value added (EVA)*, another measure of performance used by companies, is very similar to residual income.

1. When residual income is used to measure performance, the purpose is to maximize the total amount of residual income,.

2. Residual income is computed as follows when the minimum required rate of return is 20%:

Average operating assets	$100,000
Net operating income	$ 25,000
Minimum required return	
20% X $100,000	20,000
Residual income	$ 5,000

3. Residual income encourages investment in worthwhile projects that would be rejected under ROI.

4. A major disadvantage of the residual income approach is that it can't be used to compare divisions of different sizes. The reason is that it can create a bias in favor of the larger divisions, due to the larger numbers involved.

Appendix 12A: Transfer Pricing

A. A *transfer price* is the price charged by one segment of an organization for a good or service that it provides to another segment of the same organization. Three general approaches are used in setting transfer prices: (1) set transfer prices at cost, (2) set transfer prices at market price, and (3) set transfer prices at a negotiated price.

B. Many firms base transfer prices on cost—either variable cost or absorption (full) cost.

1. Although cost-based transfer prices are widely used, they have a number of disadvantages.

a. They can lead to dysfunctional decisions in a company, because they have no built-in mechanism for telling the manager when transfers should or should not be made between divisions.

b. The only division that will show any profits is the one that makes a final sale to an outside party. Other divisions will show no profits for their efforts.

c. There is no incentive for the control of costs, since one division simply passes its costs on to the next division.

2. As a partial offset to these shortcomings, advocates of cost-based transfer prices argue that they are easily understood and convenient to use.

3. If cost-based transfer prices are used, then they should be standard costs, rather than actual costs. This will avoid passing on excess costs due to inefficiency from one division to another.

C. The following formula, which is based on cost *and* market price, can be used to help determine the transfer price that should be charged:

$$\text{Transfer price} = \text{Variable cost per unit} + \text{Lost contribution margin per unit on outside sales}$$

1. The variable cost per unit in this formula refers to the variable costs incurred up to the point where the buying division receives the good or service.

2. The lost contribution margin per unit on outside sales in this formula refers to any sales that are lost by the selling division as a consequence of transferring the good or service to the buying division. This is an opportunity cost.

3. The formula represents the costs (including opportunity costs) of the selling division. As such, there is no benefit to the selling division of participating in the transfer. As a consequence, a higher transfer price may be negotiated between the selling division and the buying division. The formula provides a lower limit on the transfer price. If the buying division can acquire the good or service from an outside source, the upper limit would be the outside market price.

4. If there is idle capacity, there are no lost sales and the lost contribution margin on outside sales is zero. In this situation, the formula indicates that the lower limit on the transfer price should be simply the variable cost per unit.

REVIEW AND SELF TEST
Questions and Exercises

True or False

For each of the following statements, enter a T or an F in the blank to indicate whether the statement is true or false.

___ 1. Common costs should be allocated to product line segments on a basis of sales dollars.

___ 2. A series of segmented reports focuses on progressively smaller pieces of an organization.

___ 3. Contribution margin is basically a short-run planning tool and is especially valuable in decisions relating to temporary uses of capacity, special orders, and short-run promotional strategy.

___ 4. The terms "traceable cost" and "variable cost" are synonymous.

___ 5. As an organization is broken down into smaller segments, costs that were traceable to the larger segments may become common to the smaller segments.

___ 6. The segment margin is viewed as being the best gauge of the long-run profitability of a segment.

___ 7. A decentralized organization is one in which decision making is confined to top management.

___ 8. Residual income is equal to the difference between total revenues and operating expenses.

___ 9. Use of the ROI formula to evaluate managers may cause rejection of investment opportunities that would be beneficial to the company as a whole.

___ 10. A profit center is responsible for generating revenue, but it is not responsible for controlling costs.

___ 11. A reduction in operating assets will increase a division's ROI if sales and expenses remain unchanged.

___ 12. In computing the residual income, expenses incurred in operating corporate headquarters should be allocated to the separate divisions on the basis of sales dollars.

___ 13. Under the residual income approach, the manager seeks to maximize the rate of return on operating assets.

___ 14. An increase in total sales would typically increase the turnover of assets but it would have no effect on the margin.

___ 15. (Appendix 12A) When a division is operating at capacity, the transfer price to other divisions should include an element of opportunity cost.

___ 16. (Appendix 12A) Transfer prices based on actual cost are superior in that they provide incentive for the control of costs between transferring divisions.

___ 17. (Appendix 12A) Using cost-based transfer prices can lead to reduced overall company profits.

___ 18. (Appendix 12A) The transfer price established by the transfer pricing formula represents a lower limit for a transfer price, but the transfer price can be higher.

Multiple Choice

Choose the best answer or response by placing the identifying letter in the space provided.

___ 1. Armco, Inc., produces and sells five product lines. Which of the following costs would typically be a traceable fixed cost of a product line? a) advertising costs of the product line; b) the salary of the company's president; c) depreciation of facilities used jointly to produce several product lines; d) responses a, b, and c, are all correct.

___ 2. If a segment has a negative segment margin: a) the segment should be dropped; b) the segment should be retained only if it has a positive contribution margin; c) the segment is not covering its own traceable costs, but it still may be of benefit to the company; d) none of these.

___ 3. Rumberger, Inc. sells two products: X and Y. Data concerning the company for July follow:

	Product X	*Product Y*
Sales	$200,000	$300,000
Variable expenses	50,000	100,000
Traceable fixed expenses	80,000	150,000

In addition, there were common fixed expenses of $70,000 in July. What was the segment margin for Product X? a) $70,000; b) $120,000; c) $150,000; d) $38,000.

___ 4. Refer to the data for Rumberger, Inc. in exercise (3) above. What was the net income for the entire company? a) $120,000; b) $(4,000); c) $70,000; d) $50,000.

___ 5. Refer to the data for Rumberger, Inc. in exercise (3) above. Suppose advertising for Product Y is increased by $20,000 per month, which results in increased sales of $90,000 per month. This should have the following effect on Product Y's monthly segment margin: a) increase by $70,000; b) increase by $40,000; c) increase by $60,000; d) decrease by $20,000.

___ 6. Refer to the data for Rumberger, Inc. in exercise (5) above. What would be the effect of the increase in advertising and sales of Product Y on the company's overall net income? a) increase by $70,000; b) increase by $40,000; c) increase by $60,000; d) decrease by $20,000.

___ 7. If the level of inventory in a company is reduced, and if sales and expenses remain unchanged, one would expect the company's ROI to: a) increase; b) decrease; c) remain unchanged; d) it is impossible to tell what would happen to ROI.

___ 8. Given the following data:

Average operating assets	$ 45,000
Sales	180,000
Contribution margin	21,600
Net operating income	9,000

The company's ROI would be: a) 48%; b) 12%; c) 20%; d) 30%.

___ 9. The purpose of the residual income approach is to: a) maximize a segment's overall rate of return; b) maximize the ROI that a segment is able to get on its operating assets; c) maximize the total amount of the residual income; d) none of these.

___ 10. Given the following data:

Average operating assets	$300,000
Stockholders' equity	50,000
Sales	900,000
Net operating income	75,000
Minimum required rate of return	18%

The company's residual income would be: a) $25,000; b) $15,000; c) $21,000; d) 475,000.

___ 11. (Appendix 12A) Division A produces a part that it sells to outside customers. Data concerning this part appear below:

Selling price to outside customers	$60
Variable cost per unit	$40
Total fixed cost	$100,000
Capacity in units	20,000

Division B of the same company now purchases 5,000 units of a similar part from an outside supplier at a price of $58 per unit. If Division B wants to purchase these 5,000 units from Division A instead, and Division A has no idle capacity, then according to the formula the lower limit on the transfer price should be: a) $60; b) $58; c) $40; d) $45.

___ 12. (Appendix 12A) Refer to the data in question (11) above. If Division A has idle capacity, the transfer price should be: a) $60; b) $40; c) between $45 and $58; d) between $40 and $58.

Exercises

12-1. The following data, pertain to Bylund Company's operations for July 19X8

	Total	*Product X*	*Product Y*
Number of units sold		10,000	12,000
Selling price per unit		$20.00	$25.00
Variable cost per unit:			
Production		9.00	10.00
Selling and administrative		3.00	3.75
Fixed costs:			
Production	$ 155,000		
Selling and administrative	20,000		

Of the fixed costs, only $50,000 of the fixed production costs are traceable to the production of Product X and $75,000 are traceable to Product Y.

a. Prepare a segmented income statement for Bylund Company using the following form:

BYLUND COMPANY
Income Statement
For the Month Ended July 31

	Total		*Product X*		*Product Y*	
	Amount	*%*	*Amount*	*%*	*Amount*	*%*
Sales	$_______	_____	$ _______	_____	$ _______	_____
Less variable expenses:						
Production	$_______	_____	$ _______	_____	$ _______	_____
Selling and administrative	$_______	_____	$ _______	_____	$ _______	_____
Total variable expenses	$_______	_____	$ _______	_____	$ _______	_____
Contribution margin	$_______	_____	$ _______	_____	$ _______	_____
Less traceable fixed expenses:	$_______	_____	$ _______	_____	$ _______	_____
Product line segment margin	$_______	_____	$ _______	_____	$ _______	_____
Less common fixed expenses:						
Production	$_______	_____				
Selling and administrative	$_______	_____				
Total common fixed expenses	$_______	_____				
Net income	$_______	_____				

b. Should either Product X or Product Y be dropped? Why?

....

....

....

....

c. Product X can be enhanced by incurring an additional $25,000 in fixed production costs. Instead of raising the price of Product X to reflect the enhancement, Bylund Company would seek to increase sales. If sales increased by $80,000, should the product be enhanced?

....

....

....

....

....

....

....

....

....

12-2. Fill in the missing data for Biggerstaff, Inc.

	Total		Southwest Division		Central Division	
	Amount	%	Amount	%	Amount	%
Sales	$1,000,000	____	$ ______	____	$ ______	____
Variable expenses	$______	____	$ ______	____	$ ______	____
Contribution margin	$______	____	$ 360,000	60	$ ______	____
Traceable fixed expenses:	$______	____	$ 150,000	____	$ 200,000	____
Division segment margin..........	$______	____	$ ______	____	$ 120,000	30
Common fixed expenses..........	$______	____				
Net income..........	$ 40,000	____				

Hint: The contribution margin ratio for the Southwest Division can be used to determine its sales.

12-3. Frankel Company has the following data for its Connectors Division for last year:

Sales	$2,000,000
Net operating income	160,000
Average operating assets	800,000
Minimum rate of return	16%

a. Compute the return on investment (ROI) for the Connectors Division, using margin and turnover.

b. Compute the residual income for the Connectors Division.

12-4. Fill in the missing information for the three different companies below:

	Company 1	*Company 2*	*Company 3*
Sales	$600,000	$600,000	$______
Net operating income	60,000	______	27,000
Average operating assets	300,000	200,000	______
Margin	______	7.5%	______
Turnover	______	______	1.8
Return on investment (ROI)	______	______	27%

12-5. (Appendix 12A) Perchon Company's Regulator Division produces a small valve used by other companies as a key part in their products. Cost and sales data relating to the valve are given below:

Selling price per unit	$50
Variable costs per unit	30
Fixed costs per unit	12*

*Based on the Regulator Division's capacity of 40,000 valves per year.

Perchon Company's Boiler Division is introducing a new product that will use a valve such as the one produced in the Regulator Division. An outside supplier has quoted the Boiler Division a price of $48 per valve. The Boiler Division would like to purchase the valves from the Regulator Division instead if an acceptable transfer price can be worked out.

a. Assume that the Regulator Division is presently selling all the valves it can produce to outside customers. Use the transfer pricing formula to determine the lower limit on the transfer price:

Transfer price = Variable costs per unit + Lost contribution margin per unit on outside sales

b. From the standpoint of the entire company, should the Boiler Division purchase the valves from the Regulator Division or from the outside supplier? Explain.

....

....

....

....

c. Assume that the Boiler Division requires 10,000 valves per year and the Regulator Division is presently selling 35,000 valves per year to outside customers. What would be the impact on Perchon Company's overall profits if all 10,000 valves were acquired from the Regulator Division rather than from the outside supplier?

d. Assume that the Regulator Division has ample idle capacity to handle all the Boiler Division's needs. Use the transfer pricing formula to determine the lower limit on the transfer price.

12-6. **Critical thought writing exercise:** One criticism of ROI is that it can lead to dysfunctional decisions in a company. In what way can it lead to dysfunctional decisions, and how can the problem be avoided?

....

....

....

....

....

....

....

....

....

Answers to Questions and Exercises

True or False

1. F Common costs should never be allocated to segments since such allocations are arbitrary and could be misleading.
2. T This point is illustrated in Exhibit 12-2.
3. T Contribution margin is a short-run planning tool because the elements involved—selling price, variable expense, and volume—can be adjusted as needed in the short run.
4. F A traceable cost can be either variable or fixed.
5. T The reason that more costs become common as an organization is divided into smaller and smaller segments is that there are limits to how finely a cost can be divided.
6. T The segment margin is the best gauge of the long-run profitability of a segment because in the long run a segment must cover all of its costs—both variable and fixed.
7. F In a decentralized organization, decision making is spread through all levels of management.
8. F Residual income is the difference between net operating income and the minimum return that must be generated on operating assets.
9. T This is a major criticism of the ROI method.
10. F A profit center is responsible for controlling costs as well as generating revenues.
11. T A reduction in assets will result in an increase in the turnover figure, and an increase in the ROI.
12. F Common expenses, such as those associated with operating corporate headquarters, should not be allocated to segments when making either residual income or ROI computations.
13. F Under the residual income approach, the manager seeks to maximize the residual income figure.
14. F The margin would also typically increase, since the net operating income would generally increase more rapidly than sales (due to the effects of operating leverage).
15. T The opportunity cost is the contribution margin lost from giving up outside sales.
16. F The opposite is true. When actual cost is used as a transfer price there is little or no incentive to control costs since whatever cost is incurred can simply be transferred on to the next division.
17. T The use of cost as a transfer price provides no signal to the manager as to when transfers should or should not be made.
18. T The transfer price can be higher when the selling division has idle capacity.

Multiple Choice

1. a Since advertising costs would arise because of the existence of the various product lines and tailored to the needs of these lines, the advertising costs would be traceable fixed costs on a segmented statement.
2. c A negative segment margin means that a segment is not covering its own traceable costs. However, the segment may still be of value to the company if it is necessary to the sale of other products.

3. a The segment margin for Product X can be read directly from the segmented income statement that appears below:

	Total	*Product X*	*Product Y*
Sales	$500,000	$200,000	$300,000
Variable expenses	150,000	50,000	100,000
Contribution margin	350,000	150,000	200,000
Traceable fixed expenses	230,000	80,000	150,000
Segment margin	120,000	$ 70,000	$ 50,000
Common fixed expenses	70,000		
Net income	$ 50,000		

4. d See the segmented income statement above in the answer to exercise (3).

5. b The following statement will help in solving this exercise:

	Product Y	*Percentage of Sales*
Sales	$300,000	100 %
Variable expenses	100,000	$33\frac{1}{3}$ %
Contribution margin	200,000	$66\frac{2}{3}$ %
Traceable fixed expenses	150,000	50 %
Segment margin	$ 50,000	$16\frac{2}{3}$ %

Using the contribution margin ratio method, the $90,000 increase in sales should lead to a $60,000 (= 66 2/3% X $90,000) increase in contribution margin. This would be offset by the $20,000 increase in advertising expenses, a traceable fixed expense, to yield a net $40,000 increase in segment margin.

6. b Since there is no mention of any change in common fixed expenses, the change in the company's overall net income should be the same as the change in Product Y's segment margin.

7. a If the level of inventory is reduced, then operating assets will also be reduced. The result will be a higher turnover figure and an increase in the ROI.

8. c The computations are:

$$\text{ROI} = \frac{\$9{,}000}{\$180{,}000} \text{ X } \frac{\$180{,}000}{\$45{,}000} = 5\% \text{ X } 4 = 20\%$$

9. c Residual income has nothing to do with ROI; moreover, as residual income increases ROI frequently decreases (as shown in examples in the chapter).

10. c The computations are:

Average operating assets	$300,000
Net operating income	$ 75,000
Minimum required return (18% X $300,000)	54,000
Residual income	$ 21,000

11. a The computations are:

Transfer price = Variable costs + Lost contribution margin
Transfer price = $40 + ($60—$40 = $20)
Transfer price = $60

12. d The computations are:

Transfer price = Variable costs + Lost contribution margin
Transfer price = $40+ $ 0
Transfer price = $40

But $40 represents a lower limit for a transfer price—the price can be as high as the $58 that Division B is presently paying to the outside supplier. Thus, the transfer price should be within the range of $40 to $58 per unit.

Chapter 12

Exercises

12-1.

a.

BYLUND COMPANY
Income Statement
For the Month Ended July 31

	Total Amount	%	Product X Amount	%	Product Y Amount	%
Sales	$500,000	100	$200,000	100	$300,000	100
Less variable expenses:						
Production	210,000	42	90,000	45	120,000	40
Selling and administrative	75,000	15	30,000	15	45,000	15
Total variable expenses	285,000	57	120,000	60	165,000	55
Contribution margin	215,000	43	80,000	40	135,000	45
Less traceable fixed expenses	125,000	25	50,000	25	75,000	25
Product line segment margin	90,000	18	$ 30,000	15	$ 60,000	20
Less common fixed expenses:						
Production	30,000					
Selling and administrative	20,000					
Total common fixed expenses	50,000					
Net Income	$ 40,000					

b. Neither product should be dropped. They are both covering all of their own traceable costs and are contributing to covering the fixed common costs and to overall profits of the company.

c.

Increase in sales	$80,0000
Contribution margin ratio	X 40%
Increase in contribution margin	$ 32,000
Increase in fixed production costs	$ 25,000
Increase in net income	$ 7,000

Yes, the product should be enhanced

12-2.

	Total		*Southwest Division*		*Central Division*	
	Amount	%	*Amount*	%	*Amount*	%
Sales	$1,000,000	100	$600,000[5]	100	$400,000[6]	100
Variable expenses	320,000[10]	32	240,000[7]	40	80,000[9]	20
Contribution margin	680,000[11]	68	360,000	60	320,000[8]	80
Traceable fixed expenses:	350,000[2]	35	150,000	25	200,000	50
Division segment margin	330,000[3]	33	$210,000[1]	35	$120,000[1]	30
Common fixed expenses	290,000[4]	29				
Net income	$ 40,000	4				

Note: This problem can be solved in many different ways. The following is one sequence that can be followed:

1. $360,000 - $150,000 = $210,000
2. $150,000 + $200,000 = $350,000
3. $210,000 + $120,000 = $330,000
4. $330,000 + $40,000 = $290,000
5. $360,000 ÷ 60% = $600,000
6. $1,000,000 - $600,000 = $400,000
7. $600,000 - $360,000 = $240,000
8. $200,000 + $120,000 = $320,000
9. $400,000 - $320,000 = $80,000
10. $240,000 + $80,000 = $320,000
11. $360,000 + $320,000 = $680,000

12-3. a.

$$\text{Margin} = \frac{\text{Net operating income, \$160,000}}{\text{Sales, \$2,000,000}} = 8\%$$

$$\text{Turnover} = \frac{\text{Sales, \$2,000,000}}{\text{Average operating assets, \$800,000}} = 2.5$$

ROI = Margin X Turnover
= 8% X 2.5 = 20%

b.

Average operating assets	$800,000
Net operating income	$160,000
Minimum required return (16% X $800,000)	128,000
Residual income	$ 32,000

12-4.

	Company 1	*Company 2*	*Company 3*
Sales	$600,000*	$600,000*	$180,000
Net operating income	60,000*	45,000	27,000*
Average operating assets	300,000*	200,000*	100,000
Margin	10%	7.5%*	15%
Turnover	2	3.0	1.8*
Return on investment (ROI)	20%	22.5%	27%*

*Given

12-5.

a. Transfer Price = $30 + $20 ($50—$30 = $20) Transfer Price = $50

b. The valves should be purchased from the outside supplier, since the price will be only $48 per valve. In contrast, the company will give up $50 in revenue for each valve transferred internally rather than sold on the outside market.

c.

Regulator Division capacity	40,000 valves
Less Boiler Division's requirements	10,000 valves
Valves available for sale to outsiders	30,000 valves

Potential sales to outsiders	35,000 valves
Valves available for sale to outsiders	30,000 valves
Lost sales	5,000 valves

Cost of transferring internally:	
Variable cost $30 X 10,000	$300,000
Lost contribution margin ($50 – $30) X 5,000	100,000
Total cost of transferring internally	$400,000
Cost of purchasing from an outside supplier	$480,000

Profits will be $80,000 higher if the valves are acquired internally rather than purchased outside.

d. Transfer Price = $30 + $-0- = $30
There is no lost contribution margin, since the Regulator Division has idle capacity.

12-6. ROI can lead to dysfunctional decisions in that an investment center manager may reject an otherwise profitable investment opportunity simply because the return from the investment would reduce the investment center's overall ROI. That is, the return from the investment might be greater than the ROI being earned in the company as a whole, but less than the ROI being earned in the investment center itself. Thus, accepting the investment would benefit the company as a whole, but reduce the overall return to the investment center. This problem can be overcome by using residual income, rather than ROI, in evaluating performance in an investment center. ROI, in common with other methods such as residual income, tends to focus too much on short-term profits. For example, managers may neglect research and development since the benefits from research and development are usually delayed while the costs are immediately expensed.

Chapter 13

Relevant Costs for Decision Making

Chapter Study Suggestions

In the first few pages of the chapter, guidelines are given for identifying relevant costs. Study these pages carefully, since these guidelines are used many times in the remaining pages of the chapter to show how relevant costs can be identified in various decision-making situations.

Three decision-making situations identified in the chapter are of particular importance. These are (1) adding and dropping segments such as product lines, (2) make or buy, and (3) sell or process further. Concentrate your study on Exhibits 13-3, 13-5, and 13-7, which deal with these three topics. You must have a thorough understanding of the analytical procedure followed in each of these exhibits in order to be able to do the homework material.

CHAPTER HIGHLIGHTS

A. A *relevant cost* in a decision is a cost that should have a bearing on which alternative the manager selects. Only those costs that differ between alternatives are relevant. Costs that differ between alternatives are called *avoidable costs*.

1. There are two broad classifications of costs that are not relevant: (a) sunk costs, and (b) future costs which do not differ between alternatives. *Sunk costs* are not relevant since they have already been incurred and therefore cannot differ between alternatives.

2. To identify relevant costs, the manager should take the following steps:

a. Assemble all costs associated with each alternative being considered.

b. Eliminate sunk costs.

c. Eliminate costs that do not differ between alternatives.

d. Make a decision based on the remaining cost data. These will be the differential or avoidable costs, and hence the costs relevant to the decision to be made.

3. Costs which are relevant in one situation may not be relevant in another situation.

B. As stated above, sunk costs are never relevant in decision making since they are not avoidable; that is, they can never differ between alternatives.

1. The book value of (and depreciation on) old equipment is a sunk cost. Hence, it is not relevant in decision making.

2. However, depreciation is a sunk cost only if it relates to old equipment (e.g., equipment that has already been purchased). Thus, depreciation on new equipment would be a relevant cost in decision making.

3. Even though the book value of old equipment is not relevant in a decision, the resale value of old equipment may be relevant. In addition, if one alternative involves more wear and tear on an old machine than another alternative, that may also be relevant.

C. As stated above, future costs that do not differ between alternatives are not relevant costs.

1. For example, if maintenance costs will be the same regardless of which machine is purchased, then maintenance costs are irrelevant to the decision of which machine to purchase.

2. Relevant costs should be isolated in cost analysis for two reasons:

a. In any given situation, the irrelevant costs greatly outnumber the relevant costs. Focusing just on the relevant costs simply takes less time and effort.

b. The use of irrelevant costs intermingled with relevant costs may draw the decision maker's attention away from the matters that are really critical to the problem being studied.

D. *Adding or dropping a segment* such as a product line is a common decision. In making this decision, compare the contribution margin of the segment to the fixed costs that could be avoided by dropping the segment.

1. If the contribution margin which will be lost by dropping a product line is greater than the fixed costs which will be avoided, then the product line should be retained.

2. If the contribution margin which will be lost by dropping a product line is less than the fixed costs which will be avoided, then the line should be dropped.

3. Exhibit 13-3 illustrates an alternate approach to deciding whether to retain or drop a product line or other segment of a company. In this approach two income statements are prepared: one showing present operations, and another showing what costs and revenues would be if the product line was dropped.

4. The decision to keep or drop a product line or other segment of a company is often clouded by the allocation of common fixed costs.

a. Such allocations can make a product line or other segment *appear* to be unprofitable, when in fact the product line may be contributing substantially to the overall profits of the company.

b. Common fixed costs should never be allocated to segments of a company; segments should be charged only with those costs that are directly traceable to them, as shown in Exhibit 13-4.

E. A decision to produce a particular part internally, rather than to buy the part externally from a supplier, is often called a *make or buy decision*. The relevant costs in such a decision, as always, are the costs that differ between the alternatives.

1. Exhibit 13-5 contains an example of a make or buy decision. Notice from the exhibit that the costs that are relevant in a make or buy decision are those costs that *differ* between the make or buy alternatives.

2. Opportunity cost may be a key factor in a make or buy decision as well as in other decisions.

a. If there are no alternative uses of facilities currently being used to make a part or a product, then opportunity cost is zero and it does not need to be considered.

b. On the other hand, if buying from outside the company would free up facilities that could be used to produce something else, then an opportunity cost is present. This opportunity cost is the segment margin that could be obtained from the alternative use of the facilities; it becomes part of the cost of the "make" alternative in a make or buy decision.

F. Another common decision concerns *special orders*. Companies often have opportunities to sell products under special circumstances that don't affect their regular sales. For example, a company may receive an order on a one-time basis from an overseas customer in a market the company does not ordinarily sell in. Under such circumstances, the special order should be accepted if the incremental revenue from the special order exceeds the incremental (i.e., avoidable) costs of the order. The incremental costs would include any applicable opportunity costs.

G. A *constraint* is a scarce resource that limits the output of an organization. For example, a particular machine with a lower capacity than any other machine may be a bottleneck that limits the total output of a factory. That machine would be called a constraint and the time available on the machine would be the scarce resource.

1. To maximize total contribution margin, compute *the contribution margin per unit of the scarce resource*. The products that promise the greatest contribution margin per unit of the scarce resource should be emphasized since they generate the greatest profit from the use of the scarce resource.

2. Since the constraint limits the output from the entire organization, there can be a tremendous payoff to increasing the amount of the scarce resource that is available. This is called "elevating the constraint" and can be accomplished in a variety of ways including working overtime on the bottleneck, buying another machine, subcontracting work, and so on.

H. In some industries, such as petroleum refining, several end products are produced from a single raw material input. Such products are known as *joint products*. The *split-off point* is that point in the manufacturing process at which the joint products can be recognized as separate products.

1. Decisions as to whether a joint product should be sold at the split-off point or processed further and then sold are known as "sell or process further" decisions.

2. Costs incurred up to the split-off point are called *joint product costs*. These costs are irrelevant in decisions regarding whether a product should be processed further after the split-off point, since they are sunk costs at that point.

3. It is profitable to continue processing joint products after the split-off point so long as the incremental revenue from such processing exceeds the incremental processing costs. Exhibit 13-7 contains an example of a "sell or process further" analysis.

REVIEW AND SELF TEST
Questions and Exercises

True or False

For each of the following statements, enter a T or an F in the blank to indicate whether the statement is true or false.

___ 1. All costs are relevant in decision making, except those costs that are not avoidable.

___ 2. Variable costs are relevant costs in decision making, whereas fixed costs are not relevant.

___ 3. A sunk cost is an avoidable cost.

___ 4. Depreciation is a relevant cost if it relates to equipment that has not yet been purchased.

___ 5. Future costs are always relevant in decision making.

___ 6. Costs that are relevant in one decision situation are not necessarily relevant in another decision situation.

___ 7. If by dropping a product line a company is able to avoid more in fixed costs than it loses in contribution margin, then it will be better off if the line is eliminated.

___ 8. Allocation of common fixed costs to product lines and to other segments of a company helps the manager to see if the product line or segment is profitable.

___ 9. If a product line has a negative segment margin, it is conclusive evidence that the product line should be discontinued.

___ 10. Opportunity cost may be a key factor in a make or buy decision.

___ 11. A company should always promote the product that has the highest contribution margin per unit.

___ 12. A joint product should continue to be processed after the split-off point so long as the incremental revenue from such processing exceeds the incremental processing costs.

___ 13. Joint product costs are irrelevant in decisions regarding what to do with joint products after the split-off point.

Multiple Choice

Choose the best answer or response by placing the identifying letter in the space provided.

___ 1. All of the following costs are relevant in a make or buy decision except: a) the opportunity cost of space; b) costs that are avoidable by "buying" rather than "making"; c) variable costs of producing the item; d) costs that are differential between the "make" and "buy" alternatives; e) all of the above costs are relevant.

___ 2. One of Simplex Company's products has a contribution margin of $50,000 and fixed costs totaling $60,000. If the product is dropped, $40,000 of the fixed costs will continue unchanged. As a result of dropping the product, the company's operating income should: a) decrease by $50,000; b) increase by $30,000; c) decrease by $30,000; d) increase by $10,000.

___ 3. Halley Company produces 2,000 parts each year that are used in one of its products. The unit cost of producing this part is

Variable cost	$ 7.50
Fixed cost	6.00
Total cost	$13.50

The part can be purchased from an outside supplier at $10 per unit. If the part is purchased from the outside supplier, two-thirds of the fixed costs incurred in producing the part can be eliminated. The effect on operating income from purchasing the part would be a: a) $3,000 increase; b) $1,000 decrease; c) $7,000 increase; d) $5,000 decrease.

___ 4. Product A has a contribution margin of $8 per unit, a contribution margin ratio of 50 percent, and requires 4 machine-hours to produce. Product B has a contribution margin of $12 per unit, a contribution margin ratio of 40 percent, and requires 5 machine-hours to produce. If the constraint is machine-hours, then the company should produce and sell: a) Product A since it has the highest contribution margin ratio; b) Product B since it has the highest contribution margin per machine-hour; c) Product A since it requires fewer machine-hours per unit than does Product B; d) Product B since it has the highest contribution margin per unit.

___ 5. Sunderson Products, Inc. has received a special order for 1,000 units of a sport fighting kite. The customer has offered a price of $9.95 for each kite. The unit costs of the kite, at its normal sales level of 30,000 units per year, are detailed below:

Variable production costs	$5.25
Fixed production costs	2.35
Variable selling costs	0.75
Fixed selling and admin. costs	3.45

There is ample idle capacity to produce the special order without any increase in total fixed costs of any kind. The special order would involve lower variable selling costs—$0.15 per unit instead of $0.75 per unit. The special order would have no impact on the company's other sales. What effect would accepting this special order have on the company's operating income? a) $1,850 increase; b) $1,850 decrease; c) $4,550 increase; d) $4,550 decrease.

___ 6. Products A and B are joint products. Product A can be sold for $1,200 at the split-off point, or processed further at a cost of $600 and then sold for $1,700. Product B can be sold for $3,000 at the split-off point, or processed further at a cost of $800 and then sold for $4,000. The company should process further: a) Product A; b) Product B; c) both products; d) neither of the products.

Exercises

13-1. The most recent income statement for the men's formal wear department of Merrill's Department Store is given below:

Sales		$500,000
Less variable expenses		200,000
Contribution margin		300,000
Less fixed expenses:		
Salaries and wages	$150,000	
Insurance on inventories	10,000	
Depreciation of fixtures	65,000*	
Advertising	100,000	325,000
Net operating income (loss)		$ (25,000)

*Six year remaining useful life, with little or no current resale value.

Due to its poor showing, management is thinking about dropping the men's formal wear department. If the department is dropped, a make-work position will be found for one long-time employee who is due to retire in several years. That employee's salary is $30,000. The fixtures in the department would have no resale value and would be hauled to the county dump.

Prepare an analysis, using the following form, to determine whether the department should be dropped.

Contribution margin lost if the department is dropped		$________
Less avoidable fixed costs:		
________	$________	
________	________	
________	________	________
Increase (decrease) in operating income		$________

Based on this analysis, should the men's formal wear department be dropped?

Redo the analysis, using the alternate format shown below:

	Keep Department	*Drop Department*	*Difference: Income increase or (decrease)*
Sales	$500,000	$______	$______
Less variable expenses	200,000		
Contribution margin	300,000		
Less fixed expenses:			
Salaries and wages	150,000		
Insurance on inventories	10,000		
Depreciation of equipment	65,000		
Advertising	100,000		
Total fixed expenses	325,000		
Net operating income (loss)	$ (25,000)	$______	$______

13-2. Watson Company produces two products from a common input. Data relating to the two products are given below:

	Product A	*Product B*
Sales value at the split-off point	$60,000	$120,000
Allocated joint product costs	45,000	90,000
Sales value after further processing	90,000	200,000
Cost of further processing	20,000	85,000

Determine which of the products should be sold at the split-off point, and which should be processed further before sale. Use the form that appears below.

Sales value after further processing	$______	$______
Sales value at the split-off point		
Incremental revenue from further processing		
Less cost of further processing		
Profit (loss) from further processing	$______	$______

13-3. Petre Company is now making a small part that is used in one of its products. The company's accounting department reports the following costs of producing the part internally:

	Per Part
Direct materials	$15
Direct labor	10
Variable manufacturing overhead	2
Fixed manufacturing overhead, traceable	4
Fixed manufacturing overhead, common, but allocated	5
Total cost	$36

The traceable fixed overhead costs consist of 75 percent depreciation of special equipment, and 25 percent supervisory salaries. The special equipment has no resale value. The supervisory salaries could be avoided if production of the part were discontinued.

An outside supplier has offered to sell the parts to Petre Company for $30 each, based on an order of 5,000 parts per year. Determine whether Petre Company should accept this offer, or continue to make the parts internally? Use the following form in your answer:

	Per Unit Differential Cost		*5,000 Parts*	
	Make	*Buy*	*Make*	*Buy*
Outside purchase price		$_____		$_____
Cost of making internally:				
______________	$_____		$_____	
______________	_____		_____	
______________	_____		_____	
______________	_____		_____	
______________	_____		_____	
Total cost	$_____	$_____	$_____	$_____

13-4. **Critical thought writing exercise:** "The easiest way to distinguish between relevant and irrelevant costs is by cost behavior; variable costs are relevant costs and fixed costs are irrelevant costs." Explain why you do or do not agree with this statement.

....

....

....

....

....

....

....

....

Answers to Questions and Exercises

True or False

1. T Unavoidable costs cannot be affected by a decision and therefore are irrelevant.

2. F Fixed costs can be relevant in decision making and variable costs can be irrelevant.

3. F Sunk costs are never avoidable costs, since by definition they have already been incurred and thus can't be avoided.

4. T Depreciation on equipment that has not yet been purchased is avoidable and therefore relevant.

5. F Future costs are relevant only if they differ between alternatives; future costs that do not differ between alternatives are not relevant costs.

6. T For example, a product line manager's salary would be relevant in a decision to drop the product line, but would not be relevant in a decision about how much to spend on advertising.

7. T This statement represents one way in which a manager can determine whether a product should be dropped or retained.

8. F Allocation of common fixed costs to product lines and to other segments of a company can result in misleading data and can make a product line appear to be unprofitable when in fact it may be one of a company's best products.

9. F Even if a product line has a negative segment margin, the product's costs still must be analyzed to determine if the product should be dropped. For example, depreciation on special equipment with no resale value would be traceable to the product line, but would not be relevant in a decision to drop the product line.

10. T The opportunity cost represents the segment margin that could be obtained by best alternative use of the space currently being utilized to make an item rather than to buy it.

11. F When there is a constraint, a company should promote the product that has the highest contribution margin per unit of the scarce resource. A product might have a high contribution margin per unit, for example, but it may require a large amount of bottleneck machine time as compared to other products.

12. T Processing further under these conditions will increase profits.

13. T At the split-off point, joint product costs have already been incurred and thus they are sunk costs and not relevant in decision making.

Multiple Choice

1. e These costs are all relevant because they all represent costs which are avoidable (differential) in choosing one alternative over another.

2. c The computations are:

Contribution margin lost	$(50,000)
Less avoidable fixed costs	20,000*
Decrease in operating income	$(30,000)

*$60,000 – $40,000 = $20,000

3. a The computations are:

	Differential Cost	
	Make	*Buy*
Variable costs	$ 7.50	—
Avoidable fixed cost	4.00	—
Outside purchase price	—	$10.00
Total relevant cost	$11.50	$10.00

2,000 units X $1.50 = $3,000

4. b The computations are:

	A	*B*
Contribution margin per unit (a)	$8.00	$12.00
Machine-hours to produce (b)	4.00	5.00
CM per machine-hour (a) ÷ (b)	$2.00	$ 2.40

5. c The computations are:

Incremental revenue	
($9.95 X 1,000)	$9,950
Incremental costs:	
Variable production	
($5.25 X 1,000)	5,250
Variable selling	
($0.15 X 1,000)	150
Increase in operating income	$4,550

6. b The computations are:

	A	B
Sales value after further processing	$1,700	$4,000
Sales value at split-off	1,200	3,000
Incremental sales value	500	1,000
Incremental processing cost	600	800
Advantage (disadvantage) of further processing	$ (100)	$ 200

Exercises

13-1.

Contribution margin lost if the department is dropped		$(300,000)
Less avoidable fixed costs:		
Salaries and wages ($150,000 - $30,000)	$120,000	
Insurance on inventories	10,000	
Advertising	100,000	230,000
Decrease in overall company net operating income		$ (70,000)

Based on the analysis above, the department should not be dropped. The solution using the alternate format appears below:

	Keep Department	*Drop Department*	*Difference: Income increase or (decrease)*
Sales	$500,000	$ -0-	$(500,000)
Less variable expenses	200,000	-0-	200,000
Contribution margin	300,000	-0-	$(300,000)
Less fixed expenses:			
Salaries and wages	150,000	30,000	120,000
Insurance on inventories	10,000	-0-	10,000
Depreciation of fixtures	65,000	65,000*	-0-
Advertising	100,000	-0-	100,000
Total fixed expenses	325,000	95,000	230,000
Net operating income (loss)	$(25,000)	$(95,000)	$ (70,000)

* If the department were dropped, the remaining book value of the fixtures would be written off at once. If the department were not dropped, the remaining book value would be written off over a number of years in the form of depreciation charges. In either case, the entire remaining book value will eventually flow through the income statement as charges in one form or another.

13-2.

	Product A	*Product B*
Sales value after further processing	$ 90,000	$200,000
Sales value at the split-off point	60,000	120,000
Incremental revenue from further processing	30,000	80,000
Less cost of further processing	20,000	85,000
Profit (loss) from further processing	$ 10,000	$ (5,000)

13-3.

	Per Unit Differential Costs		*5,000 Parts*	
	Make	*Buy*	*Make*	*Buy*
Outside purchase price		$30		$150,000
Cost of making internally:				
Direct materials	$15		$ 75,000	
Direct labor	10		50,000	
Variable manufacturing overhead	2		10,000	
Fixed manufacturing overhead, traceable	1*		5,000	
Fixed manufacturing overhead, common, but allocated	-	-	-	-
Total cost	$28	$30	$140,000	$150,000
Difference in favor of making		$2		$10,000

*$4 X 25% = $1. The depreciation on the equipment and the common fixed overhead would not be avoidable costs.

13-4. This statement is not true. Variable costs are not automatically relevant costs, and fixed costs are not automatically irrelevant costs. Whether a cost is relevant depends on whether the cost is avoidable. A fixed cost can be avoidable, the same as a variable cost can be avoidable. On the other hand, a variable cost may not be avoidable in a particular decision situation and therefore not relevant to the decision. For example, the variable costs in already manufactured obsolete goods would not be relevant in a decision as to whether the goods should be sold at a discount price or simply junked.

Chapter 14

Capital Budgeting Decisions

Chapter Study Suggestions

To understand the material in this chapter, it is essential that you have a solid understanding of the concept of present value. If you have not worked with present value before, study Appendix 14A, "The Concept of Present Value," until you thoroughly understand what present value is and how it is computed. Then turn to Review Problem 1 at the end of the chapter and work it out step by step.

Once you understand present value, you will be ready to tackle the capital budgeting methods illustrated in the chapter. The first of these methods is called the net present value method. Exhibits 14-1 and 14-4 illustrate this method. Follow through each number in the exhibits, and trace the factors back to the tables given at the end of the chapter. Unless you do this, you won't really understand what is going on. Also note the format in which the data are presented. You should use a similar format in your own work unless otherwise directed by your instructor.

The second method presented for capital budgeting is called the internal rate of return method. It is illustrated in Example D. This method is similar to the net present value method in that both methods are based on discounting future cash flows.

There are two methods of making capital budgeting decisions that do not discount future cash flows. These are the payback method and the simple rate of return method. Formulas are provided for both methods. Pay particular attention to the formula for the simple rate of return. It can be tricky to apply.

CHAPTER HIGHLIGHTS

A. The term *capital budgeting* is used to describe planning and financing major capital outlays that commit the company for some time into the future such as purchasing new equipment, building a new facility, or introducing a new product line.

1. Capital budgeting usually involves investment—committing funds now so as to obtain cash inflows in the future.

2. Capital budgeting decisions fall into two broad categories:

a. *Screening decisions:* Decisions relating to whether or not a proposed project meets some preset criterion for acceptance.

b. *Preference decisions*: Decisions relating to the selection of a proposed project from among several competing projects.

B. Because business investments tend to be long-term in nature, a business should pay particular attention to the time value of money in investment decisions.

1. *Discounted cash flow methods* give full recognition to the time value of money, and at the same time provide for full recovery of original capital.

2. There are two methods that use discounted cash flows—the *net present value method* and the *internal rate of return method.*

C. The net present value method is illustrated in Example A (Exhibit 14-1) and in Example C (Exhibit 14-4). The basic steps in this method are:

1. Determine the required investment.

2. Determine the future cash inflows and outflows that result from the investment.

3. Use the *present value tables* to find the appropriate *present value factors.*

a. The values (or factors) in the present value tables depend upon the discount rate and the number of periods (usually years).

b. The *discount rate* in present value analysis is the company's required rate of return, which is often the company's cost of capital. The *cost of capital* is a broad concept involving a blending of the cost of all sources of capital funds, both debt and equity. The details of the cost of capital are covered in finance classes.

4. Multiply the cash flows by their present value factors and sum the results. The end result (which is net of the initial investment) is called the *net present value* of the project.

5. In a screening decision, if the net present value is positive, the investment should be accepted. If the net present value is negative, the investment should be rejected.

D. Discounted cash flow analysis is based entirely on *cash flows*—not on accounting net income. Accounting net income must be ignored in cash flow analysis.

1. Typical cash flows associated with an investment are:

a. Typical cash outflows include: initial investment (including installation costs); increased working capital needs; repairs and maintenance; and incremental operating costs.

b. Typical cash inflows include: incremental revenues; reductions in costs; salvage value; and release of working capital at the end of the project.

2. Depreciation is not a cash flow and therefore is not part of the analysis. (However, depreciation can affect taxes, which is a cash flow. This aspect of depreciation is covered in Chapter 15.)

3. Quite often, a project requires an infusion of cash (i.e., working capital) in order to finance inventories, receivables, and other working capital items. Typically, at the end of the project these working capital items can be liquidated (i.e., the inventory can be sold) and the cash invested in these items recovered. Thus, working capital is counted as a cash outflow at the beginning of a project and as a cash inflow at the end of the project.

4. Two simplifying assumptions are commonly made in discounted cash flow analysis:

a. All cash flows occur at the *end* of a period.

b. All cash flows generated by an investment project are immediately reinvested at a rate of return equal to the discount rate.

E. The internal rate of return method is another discounted cash flow method used in capital budgeting decisions.

1. The *internal rate of return* is the rate of return promised by an investment project over its useful life; it is the discount rate for which the net present value of a project is zero.

2. When the cash flows are the same every year, the following formula can be used to find the internal rate of return:

$$\frac{\text{Investment required}}{\text{Net annual cash inflows}} = \text{Factor of the internal rate of return}$$

For example, assume an investment of $3,791 is made in a project that will last five years and has no salvage value. Also assume that the annual cash inflow from the project will be $1,000.

$$\frac{\$3{,}791}{\$1{,}000} = 3.791 \text{ Factor}$$

From Table 14C-4 in Appendix 14C, scanning along the 5 year row, it can be seen that this factor represents a 10 percent rate of return. Therefore, the internal rate of return is 10 percent. (You may want to verify that this calculation is correct by computing the net present value of the investment, which should be zero.)

3. If the factor computed in (3) above falls between two factors in the present value table, interpolation is used to estimate the true internal rate of return. The interpolation process is illustrated in the chapter.

4. If the cash flows are not the same every year, the internal rate of return is found using trial and error. The internal rate of return is whatever discount rate makes the net present value of the project equal zero.

5. In a screening decision, the internal rate of return is compared to the required rate of return. If the internal rate of return is less than the required rate of return, the project is rejected. If it is greater than or equal to the required rate of return, the project is accepted.

F. Two common approaches used in the net present value method are the *total-cost* approach and the *incremental-cost* approach.

1. The total-cost approach is the most flexible and the most widely used method. Exhibit 14-7 shows this approach. Note in Exhibit 14-7 that *all* cash inflows and *all* cash outflows are included in the solution under each alternative.

2. The incremental-cost approach is a simpler and more direct route to a decision. This approach focuses on differential costs. Exhibit 14-8 shows this approach.

3. If done correctly, the difference in the net present values between the alternatives under the total-cost approach will equal the net present value under the incremental-cost approach. In other words, the two approaches should lead to exactly the same conclusion.

G. Sometimes no revenue or cash inflow is directly involved in a decision. In this situation, the company will select the *least-cost* alternative. The least cost can be determined by either the total-cost approach or the incremental approach. Exhibits 14-9 and 14-10 illustrate least-cost decisions.

H. It is often difficult to quantify all the benefits involved in an investment in automation—particularly the intangible benefits.

1. The reduction in direct labor cost from automation may be easy to quantify. Intangible benefits, such as greater throughput or greater flexibility in operations, are usually very difficult to quantify. It would be a mistake to ignore these intangible benefits simply because they are difficult to quantify.

2. The difficulty can often be resolved by computing how large the intangible benefits would have to be in order to make the investment attractive. The steps in this approach are:

a. Compute the net present value of the tangible costs and benefits. If the result is positive, the investment is accepted immediately since the intangible benefits simply make it even more attractive.

b. If the net present value of the tangible costs and benefits is negative, compute the additional net annual cash inflows that would make the net present value positive.

c. If the intangible benefits are likely to be at least as large as the required additional net annual cash inflows computed in (2), then accept the project.

I. There are two other capital budgeting methods considered in the chapter. These methods do not involve discounting cash flows One of these is the payback method.

1. The *payback method* computes the time period required for an investment project to recoup its own initial cost out of the cash receipts it generates. The payback period is expressed in years. When the cash inflows from the project are the same every year, the following formula can be used:

$$\text{Payback period} = \frac{\text{Investment required}}{\text{Net annual cash inflows}}$$

a. In computing the "Investment Required," if new equipment is replacing old equipment, then the cost of the new equipment should be reduced by any salvage value obtained from the old equipment.

b. In computing the "Net Annual Cash Inflow," if new equipment is replacing old equipment, then only the incremental cash inflow provided by the new equipment over the old equipment should be used.

c. Note that this is the same formula as the one that is used in internal rate of return calculations.

2. The payback method is not a measure of profitability. Rather it is a measure of how long it takes for a project to recoup its own investment cost.

3. Major defects in the payback method are that it ignores the time value of money, and that it ignores all cash flows that occur once the initial cost has been recovered. However, the payback method can be useful in industries where project lives are very short and uncertain.

J. Another capital budgeting method that does not involve discounted cash flow is the simple rate of return method.

1. The simple rate of return method focuses on accounting net income, rather than on cash flows. The formula for its computation is:

$$\text{Simple rate of return} = \frac{\text{Incremental revenues} - \text{Incremental expenses}}{\text{Initial investment}}$$

If new equipment is replacing old equipment, then the "Initial Investment" in the new equipment is the cost of the new equipment reduced by any salvage value obtained from the old equipment.

2. A major defect of the simple rate of return method is that it does not consider the time value of money. Therefore, the rate of return computed by this method will not be an accurate guide as to the profitability of an investment project.

Appendix 14A: The Concept of Present Value

A. Since most business investments extend over long periods, it is important to recognize the time value of money in capital budgeting analysis. Essentially, a dollar received today is more valuable than a dollar received in the future. There are two reasons for this:

1. The first reason is that the dollar received today can be invested and earn an immediate return.

2. The second reason is that there is uncertainty about the future, and therefore a dollar in the future may never be received.

B. Present value analysis makes it possible for the manager to recognize the time value of money in capital budgeting decisions.

1. Present value analysis involves expressing a future cash flow in terms of present dollars. When a future cash flow is expressed in terms of its present value, the process is called *discounting*.

2. Use Table 14C-3 in Appendix 14C to determine the present value of a single sum to be received in the future. This table contains factors for various rates of interest for various periods, which when multiplied by the future sum, will give the sum's present value.

3. Use Table 14C-4 in Appendix 14C to determine the present value of an *annuity*, or stream, of cash flows. This table contains factors that, when multiplied by the stream of cash flows, will give the stream's present value. Be careful to note that this annuity table is for a very specific type of annuity in which the first payment occurs at the end of the first year.

Appendix 14B: Inflation and Capital Budgeting

A. Inflation has an impact on the numbers that are used in a capital budgeting analysis—both the cash flows and the discount rate.

B. Under certain conditions, it doesn't make any difference whether you adjust both the cash flows and the discount rate for inflation or whether you do not adjust them for inflation. However, you must be consistent. If there is any adjustment made for inflation, both the cash flows and the discount rate must be adjusted for inflation.

C. For the sake of simplicity, we assume in Chapters 14 and 15 that there is no inflation.

REVIEW AND SELF TEST
Questions and Exercises

True or False

For each of the following statements, enter a T or an F in the blank to indicate whether the statement is true or false.

___ 1. Under the net present value method, the present value of all cash inflows associated with an investment project are compared to the present value of all cash outflows, with the difference, or net present value, determining whether or not the project is an acceptable investment.

___ 2. One key shortcoming of discounted cash flow methods is that they do not provide for the recovery of the original investment.

___ 3. Although depreciation is an important element in the computation of accounting net income, it is not used in capital budgeting computations, since it does not involve a cash flow.

___ 4. Although a cash outlay for a noncurrent asset such as a machine would be considered in a capital budgeting analysis, a cash outlay for a working capital item such as inventory would not be considered.

___ 5. In discounted cash flow analysis, cash flows are ordinarily assumed to occur uniformly throughout a period.

___ 6. The internal rate of return is the discount rate for which a project's net present value is zero.

___ 7. The internal rate of return method is simpler to use, makes it easier for the manager to adjust for risk, and provides more usable information than the net present value method.

___ 8. In present value analysis, the higher the discount rate, the higher is the present value of a given future cash inflow.

___ 9. In comparing two investment alternatives, the total-cost approach provides the same ultimate answer as the incremental-cost approach.

___ 10. If an investment in automated equipment can't be justified by a reduction in direct labor cost, then the investment probably shouldn't be made.

___ 11. The simple rate of return method explicitly takes depreciation into account.

___ 12. The payback method does not consider the time value of money.

___ 13. The present value of a cash inflow to be received in 5 years is greater than the present value of the same sum to be received in 10 years.

Multiple Choice

Choose the best answer or response by placing the identifying letter in the space provided.

The following data relate to questions 1 and 2.

Peters Company is considering the purchase of a machine to further automate its production line. The machine would cost $30,000, and have a ten-year life with no salvage value. It would save $8,000 per year in labor costs, but would increase power costs by $1,000 annually. The company's required rate of return is 12%.

___ 1. The present value of the net annual cost savings would be: a) $39,550; b) $45,200; c) $5,650; d) $70,000.

___ 2. The net present value of the proposed machine would be: a) $(15,200); b) $5,650; c) $9,550; d) $30,000.

___ 3. Acme Company is considering investing in a new machine that costs $84,900, and which has a useful life of 12 years with no salvage value. The machine will generate $15,000 annually in net cash inflows. The internal rate of return on the machine is: a) 8%; b) 10%; c) 12%; d) 14 %.

___ 4. White Company's required rate of return is 12%. The company is considering an investment opportunity that would yield a return of $10,000 in five years. What is the most that the company should be willing to invest in this project? a) $36,050; b) $5,670; c) $17,637; d) $2,774.

___ 5. Dover Company is considering an investment project in which a working capital investment of $30,000 would be required. The investment would provide cash inflows of $10,000 per year for six years. If the company's required rate of return is 18 percent, and if the working capital is released at the end of the project, then the project's net present value is: a) $4,980; b) $(4,980); c) $16,080; d) $(12,360).

___ 6. Whiting Company has completed a net present value analysis for a project that shows a $113,000 *negative* net present value. This project involves a purchase of automated equipment that would have a 10-year useful life. The company's required rate of return is 12%. What amount of cash inflow each year would have to be provided by the intangible benefits associated with the project in order for the project to be acceptable? a) $11,300; b) $13,560; c) $18,000; d) $20,000

___ 7. Frumer Company has purchased a machine that cost $30,000, that will save $6,000 per year in cash operating costs, and that has an expected life of 15 years with zero salvage value. The payback period on the machine will be: a) 2 years; b) 7.5 years; c) 5 years; d) 0.2 years.

___ 8. Refer to the data in question (7) above. The simple rate of return on the machine is approximately: a) 20%; b) 13.3%; c) 18%; d) 10%.

Exercises

14-1. You have recently won $100,000 in a contest. You have been given the option of receiving $100,000 today or receiving $12,000 at the end of each year for the next 20 years.

a. If you can earn 8% on investments, which of these two options would you select? (Note: The net present value method assumes that any cash flows are reinvested at a rate of return equal to the discount rate. Therefore, to answer this question you can compare the net present values of the cash flows under the two alternatives using 8% as the discount rate.)

Item	*Year(s)*	*Amount of Cash Flows*	*8 Percent Factor*	*Present Value of Cash Flows*
Receive the annuity	_____	$ ________	________	$__________
Receive the lump sum	_____	________	________	__________
Net present value in favor of ________________				$__________

b. If you can earn 12% on investments, which of these two options would you select?

Item	*Year(s)*	*Amount of Cash Flows*	*12 Percent Factor*	*Present Value of Cash Flows*
Receive the annuity	_____	$ ________	________	$__________
Receive the lump sum	_____	________	________	__________
Net present value in favor of ________________				$__________

14-2. Lynde Company has been offered a contract to provide a key replacement part for the Army's main attack helicopter. The contract would expire in eight years. The projected cash flows that result from the contract are given below:

Cost of new equipment	$300,000
Working capital needed	100,000
Net annual cash inflows	85,000
Salvage value of equipment in eight years	50,00

The company's required rate of return is 16 percent. The working capital would be released for use elsewhere at the end of the project.

Complete the analysis below to determine whether the contract should be accepted.

Item	*Year(s)*	*Amount of Cash Flows*	*16 Percent Factor*	*Present Value of Cash Flows*
Cost of new equipment	_____	$________	________	$________
Working capital needed	_____	________	________	________
Net annual cash inflows	_____	________	________	________
Salvage value of equipment	_____	________	________	________
Working capital released	_____	________	________	________
Salvage value of equipment	_____	________	________	________
Net present value				$________

Should the contract be accepted? Explain.

....

....

....

....

14-3. Swift Company is considering the purchase of a new machine that will cost $20,000. The machine will provide revenues of $9,000 per year. Out-of-pocket operating costs will be $6,000 per year. The new machine will have a useful life of 10 years and will have zero salvage value. The company's required rate of return is 12 percent.

a. What is the internal rate of return? (Interpolate if necessary.)

Annual revenue .... $__________

Annual operating costs........................... __________

Net annual cash inflow.......................... $__________

$$\frac{\text{Investment required}}{\text{Net annual cash inflows}} = \frac{\text{Factor of the}}{\text{internal rate of return}}$$

__________ = __________

	Present Value Factor	
____% factor	________	________
True factor	________	
____% factor		________
Difference	________	________

Internal rate of return = ____% + (____ x 2%) =

b. Should the company buy the new machine? Why or why not?

....

....

....

....

14-4. Harlan Company would like to purchase a new machine that makes wonderfully smooth fruit sorbet that the company can sell in the premium frozen dessert sections of supermarkets. The machine costs $450,000 and has a useful life of ten years with a salvage value of $50,000. Annual revenues and expenses resulting from the new machine follow:

Sales revenue		$300,000
Less operating expenses:		
Advertising	$100,000	
Salaries of operators	70,000	
Maintenance	30,000	
Depreciation	40,000	240,000
Net income		$ 60,000

a. Harlan Company will not invest in new equipment unless it promises a payback period of 4 years or less. Compute the payback period on the sorbet machine.

Computation of the net annual cash inflow:

Net income	$__________
Add: Noncash deduction for depreciation	__________
Net annual cash inflow	$__________

Computation of the payback period:

$$\frac{\text{Investment required}}{\text{Net annual cash inflows}} = \text{Payback period}$$

$$\frac{\_\_\_\_\_\_\_\_\_\_}{\_\_\_\_\_\_\_\_\_\_} = \_\_\_\_\_\_ \text{ years}$$

According to Harlan's criterion, should the machine be purchased? Explain.

....

....

....

b. Compute the simple rate of return promised by the new machine.

$$\frac{\text{Incremental revenues} - \text{Incremental expenses}}{\text{Initial investment}} = \text{Simple rate of return}$$

$$\frac{\_\_\_\_\_\_\_\_\_\_}{\_\_\_\_\_\_\_\_\_\_} = \_\_\_\_\_\_ \%$$

14-5. **Critical thought writing exercise:** As the discount rate increases, the present value of a given future sum also increases. Do you agree? Why or why not?

Answers to Questions and Exercises

True or False

1. T Exhibit 14-4 illustrates this point.

2. F Discounted cash flow methods do provide for recovery of original investment, as illustrated in Exhibit 14-3.

3. T The cash flow occurs when equipment is purchased; depreciation is an expense that involves no cash flow.

4. F A cash outlay for a working capital item represents an investment, the same as a cash outlay for a machine; thus, it would be considered in a capital budgeting analysis.

5. F Cash flows are assumed to occur at the end of a period.

6. T This statement is true by definition; the principle involved is illustrated in Exhibit 14-5.

7. F The opposite is true—the net present value method is the method that is simpler to use, and so forth.

8. F The opposite is true—the higher the discount rate, the lower is the present value of a given future cash inflow.

9. T The total-cost approach and the incremental-cost approach are just different ways of obtaining the same result.

10. F Only rarely will a reduction in direct labor cost justify an investment in automated equipment. Typically, the justification for such an investment will come from intangible benefit such as greater throughput or greater flexibility in operations.

11. T This point is illustrated in formulas (3) and (4) in the text.

12. T This is a major defect of the payback method—dollars are given the same weight regardless of the year in which they are received.

13. T When discounting a single sum, the shorter the time period, the greater the present value.

Multiple Choice

1. a The computations are:

Savings in labor costs	$ 8,000
Less increased power costs	1,000
Net cost savings	$ 7,000
Present value factor for 12% for 10 years (Table 14C-4)	x 5.650
Present value of cost savings	$39,550

2. c The computations are:

Investment in the machine	$(30,000)
Present value of cost savings	39,550
Net present value	$ 9,550

3. d The computations are:

$$\frac{\text{Investment required}}{\text{Net annual cash inflows}} = \text{Factor of the internal rate of return}$$

$$\frac{\$84{,}900}{\$15{,}000} = 5.660 \text{ Factor}$$

Looking at the 12-year row in the annuity Table 14C-4, a factor of 5.660 equals a return of 14%.

4. b The computations are:

Return in 5 years	$10,000
Factor for 12% for 5 years (Table 14C-3)	x 0.567
Present value	$ 5,670

This is the maximum amount the company is willing to invest since if it were to invest more than $5,670, the net present value of the investment would be negative.

5. c The computations are:

	Year(s)	*Amount*	*18% Factor*	*Present Value*
Working capital investment	Now	$(30,000)	1.000	$(30,000)
Cash inflow	1-6	10,000	3.498	34,980
Working capital released	6	30,000	0.370	11,100
Net present value				$ 16,080

6. d The computations are:

$$\frac{\text{Net present value } \$(113{,}000)}{\text{Factor, } 5.650} = \$20{,}000$$

7. c The computation is:

$$\text{Payback period} = \frac{\text{Investment required}}{\text{Net annual cash inflows}}$$

$$= \frac{\$30{,}000}{\$6{,}000} = 5 \text{ years}$$

8. b The computation is:

$$\text{Simple rate of return} = \frac{\text{Incremental revenues} - \text{Incremental expenses}}{\text{Initial investment}}$$

$$= \frac{\$6{,}000^{*} - \$2{,}000^{**}}{\$30{,}000} = 13.3\%$$

* The "incremental revenue" is the cost savings of $6,000 per year.
** The incremental expense is the annual depreciation charge of $2,000 = $30,000 ÷ 15 years.

Exercises

14-1. a. The annuity is preferable if the discount rate is 8 percent:

Item	*Year(s)*	*Amount of Cash Flows*	*8 Percent Factor*	*Present Value of Cash Flows*
Receive the annuity	1-20	$ 12,000	9.818	$117,816
Receive the lump sum	Now	100,000	1.000	100,000
Net present value in favor of the annuity				$ 17,816

b. The lump sum is preferable if the discount rate is 12 percent:

Item	*Year(s)*	*Amount of Cash Flows*	*12 Percent Factor*	*Present Value of Cash Flows*
Receive the annuity	1-20	$ 12,000	7.469	$ 89,628
Receive the lump sum	Now	100,000	1.000	100,000
Net present value in favor of the lump sum				$ 10,372

14-2.

Item	*Year(s)*	*Amount of Cash Flows*	*16 Percent Factor*	*Present Value of Cash Flows*
Cost of new equipment	Now	($300,000)	1.000	($300,000)
Working capital needed	Now	(100,000)	1.000	(100,000)
Net annual cash receipts	1-8	85,000	4.344	369,240
Salvage value of equipment	8	50,000	0.305	15,250
Working capital released	8	100,000	0.305	30,500
Net present value				$ 14,990

Yes, the contract should be accepted. The net present value is positive, which means that the contract will provide more than the company's 16 percent required rate of return.

14-3. a.

Annual revenue	$9,000
Annual operating costs	6,000
Incremental cash inflow	$3,000

$$\frac{\text{Investment required}}{\text{Net annual cash inflows}} = \text{Factor of the internal rate of return}$$

$$= \frac{\$20,000}{\$3,000} = 6.667$$

Since the 6.667 factor falls between the 8 percent and 10 percent rates of return in Table 14C-4, it will be necessary to interpolate to find the exact rate of return:

	Present Value Factor	
8% factor	6. 710	6.710
True factor	6.667	
10% factor		6.145
Difference	0.043	0.565

$$\text{Internal rate of return} = 8\% + \left(\frac{0.043}{0.565} \times 2\%\right) = 8.15\%$$

b. No, the machine should be rejected since the 8.15% internal rate of return is less than the 12% required rate of return.

14-4. a. The net annual cash inflow would be:

Net income	$ 60,000
Add: Noncash deduction for depreciation	40,000
Net annual cash inflow	$100,000

The payback period would be:

$$\text{Payback period} = \frac{\text{Investment required}}{\text{Net annual cash inflows}} = \frac{\$450,000}{\$100,000} = 4.5 \text{ years}$$

The machine would not be purchased since it will not provide the 4 year payback period required by the company.

b. The simple rate of return would be:

$$\text{Simple rate of return} = \frac{\text{Incremental revenues} - \text{Incremental expenses}}{\text{Initial investment}} = \frac{\$300,000 - \$240,000}{\$450,000} = 13.3\%$$

14-5. No. As the discount rate increases, the present value of a given future sum decreases. As the discount rate increases, less must be set aside today to yield a given future sum. This is the power of compounding interest. For example, the factor for a discount rate of 12 percent for a single sum to be received ten years from now is 0.322, whereas the factor for a discount rate of 14 percent over the same period is 0.270. If the sum to be received in ten years is $10,000, the present value in the first case is $3,220, but only $2,700 in the second case. Thus, as the discount rate increases, the present value of a given sum decreases.

Chapter 15

Further Aspects of Investment Decisions

Chapter Study Suggestions

This chapter builds on the discounted cash flow methods introduced in Chapter 14 and discusses the impact of income taxes on capital budgeting decisions. Make sure you understand and remember the formulas in Exhibit 15-3 showing the computation of after-tax cost and after-tax benefit. In addition, you should memorize the formula for the tax shield associated with depreciation. Exhibit 15-7 provides a comprehensive illustration of the computation of net present value. Study this exhibit and the related text material with special care; the computations on the exhibit are complex and will take some time to digest.

Two methods are illustrated in the chapter for ranking investment projects according to preference. These are: 1) the internal rate of return method, and 2) the profitability index. Notice that the profitability index is based on the net present value concepts discussed in the preceding chapter.

CHAPTER HIGHLIGHTS

A. Income taxes affect cash flows and therefore should generally be considered in capital budgeting. However, nonprofit entities such as hospitals, schools, or governmental units are not subject to income taxes and may use the simpler approaches illustrated in Chapter 14.

B. Both the cost and benefits of a project should be estimated on an after-tax basis.

1. The true cost of a tax-deductible item is the amount of the payment net of any reduction in income taxes due to the payment. An expenditure net of its tax effects is known as *after-tax cost.* For example, assume that a company needs to overhaul a machine at a cost of $6,000. The cost of the overhaul is a tax-deductible expense. If the income tax rate is 30%, the after-tax cost of the overhaul is:

Cost of overhaul	$6,000
Reduction in taxes due to the overhaul (30% x $6,000)	(1,800)
After-Tax Cost	$4,200

2. The formula that will give the net after-tax cash inflow for any tax-deductible expenditure is:

$$(1 - \text{Tax rate}) \times \frac{\text{Tax deductible}}{\text{cash expense}} = \text{After–tax cost}$$

3. Not all cash outflows are tax deductible expenses.

a. For example, an investment in working capital is not tax-deductible. It is not an expense since such an investment involves transforming one asset (such as cash) into another asset (such as inventory).

b. The purchase cost of a depreciable asset *is not* a tax deductible item in the period in which it is purchased. However, depreciation on the asset *is* tax deductible. (See section D below.)

C. As with cash expenditures, taxable cash receipts must also be placed on an after-tax basis.

1. A cash receipt net of its tax effect is known as *after-tax benefit*. For example, assume that a company receives $100,000 from sale of services. If the tax rate is 30%, the after-tax benefit is:

Revenue	$ 100,000
Income tax payment required (30% x $100,000)	(30,000)
After-Tax Benefit	$ 70,000

2. The formula that will give the net after-tax cash inflow from revenue or other taxable cash receipts is:

$$(1 - \text{Tax rate}) \times \frac{\text{Taxable cash}}{\text{receipt}} = \text{After–tax benefit}$$

3. The same formula can be used when a project promises cash cost savings rather than additional revenues. The cost savings can be treated the same as a revenue item in determining the net after-tax cash inflow.

4. Not all cash receipts are taxable. For example, the release of working capital at the termination of an investment project is not a taxable cash inflow.

D. Depreciation is not a cash outflow. However, depreciation deductions do affect the amount of taxes that a firm will pay.

1. The depreciation deduction acts as a *tax shield*. Depreciation deductions shield revenues from taxation and lower the amount of income taxes that a company has to pay.

2. The formula used to compute the tax savings from the depreciation tax shield is:

$$\text{Tax rate} \times \frac{\text{Depreciation}}{\text{deduction}} = \frac{\text{Tax savings from the}}{\text{depreciation tax shield}}$$

E. In the United States, taxpayers must use the Modified Accelerated Cost Recovery System, MACRS, to depreciate assets for tax purposes. (MACRS does not have to be used for financial reporting purposes and usually isn't.)

1. Under MACRS, assets are placed into one of eight property classes according to their useful lives. See Exhibit 15-4 in the text for details.

2. Under MACRS, the *half-year convention* must be observed, which means that only one half year's depreciation can be taken in the first and last year of the asset's life. In effect, this adds a full year to the recovery period, as shown in Exhibit 15-5.

3. Under MACRS, salvage value is not considered in computing depreciation deductions.

4. There are two methods of determining the depreciation deduction: the MACRS tables and the optional straight-line method.

a. The MACRS tables, which are based on accelerated depreciation methods, are reproduced in Exhibit 15-5.

b. Under the optional straight-line method, taxpayers can depreciate an asset evenly over its property class life—with the exception of the first and last years which are depreciated at half the usual rate.

c. Generally, the MACRS tables should be used since they allow more rapid write-offs of the original cost of assets and therefore usually yield a higher present value.

5. If an asset is disposed of after it has been fully depreciated for tax purposes, any proceeds are fully taxable since the MACRS tables and the optional straight-line methods assume zero salvage value.

F. Exhibit 15-7 contains a comprehensive example of income taxes and capital budgeting. Follow this example carefully step by step.

1. Notice that all cash flows involving tax deductible expenses and taxable receipts have been placed on an after-tax basis by multiplying the cash flow in each case by one minus the tax rate.

2. Also notice that the depreciation deductions are multiplied *by the tax rate itself* to determine the tax savings (cash inflow) resulting from the tax shield. *These two points should be studied with great care until both are thoroughly understood.*

G. Preference decisions involve the ranking of investment projects. Such a ranking is necessary whenever there are limited funds available for investment.

1. Preference decisions are sometimes called *ranking* decisions or *rationing* decisions because they ration limited investment funds among competing investment opportunities.

2. When using the internal rate of return to rank competing investment projects, the preference rule is: *The higher the internal rate of return, the more desirable the project.*

3. If the net present value method is used to rank competing investment projects, the net present value of one project should not be compared directly to the net present value of another project, unless the investments in the projects are of equal size.

a. To make a valid comparison between projects that require different investment amounts, a *profitability index* is computed. The formula for the profitability index is:

$$\frac{\text{Present value of cash inflows}}{\text{Investment required}} = \text{Profitability index}$$

This is basically an application of the idea from Chapter 13 of utilization of a scarce resource. In this case, the scarce resource is the investment funds. The profitability index is similar to the contribution margin per unit of the scarce resource.

b. The preference rule when using the profitability index is: *The higher the profitability index, the more desirable the project.*

4. The profitability index is conceptually superior to the internal rate of return as a method of making preference decisions because the profitability index will always give the correct signal as to the relative desirability of alternatives, even if alternatives have different lives and different patterns of earnings. In contrast, the internal rate of return method may incorrectly rank some potential projects.

REVIEW AND SELF TEST
Questions and Exercises

True or False

For each of the following statements, enter a T or an F in the blank to indicate whether the statement is true or false.

___ 1. The after-tax cost of a tax-deductible item is computed by the formula: Tax rate x Cash expense = After-tax cost.

___ 2. The half-year convention must be used with the MACRS tables, but not with the optional straight-line method.

___ 3. Since salvage value is not considered when computing depreciation under MACRS, any salvage value received on sale of an asset is taxed as income.

___ 4. The MACRS tables allow a greater total amount of depreciation to be taken over the life of an asset than is allowed under the optional straight-line method.

___ 5. The release of working capital at the end of an investment project would be a taxable cash inflow.

___ 6. A company can use one depreciation method for tax purposes and an entirely different method in preparing financial statements.

___ 7. In general, a larger present value of tax savings from the depreciation tax shield will result from using the MACRS tables than from the optional straight-line method.

___ 8. In ranking investment projects, a project with a high net present value should always be ranked above a project with a lower net present value.

___ 9. In preference decision situations, the net present value and internal rate of return methods may yield conflicting rankings of projects.

___ 10. The profitability index is computed by dividing a project's net present value by the investment required in the project.

___ 11. Under the optional straight-line method, an asset is depreciated over its useful life rather than over its MACRS property class life.

___ 12. The depreciation method that is used for financial statement purposes should also be used in discounted cash flow analysis.

Multiple Choice

Choose the best answer or response by placing the identifying letter in the space provided.

___ 1. A project is being considered in which the annual cash operating expenses are $20,000. If the company's tax rate is 30 percent, what is the after-tax cost of the operating expenses? a) $6,000; b) $14,000; c) $20,000; d) $60,000.

___ 2. A project is being considered in which the annual cash revenues are $80,000. If the company's tax rate is 30 percent, what is the after-tax benefit of the revenues? a) $0; b) $24,000; c) $56,000; d) $80,000.

___ 3. Kinnard Inc.'s depreciation deduction last year was $50,000 and its tax rate was 30 percent. The company's tax savings from the depreciation tax shield for the year was: a) $15,000; b) $35,000; c) $50,000; d) $30,000.

___ 4. Leeds Company has purchased a machine that cost $90,000, has an $8,000 salvage value, and is in the MACRS 5-year property class. The machine was purchased on December 1 of the current year. If the optional straight-line method is used, the depreciation in the first year will be: a) $1,600; b) $18,000; c) $16,400; d) $9,000.

___ 5. Refer to the data in question (4) above. If the MACRS tables are used to compute depreciation deductions, the depreciation in the *second* year will be: a) $9,000; b) $16,400; c) $28,800; d) $18,000.

___ 6. Polar Company is studying a project that would require a $200,000 working capital investment. If the company's tax rate is 30 percent, then the initial investment in working capital should be shown in the capital budgeting analysis as a cash outflow of: a) $200,000; b) $140,000; c) $60,000; d) $0.

___ 7. Refer to the data in question (6) above. The working capital would be released for use elsewhere at the end of the project in four years. The company's after-tax cost of capital is 10%. What is the approximate present value of the after-tax cash flows associated with the release of the working capital? a) $200,000; b) $95,600; c) $136,600; d) $0.

___ 8. A project requires an investment of $40,000, has a present value of cash inflows of $50,000, and has a net present value of $10,000. The project's profitability index would be: a) 0.80; b) 1.25; c) 4.0; d) 1.00.

Exercises

15-1. Martin Company is acquiring a new copier for use in its office. The following data relate to the new copier:

Cost of the new copier	$150,000
Annual savings in cash operating costs	40,000
Salvage value of the new copier	6,000
Overhaul of the new copier required in the third year	5,000
Life of the new copier	8 years

The new copier would replace an old machine that has a remaining book value (for tax purposes) of $18,000. The old machine can be sold now for $10,000. The company's tax rate is 30 percent.

a. Compute the after-tax savings in annual cash operating costs. $__________

b. Compute the after-tax cost of the overhaul required in the third year. $__________

c. Compute the tax savings from the depreciation tax shield for each year and in total. The company uses the MACRS tables and the copier is in the 5-year property class.

Year	*Cost*	*MACRS Percentage*	*Depreciation Deduction*	*Tax Rate*	*Tax Shield: Income Tax Savings*
1	$150,000	______	______	30.0%	______
2	______	______	______	______	______
3	______	______	______	______	______
4	______	______	______	______	______
5	______	______	______	______	______
6	______	______	______	______	______
Total					______

d. Compute the after-tax benefit from the salvage value of the new copier. $____________

e. Compute the after-tax cash inflow from sale of the old machine. (This is a tough question. See the computations in Exhibit 15-8 in the text for an example.)

Cash received from the sale		$ ____________
Tax savings from loss on sale:		
Current book value	$ ____________	
Sale price now	____________	
Loss on disposal	____________	
Multiply by the tax rate	x 0.30	
Tax savings from loss		____________
Total cash inflows...		$____________

15-2. Marvel Company has $60,000 to invest and is considering two alternatives:

	Investment X	*Investment Y*
Cost of equipment	$60,000	—
Working capital needed	—	$60,000
Annual cash inflows	20,000	20,000
Salvage value	3,000	—
Life of the project...........................	5 years	5 years

The company's cost of capital is 12 percent, and the tax rate is 30 percent.

a. Compute the net present value of each investment using the form that appears below. The equipment is in the MACRS 3-year property class. The company uses the optional straight-line method of depreciation for tax purposes.

Items and computations				*Year(s)*	*(1) Amount*	*(2) Tax effect*	*(1) x (2) After-tax cash flows*	*12 percent factor*	*Present value of cash flows*
Investment X:									
Cost of equipment				______	________	________	________	______	________
Annual cash inflows				______	________	________	________	______	________
Depreciation deductions:									
Year	*Cost*	*Dep 'n percentage*	*Dep 'n deduction*						
1	________	______	________	______	________	________	________	______	________
2	________	______	________	______	________	________	________	______	________
3	________	______	________	______	________	________	________	______	________
4	________	______	________	______	________	________	________	______	________
Salvage value				______	________	________	________	______	________
Net present value									========
Investment Y:									
Working capital needed				______	________	________	________	______	________
Annual cash inflows				______	________	________	________	______	________
Working capital released				______	________	________	________	______	________
Net present value									========

b. Compute the profitability index for each investment.

$$\frac{\text{Present value of cash inflows}}{\text{Investment required}} = \text{Profitability index}$$

Investment X: ______________________ = __________
____

Investment Y: ______________________ = __________
____

15-3. **Critical thought writing exercise:** On an income statement, cash expenses and depreciation expenses are added together and deducted from revenues to determine net income. Assume that a company has cash operating expenses of $50,000 and depreciation expenses of $20,000. Can these amounts be added together and treated as one in a capital budgeting analysis, or should they be kept separate? Explain your answer.

Answers to Questions and Exercises

True or False

1. F The formula is: (1 - Tax rate) x Cash expense = After-tax cost.

2. F The half-year convention must be observed with either the MACRS tables or the optional straight-line method.

3. T The salvage value is fully taxable as income since the taxpayer will already have fully depreciated the asset.

4. F The same total amount of depreciation (equal to the original cost of the asset) is taken regardless of the depreciation method used. This point is illustrated in Exhibit 15-6 (where a total of $300,000 depreciation is taken under both methods).

5. F The release of working capital would simply be a return of the taxpayer's original investment and thus would not be taxable as income.

6. T The depreciation method used for tax purposes has no bearing on the method(s) that can be used in preparing financial statements.

7. T This point is illustrated in Exhibit 15-6.

8. F Net present value can't be used in ranking projects when investment funds are limited, since one project may have a higher net present value than another simply because it is larger and requires a greater investment. When the net present value method is used, the profitability index should be used to compare projects.

9. T See the example in the text in the section "Comparing the Preference Rules."

10. F The profitability index is computed by dividing the present value of an asset's total cash inflows by the investment required.

11. F Under the optional straight-line method, a taxpayer depreciates an asset over its MACRS property class life.

12. F In discounted cash flow analysis, a taxpayer should use the depreciation method that is used for tax purposes. The only bearing depreciation has on discounted cash flow analysis is the reduction in tax payments.

Multiple Choice

1. b (1–0.30) x $20,000 = $14,000

2. c (1–0.30) x $80,000 = $56,000

3. a 0.30 x $50,000 = $15,000

4. d The computations are:
$90,000 ÷ 5 years = $18,000;
$18,000 x 1/2 = $9,000.

5. c From Exhibit 15-5, the depreciation rate for the second year for the 5-year property class is 32.0%. Therefore, the second year's depreciation would be 32.0% of $90,000 or $28,800.

6. a Working capital represents an investment, not an expense, so there is no effect on taxes. This point is discussed in connection with Exhibit 15-7.

7. c The release of working capital does not affect taxes. Therefore, the entire $200,000 represents an after-tax cash flow. The present value factor for four periods at 10% per period is 0.683, so the present value of the $200,000 is 0.683 x $200,000 or $136,600.

8. b $50,000 ÷ $40,000 = 1.25

Exercises

15-1. a. (1 – Tax rate) x Taxable cash receipt = After-tax benefit
(1 - 0.30) x $40,000 = $28,000

b. (1 – Tax rate) x Tax deductible cash expense = After-tax cost
(1 - 0.30) x $5,000 = $3,500

c.

Year	*Cost*	*MACRS Percentage*	*Depreciation Deduction*	*Tax Rate*	*Tax Shield: Income Tax Savings*
	(1)	*(2)*	*(1) x (2) = (3)*	*(4)*	*(3) x (4)*
1	$150,000	20.0	$30,000	30%	$ 9,000
2	$150,000	32.0	48,000	30%	14,400
3	$150,000	19.2	28,800	30%	8,640
4	$150,000	11.5	17,250	30%	5,175
5	$150,000	11.5	17,250	30%	5,175
6	$150,000	5.8	8,700	30%	2,610
					$45,000

d. (1 – Tax rate) x Taxable cash receipt = After-tax benefit
(1 - 0.30) x $6,000 = $4,200

e. Cash flow from disposal of the old machine:

Cash received from sale		$10,000
Tax savings from loss on sale:		
Current book value	$18,000	
Sale price now	10,000	
Loss on disposal	8,000	
Multiply by the tax rate	x 30%	
Tax savings from loss		2,400
Total net cash inflow		$12,400

15-2. a.

Items and computations	Year(s)	(1) Amount	(2) Tax effect	(1) x (2) After-tax cash flows	12 percent factor	Present value of cash flows
Investment X:						
Cost of equipment	Now	$(60,000)	—	$(60,000)	1.000	$(60,000)
Annual cash inflows	1-5	20,000	1- 30%	14,000	3.605	50,470
Depreciation deductions:						

Year	Cost	Dep 'n percentage	Dep 'n deduction	Year(s)	(1) Amount	(2) Tax effect	(1) x (2) After-tax cash flows	12 percent factor	Present value of cash flows
1	$60,000	16.7%	$10,000	1	10,000	30%	3,000	0.893	2,679
2	60,000	33.3	20,000	2	20,000	30%	6,000	0.797	4,782
3	60,000	33.3	20,000	3	20,000	30%	6,000	0.712	4,272
4	60,000	16.7	10,000	4	10,000	30%	3,000	0.636	1,908

Items and computations	Year(s)	(1) Amount	(2) Tax effect	(1) x (2) After-tax cash flows	12 percent factor	Present value of cash flows
Salvage value	5	3,000	1-30%	2,100	0.567	1,191
Net present value						$ 5,302
Investment Y:						
Working capital needed	Now	$(60,000)	—	$(60,000)	1.000	$(60,000)
Annual cash inflows	1-5	20,000	1- 30%	14,000	3.605	50,470
Working capital released	5	60,000	—	60,000	0.567	34,020
Net present value.						$ 24,490

b. Investment X: $\frac{\$65,302}{\$60,000}$ = 1.09 (rounded) Investment Y: $\frac{\$84,490}{\$60,000}$ = 1.41 (rounded)

15-3. The two amounts should be kept separate. The after-tax cash flows are very different for cash expenses and for depreciation. The after-tax cash outflows for deductible cash expenses are measured by multiplying the cash expenses by one minus the tax rate. By contrast, depreciation expenses trigger a cash inflow through the depreciation tax shield. The amount of the inflow is measured by multiplying the depreciation expenses by the tax rate itself.

Chapter 16

Service Department Costing: An Activity Approach

Chapter Study Suggestions

There are three key exhibits in this chapter—Exhibits 16-2, 16-4, and 16-7. Exhibit 16-2 illustrates the direct method and Exhibit 16-4 illustrates the step method of allocating service department costs to operating departments. Follow the computations in the exhibits through step-by-step, and note the difference in the way the two methods handle the cost data.

Exhibit 16-7 expands on Exhibits 16-2 and 16-4 by showing how breaking costs down into their variable and fixed components can make the allocations more meaningful. Spend the bulk of your study time on the sections titled, "Allocating costs by behavior," and "A summary of cost allocation guidelines." Then note from Exhibit 16-7 how the ideas in these two sections are implemented in an extended allocation problem. This is a very important exhibit, since it is the basis for many of the longer, more difficult homework problems.

CHAPTER HIGHLIGHTS

A. The two broad classes of departments within an organization are operating departments and service departments.

1. *Operating departments* include those departments or units where the central purposes of the organization are carried out. Examples of such departments or units include the surgery department in a hospital, the shoe department in a department store, and producing departments in a manufacturing firm.

2. *Service departments* do not engage directly in operating activities. Rather, they provide service or assistance to other departments. Examples of service departments include the cafeteria in a hospital, the billing department in a department store, and the purchasing department in a factory.

3. The costs of service departments are typically allocated to operating departments. These allocated costs are then added to the overhead costs of the operating departments and included in predetermined overhead rates.

B. There are three major methods for allocating service department costs—the direct method, the step method, and the reciprocal method. The methods differ mainly in how they treat services that service departments provide to each other. These services are called *interdepartmental services* or *reciprocal services*.

C. The *direct method* is the simplest, and the least accurate, of the three methods. When the direct method is used, reciprocal services are ignored and service department costs are allocated directly to operating departments. For example, a hospital's custodial staff cleans administrative offices as well as operating rooms and hospital wards. However, in the direct method none of the custodial costs are allocated to the administrative department. Instead, all the custodial costs are allocated *directly* to the operating departments that generate revenue.

D. The *step method*, or *step-down method*, is slightly more complex that the direct method, but it is also more accurate.

1. In the step method, a specific order is selected for allocating the service department costs. Usually, service departments are ranked in terms of the amount of service they provide to other service departments, with the service department that provides the greatest service to the other service departments ranked first.

2. The costs of the first service department are allocated to *all the* other departments, both service and operating departments. Once the first service department's costs have been allocated, it is ignored in subsequent allocations.

3. Then the costs of the next service department are allocated to the *remaining* service departments as well as to the operating departments. However, any services provided by the second service department to the first service department are ignored. No costs are allocated back to the first service department.

4. The allocation proceeds in this manner, stepping through all the service departments. In each step, the next service department's costs are allocated to the remaining service departments as well as to the operating departments. Once a service department's costs have been allocated, the service department is ignored.

5. By following this procedure, the step method takes into account some of the reciprocal services, but not all of them.

E. The *reciprocal method* is the most complex, and the most accurate method of the three methods for allocating service department costs. The reciprocal method takes all of the reciprocal services fully into account. However, the reciprocal method is seldom used in practice because of its complexity and therefore we have not covered it in any detail in the book.

F. Whenever possible, service department costs should be separated into fixed and variable classifications and allocated separately to the other departments that use those services. By allocating fixed and variable costs separately, a company can avoid possible inequities in allocation as well as provide data which are more useful for planning and controlling operations.

1. The variable costs of providing services should be charged to other departments using as an allocation base whatever it is that causes the variable cost to vary. For example, if maintenance costs increase and decrease in proportion to machine hours, then machine hours should be used as the allocation base for maintenance costs.

a. At the beginning of the period, charges to departments that use the services should be computed by multiplying *budgeted* rates (e.g., $2.75 per machine hour) by *budgeted* activity of the other departments (e.g., 1,200 budgeted machine hours). These allocations, or charges, are used for planning.

b. At the end of the period, charges to the departments that use the services should be computed by multiplying *budgeted* rates (*not actual* rates) by *actual* activity. These charges are used for performance evaluation. If actual rates were used, the other departments would implicitly be held responsible for inefficiencies in the service department.

2. The fixed costs of service departments represent the cost of having long-run service capacity available. These costs are best allocated to consuming departments on the basis of *predetermined, lump-sum* amounts.

a. When allocating fixed costs, the *budgeted* (not actual) costs should be allocated on the basis of either *long-run average* activity or *peak period* requirements (not budgeted or actual activity). The reason for this is that the level of the fixed costs is usually determined by management's planning for the long run or for peak period activity. Management wants to make sure that there is enough capacity to handle peak period needs.

b. Once set, lump-sum allocations of fixed costs will not change between the beginning and the end of the period.

c. A company should not allocate fixed costs with a variable allocation base such as sales dollars. An inequity may arise since fixed costs allocated to one department will be affected by what happens in other departments.

3. Any difference between the actual service department costs and the costs charged to the operating departments at the end of the period should be retained in the service department as a spending variance.

G. In summary, the guidelines for allocating service department costs are:

1. If possible, the distinction between variable and fixed costs should be maintained.

2. Variable costs should be allocated at the budgeted rate, using as an allocation base whatever activity causes the incurrence of the cost.

3. Fixed costs should be allocated in predetermined, lump-sum amounts.

4. If it is not feasible to maintain a distinction between variable and fixed costs in a service department, the costs of the department should be allocated to consuming departments according to that base which appears to provide the best measure of benefits received.

5. Where feasible, reciprocal services between departments should be recognized.

REVIEW AND SELF TEST
Questions and Exercises

True or False

For each of the following statements, enter a T or an F in the blank to indicate whether the statement is true or false.

___ 1. The overhead rates used in operating departments should include allocated costs from service departments.

___ 2. The direct method of allocating service department costs fully accounts for all reciprocal services among service departments.

___ 3. When allocating a service department's costs under the direct method, one should never include the service department being allocated in the allocation base. (e.g., The meals served to cafeteria workers should not be included in the allocation base for the cafeteria.)

___ 4. When allocating a service department's costs under the step method, one *should* include the service department being allocated in the allocation base.

___ 5. The direct method of cost allocation is much simpler than the step method, in that services provided between service departments are ignored.

___ 6. The reciprocal method is generally considered to be more accurate than the step method of service department allocation.

___ 7. The order in which service departments are allocated makes a difference in the costs that are allocated to a particular operating department when the direct method is used.

___ 8. In allocating costs by the step method, the allocation sequence typically begins with the service department that provides the greatest amount of service to other departments.

___ 9. Variable costs of service departments should be allocated to operating departments in predetermined, lump-sum amounts.

___ 10. If a variable allocation base (such as direct labor hours) is used to allocate fixed service department costs, inequities may result in the amount of cost allocated to the various operating departments.

___ 11. Budgeted costs, rather than actual costs, should always be allocated from service departments to operating departments.

___ 12. Sales dollars represent a good allocation base, because sales dollars are easy to work with and show a department's "ability to pay."

Multiple Choice

Choose the best answer or response by placing the identifying letter in the space provided.

The following data are used in multiple choice questions 1 through 6.

Oscar Company has two service departments, personnel and custodial, and two operating departments, A and B. Budgeted data for the current year appears below:

	Service Departments		*Operating Departments*	
	Personnel	*Custodial*	*A*	*B*
Overhead costs	$800	$600	$2,000	$5,000
Employees	2	18	30	50
Space occupied in thousands of sq. ft.	20	10	40	80

Personnel costs are allocated on the basis of employees. Custodial costs are allocated on the basis of space occupied. The company makes no distinction between fixed and variable costs in its service department allocations.

___ 1. If the direct method of service department allocation is used, how much Personnel Department cost would be allocated to Operating Department A? a) $240; b) $300; c) $0; d) $800.

___ 2. If the direct method of service department allocation is used, how much Personnel Department cost would be allocated back to the Personnel Department? a) $16; b) $800; c) $0; d) $200.

___ 3. If the direct method of service department allocation is used, what would be the total overhead cost in Operating Department B after the allocations have been completed? a) $5,900; b) $900; c) $5,000; d) $6,400.

___ 4. If the step method of service department allocation is used and Personnel Department costs are allocated first, how much Personnel Department cost would be allocated to the Custodial Department? a) $146.94; b) $0; c) $144; d) $200.

___ 5. If the step method of service department allocation is used and Personnel Department costs are allocated first, how much Custodial Department cost would be allocated to the Personnel Department? a) $80; b) $0; c) $99.59; d) $150.

___ 6. If the step method of service department allocation is used and Personnel Department costs are allocated first, how much Custodial Department cost would be allocated to Operating Department A? a) $0; b) $150; c) $248.94; d) $171.43.

The following information applies to multiple choice questions 7 through 11.

Data for Wasatch Company's two operating departments follow:

	Budgeted Machine Hours Requirements	*Peak Period*
Operating Department #1	15,000	40%
Operating Department #2	25,000	60
Total Machine Hours	40,000	100%

The Wasatch Company has a Repair Department that serves these two operating departments. The variable repair costs are budgeted at $0.20 per machine hour. Fixed costs are budgeted at $12,000 per year. Fixed repair costs are allocated to operating departments on the basis of peak period requirements.

At the end of the year, the actual machine hours worked by the operating departments were 16,000 hours for Department #1 and 24,000 hours for Department #2. The actual Repair Department costs were $8,600 variable and $13,000 fixed.

___ 7. The amount of variable repair cost allocated to Department #l at the beginning of the year should be: a) $3,000; b) $5,000; c) $4,800; d) $7,200.

___ 8. The amount of fixed repair cost allocated to Department #2 at the beginning of the year should be: a) $3,000; b) $5,000; c) $4,800; d) $7,200.

___ 9. The amount of variable repair cost allocated to Department #1 at the end of the year should be: a) $4,800; b) $5,200; c) $3,200; d) $7,200.

___ 10. The amount of fixed repair cost allocated to Department #2 at the end of the year should be: a) $4,800; b) $7,800; c) $3,200; d) $7,200.

___ 11. The amount of actual repair costs not allocated to the operating departments and retained in the Repair Department at the end of the year as a spending variance should be: a) $600; b) $1,600; c) $1,000; d) $1,400.

Chapter 16

Exercises

16-1. Piney Company has three service departments and two operating departments. Following are costs and other data relating to these departments:

	Service Departments			Operating Departments	
	Janitorial	*Cafeteria*	*Engineering*	*Assembly*	*Finishing*
Overhead costs	$60,000	$42,600	$75,000	$230,000	$300,000
Square feet	1,500 sq. ft.	2,000 sq. ft.	1,000 sq. ft.	4,000 sq. ft.	3,000 sq. ft.
Number of employees	15	12	50	200	400

The Janitorial Department performs the greatest amount of service to the other departments, followed by the Cafeteria, with the Engineering Department last. The company allocates Janitorial costs on the basis of square feet. The Cafeteria and Engineering costs are allocated on the basis of the number of employees. The company makes no distinction between variable and fixed service department costs in its allocations of service department costs.

Allocate service department costs to the operating departments using the step method.

	Service Departments			Operating Departments	
	Janitorial	*Cafeteria*	*Engineering*	*Assembly*	*Finishing*
Overhead costs	$ 60,000	$ 42,600	$ 75,000	$ 230,000	$ 300,000
Allocations:					
Janitorial	______	______	______	______	______
Cafeteria		______	______	______	______
Engineering			______	______	______
Total	$______	$______	$______	$______	$______

16-2. Refer to the data in Exercise 16-1. Allocate the service department costs to the operating departments using the direct method.

	Service Departments			Operating Departments	
	Janitorial	*Cafeteria*	*Engineering*	*Assembly*	*Finishing*
Overhead costs	$ 60,000	$ 42,600	$ 75,000	$ 230,000	$ 300,000
Allocations:					
Janitorial	______			______	______
Cafeteria		______		______	______
Engineering			______	______	______
Total	$______	$______	$______	$______	$______

16-3. The municipal motor pool provides cars on loan to city employees who must travel on official business. The city has three departments that use this service—Public Safety, General Administration, and Sanitation. Data concerning these departments' annual use of the motor pool (in thousands of miles driven) appear below:

	Public Safety	*General Administration*	*Sanitation*
Budgeted use (thousands of miles)............	600	800	200
Actual use (thousands of miles)............	500	900	250
Peak period requirements............	35%	50%	15%

The motor pool's budgeted annual fixed costs are $330,000. Peak period requirements determine the level of the fixed costs. Budgeted variable costs are $80 per thousand miles driven.

a. How much of the motor pool's budgeted costs should be allocated to Public Safety at the beginning of the year for planning purposes?

b. Suppose the motor pool's actual costs for the year were $345,000 for fixed costs and $138,000 for variable costs. How much of this actual cost should be allocated to Public Safety at the end of the year for performance evaluation purposes?

16-4. **Critical thought writing exercise:** "Since sales dollars is a measure of ability to pay, it is probably the most equitable base for allocating service department costs to operating departments." Explain why you do or do not agree with this statement.

Answers to Questions and Exercises

True or False

1. T Service department costs are charged to products and services through the overhead rates of operating departments.

2. F The direct method entirely ignores reciprocal services among service departments.

3. T If the service department being allocated is included in the allocation base, then some of the cost will be allocated back to the service department.

4. F See the answer to (3) above.

5. T See Exhibit 16-2.

6. T The reciprocal method fully accounts for all reciprocal services among service departments.

7. F The order of allocation doesn't make any difference in the direct method. The order of allocation does, however, make a difference in the step method.

8. T This statement describes the procedure followed using the step method.

9. F Fixed costs—not variable costs—should be allocated in predetermined, lump-sums.

10. T The inequities that can result are discussed in the section of the chapter titled "Pitfalls in allocating fixed costs."

11. T Budgeted, rather than actual, costs should be allocated in order to avoid passing inefficiencies on from one department to another.

12. F As discussed in the text, sales dollars is a poor allocation base.

Multiple Choice

1. d Allocation base = 30 + 50 = 80
Allocation: (30/80) X $800 = $300

2. c Even though the Personnel Department has two employees, none of its costs are charged to itself in the direct method or in the step method.

3. a

Original overhead cost in Operating Department B	$5,000
Allocated Personnel Dept. cost: (50/80) X $800	500
Allocated Custodial Dept. cost: (80/120) X $600	400
Total	$5,900

4. a Allocation base = 18 + 30 + 50 = 98
Allocation: (18/98) X $800 = $146.94

5. b In the step method, once a service department's costs have been allocated, the department is ignored in subsequent allocations.

6. c This problem requires two steps:

Original Custodial cost	$600.00
Allocated from Personnel *..........	146.94
Custodial cost to be allocated..........	$746.94

*See the answer to question (4) above.

Allocation base = 40 + 80 = 120
Allocation: (40/120) X $746.94 = $248.98

7. a The computations are:
15,000 hours X $0.20 = $3,000.

8. d 60% X $12,000 = $7,200.

9. c The computations are:
16,000 hours X $0.20 = $3,200.
The budgeted rate is still used.

10. d Fixed costs should be allocated in predetermined, lump-sum amounts and the allocation at the end of the year should be the same as at the beginning of the year.

11. b The computations are:

Actual costs ($8,600 + $13,000)..........		$21,600
Allocated costs:		
Variable *..........	$8,000	
Fixed**	12,000	20,000
Unallocated		$ 1,600

*(16,000 hrs. + 24,000 hrs.) X $0.20 = $8,000
** The budgeted amount

Chapter 16

Exercises

16-1.

	Service Departments			*Operating Departments*	
	Janitorial	*Cafeteria*	*Engineering*	*Assembly*	*Finishing*
Overhead costs	$60,000	$42,600	$75,000	$230,000	$300,000
Allocations:					
Janitorial [1]	(60,000)	12,000	6,000	24,000	18,000
Cafeteria [2]		(54,600)	4,200	16,800	33,600
Engineering [3]			(85,200)	28,400	56,800
Total	$ -0-	$ -0-	$ -0-	$299,200	$408,400

$$^1 \frac{\text{Janitorial cost}}{\text{Total square feet}} = \frac{\$60{,}000}{10{,}000 \text{ square feet}} = \$6 \text{ per square foot}$$

$$^2 \frac{\text{Cafeteria cost}}{\text{Number of employees}} = \frac{\$54{,}600}{650 \text{ employees}} = \$84 \text{ per employee}$$

$$^3 \frac{\text{Engineering cost}}{\text{Number of employees}} = \frac{\$85{,}200}{600 \text{ employees}} = \$142 \text{ per employee}$$

16-2.

	Service Departments			*Operating Departments*	
	Janitorial	*Cafeteria*	*Engineering*	*Assembly*	*Finishing*
Overhead costs	$60,000	$42,600	$75,000	$230,000	$300,000
Allocation:					
Janitorial [1]	(60,000)			34,286	25,714
Cafeteria [2]		(42,600)		14,200	28,400
Engineering [3]			(75,000)	25,000	50,000
Total	$ -0-	$ -0-	$ -0-	$303,486	$404,114

$$^1 \frac{\text{Janitorial cost}}{\text{Total square feet}} = \frac{\$60{,}000}{7{,}000 \text{ square feet}} = \$8.57 \text{ per square foot}$$

$$^2 \frac{\text{Cafeteria cost}}{\text{Number of employees}} = \frac{\$42{,}600}{600 \text{ employees}} = \$71 \text{ per employee}$$

$$^3 \frac{\text{Engineering cost}}{\text{Number of employees}} = \frac{\$75{,}000}{600 \text{ employees}} = \$125 \text{ per employee}$$

16-3. a. Variable cost allocation:

Budgeted activity X budgeted rate	
600 thousand miles X $80	$ 48,000
Fixed cost allocation:	
% of peak period requirement X budgeted fixed cost	
35% X $330,000	115,500
Total	$163,500

b. Variable cost allocation:

Actual activity X budgeted rate	
500 thousand miles X $80	$ 40,000
Fixed cost allocation:	
% of peak period requirement X budgeted fixed cost	
35% X $330,000	115,500
Total	$155,500

16-4. Sales dollars is not a good base for allocating service department costs to other departments. This is because there generally is no cause-and-effect relationship between sales in operating departments and the incurrence of costs in the service departments. Thus, if sales dollars is used to allocate service department costs to other departments, inequities can result in the allocations. The amount of cost allocated to a given department will depend in large part on what is happening in other departments. A drop in sales in one department will result in it being relieved of allocated costs, and these costs will be shifted to other departments. As a consequence, the better departments will be penalized for lack of effectiveness elsewhere that is beyond their control.

Chapter 17

"How Well Am I Doing?" Statement of Cash Flows

Chapter Study Suggestions

This chapter shows how to prepare a statement of cash flows. The statement of cash flows is constructed primarily by examining changes in balance sheet accounts. There are three key exhibits in the chapter. The first, Exhibit 17-2, indicates which changes in the various balance sheet items are considered to be sources of cash and which are considered to be uses of cash. The second key exhibit is Exhibit 17-7, which provides guidelines for classifying transactions as operating, investing, and financing activities. Once the transactions have been classified as sources or uses and as operating, investing, or financing activities, it is fairly straight-forward to put together a statement of cash flows. However, there are many details to keep track of. Therefore, we recommend a systematic approach based on a worksheet such as the one in Exhibit 17-10.

CHAPTER HIGHLIGHTS

A. The purpose of the statement of cash flows is to highlight the major activities that have provided and used cash during the period.

B. The term *cash* is broadly defined to include both cash and cash equivalents. Cash equivalents consist of short-term, highly liquid investments such as treasury bills, commercial paper, and money market funds that are made solely for the purpose of generating a return on cash that is temporarily idle.

C. A period's net cash flow is equal to the change in the cash account during the period. (Remember that cash is taken to mean cash and cash equivalents when talking about the statement of cash flows.) Exhibit 17-1 shows that the change in cash during a period can be expressed in terms of the changes in all of the noncash balance sheet accounts. The statement of cash flows is based on this fact. The statement is basically a listing of changes in the noncash balance sheet accounts.

D. The changes in the noncash account balances can be classified as *sources* and *uses*. On the statement of cash flows, sources positively affect cash flow and uses negatively affect cash flow.

1. The following are classified as "sources":

a. Net income (part of the change in the retained earnings account).

b. Decreases in noncash assets.

c. Increases in liabilities.

d. Increases in capital stock accounts.

2. The following are classified as "uses":

a. Increases in noncash assets.

b. Decreases in liabilities.

c. Decreases in capital stock accounts.

d. Dividends paid to shareholders (part of the change in the retained earnings account).

3. The "sources" and "uses" usually make intuitive sense. For example, an increase in inventory (a noncash asset) implicitly requires cash and is considered to be a "use." As another example, if a company borrows money, it would be classified as a source of cash since it involves an increase in a liability.

E. The FASB requires that the statement of cash flows be divided into three sections. These sections relate to *operating activities, investing activities, and financing activities.*

1. As a general rule, operating activities are those activities that enter into determination of net income. These activities include:

a. Net income (or net loss).

b. Changes in current assets.

c. Changes in noncurrent assets that affect net income, such as depreciation and amortization.

d. Changes in current liabilities (except for debts to lenders and dividends).

e. Changes in noncurrent liabilities that affect net income, such as interest on debt.

2. Investing activities consist of changes in noncurrent assets that are not included in net income.

3. As a general rule, financing activities consist of any transactions involving borrowing from creditors (other than the payment of interest), and any transactions involving the owners of a company. Specific financing activities include:

a. Changes in current liabilities that are debts to lenders rather than obligations to suppliers, employees, or a government.

b. Changes in noncurrent liabilities that are not included in net income.

c. Changes in capital stock accounts.

d. Dividends paid to the company's shareholders.

F. Companies sometimes acquire assets or dispose of liabilities through *direct exchange transactions.* Examples include the issue of capital stock in exchange for property and equipment and the conversion of long-term debt into common stock.

1. Direct exchanges affect only non-current balance sheet accounts and have no effect on cash.

2. Direct exchanges are not reported on the statement of cash flows itself. However, they must be disclosed in a separate schedule accompanying the statement of cash flows.

G. For both financing and investing activities, items on the statement of cash flows must be presented in gross amounts rather than in net amounts. For example, if a company issues $100,000 of common stock and then uses the cash to pay off $100,000 of long-term debt, the two amounts must be shown separately. (This is not a direct exchange transaction because the common stock was issued for cash and then the cash was used to retire the debt.)

H. The net result of the cash inflows and outflows arising from operating activities is referred to as the *net cash provided by operating activities.* This figure can be computed using the *direct method* or the *indirect method.*

1. Under the direct method, the income statement is reconstructed on a cash basis from top to bottom. This method is discussed in Appendix 17A.

2. Under the indirect method, the net cash provided by operations is computed by starting with net income and adjusting it to a cash basis. The steps to follow in this adjustment process are illustrated in Exhibit 17-8 and explained in Exhibit 17-9.

3. The direct and indirect methods yield exactly the same figure for the net cash provided by operating activities.

4. The FASB recommends that the direct method be used, but almost all companies use the indirect method. The major reason for this is probably that following the FASB's recommendation in this matter involves more work and more disclosures.

I. Carefully study Exhibit 17-10, which illustrates the mechanics of putting together a worksheet. Make sure you understand each of the entries on this worksheet. Once this worksheet has been completed, the statement of cash flows can be easily constructed.

J. Carefully study Exhibit 17-12, which illustrates the format of the statement of cash flows. Make sure you can construct this statement using the worksheet in Exhibit 17-10.

Appendix 17A: The Direct Method

A. The direct method reconstructs the income statement from the top down. See Exhibit 17A-1 for an example.

1. To adjust revenue to a cash basis:

a. Subtract (add) any increase (decrease) in accounts receivable.

2. To adjust cost of goods sold to a cash basis:

a. Add (subtract) any increase (decrease) in inventory.

b. Subtract (add) any increase (decrease) in accounts payable.

3. To adjust operating expenses to a cash basis:

a. Add (subtract) any increase (decrease) in prepaid expenses.

b. Subtract (add) any increase (decrease) in accrued liabilities.

c. Subtract the period's depreciation and amortization charges.

4. To adjust income tax expense to a cash basis:

a. Subtract (add) any increase (decrease) in taxes payable.

b. Subtract (add) any increase (decrease) in deferred taxes.

REVIEW AND SELF TEST
Questions and Exercises

True or False

For each of the following statements, enter a T or an F in the blank to indicate whether the statement is true or false.

___ 1. Cash equivalents consist of any investments in stocks, bonds, treasury bills, or money market funds.

___ 2. Dividends received on stock held as an investment are included in the operating activities section of the statement of cash flows.

___ 3. Interest paid on amounts borrowed is included in the financing activities section of the statement of cash flows.

___ 4. Lending money to another entity (such as to a subsidiary) is classified as a financing activity.

___ 5. The payment of cash dividends to the company's stockholders is classified as a financing activity.

___ 6. All forms of debt, including accounts payable, short-term borrowing, and long-term borrowing, are classified as financing activities on the statement of cash flows.

___ 7. For both financing and investing activities, items on the statement of cash flows should be presented in gross amounts rather than in net amounts.

___ 8. Generally, the direct and indirect methods will yield different figures for the net cash provided by operating activities.

___ 9. Only changes in noncurrent accounts (assets, liabilities, and owners' equity) are analyzed in preparing a statement of cash flows.

___ 10. The cash account will always increase during the year if a company is profitable.

___ 11. (Appendix 17A) The income statement is reconstructed on a cash basis from top to bottom under the direct method of computing the net cash provided by operating activities.

___ 12. (Appendix 17A) In computing the net cash provided by operating activities, depreciation is added to net income under the indirect method, but it is deducted from operating expenses under the direct method.

Multiple Choice

Choose the best answer or response by placing the identifying letter in the space provided.

___ 1. For purposes of constructing a statement of cash flows, an increase in inventory would be classified as: a) a source and an operating activity; b) a use and an operating activity; c) a source and an investing activity; d) a use and an investing activity.

___ 2. An increase in accounts payable would be classified as: a) a source and an operating activity; b) a use and an operating activity; c) a source and a financing activity; d) a use and a financing activity.

___ 3. An increase in bonds payable would be classified as: a) a source and an investing activity; b) a use and an investing activity; c) a source and a financing activity; d) a use and a financing activity.

___ 4. An increase in long-term investments would be classified as: a) a source and an investing activity; b) a use and an investing activity; c) a source and a financing activity; d) a use and a financing activity.

___ 5. Cash dividends paid to the company's stockholders would be classified as: a) a source and an operating activity; b) a use and an operating activity; c) a source and a financing activity; d) a use and a financing activity.

___ 6. An increase in the company's common stock account would be classified as: a) a source and an investing activity; b) a use and an investing activity; c) a source and a financing activity; d) a use and a financing activity.

Exercises

17-1. Ingall Company's comparative balance sheet and income statement for the most recent year follow:

INGALL COMPANY
Comparative Balance Sheet
(dollars in millions)

	Ending Balance	*Beginning Balance*
Assets		
Cash	$ 14	$ 10
Accounts receivable	21	15
Inventory	50	43
Prepaid expenses	2	6
Plant and equipment	190	140
Less accumulated depreciation	(65)	(54)
Long-term investments	70	90
Total assets	$282	$250
Liabilities and Stockholders' Equity		
Accounts payable	$ 26	$ 25
Accrued liabilities	10	12
Taxes payable	13	18
Bonds payable	50	40
Deferred income taxes	36	31
Common stock	80	70
Retained earnings	67	54
Total liabilities and stockholders' equity	$282	$250

INGALL COMPANY
Income Statement
(dollars in millions)

Sales	$230
Less cost of goods sold	120
Gross margin	110
Less operating expenses	70
Net operating income	40
Gain on sale of long-term investments	5
Income before taxes	45
Less income taxes	14
Net income	$ 31

Notes: Dividends of $18 million were declared and paid during the year. The gain on sale of long-term investments was from the sale of investments for $25 million in cash. These investments had an original cost of $20 million. There were no retirements or disposals of plant or equipment during the year.

Using the blank form on the following page, prepare a worksheet like Exhibit 17-10 for Ingall Company.

INGALL COMPANY
Statement of Cash Flows Worksheet

	Change	*Source or use?*	*Cash Flow Effect*	*Adjust-ments*	*Adjusted Effect*	*Classi-fication*
Assets (except cash and cash equivalents)						
Current assets:						
Accounts receivable	____	____	____		____	____
Inventory	____	____	____		____	____
Prepaid expenses	____	____	____		____	____
Noncurrent assets:						
Plant and equipment	____	____	____		____	____
Long-term investments	____	____	____	____	____	____
Liabilities, Contra-assets, and Stockholders' Equity						
Contra-assets:						
Accumulated depreciation	____	____	____		____	____
Current liabilities:						
Accounts payable	____	____	____		____	____
Accrued liabilities	____	____	____		____	____
Taxes payable	____	____	____		____	____
Noncurrent liabilities:						
Bonds payable	____	____	____		____	____
Deferred income taxes	____	____	____		____	____
Stockholders' equity:						
Common stock	____	____	____		____	____
Retained earnings						
Net income	____	____	____		____	____
Dividends	____	____	____		____	____
Additional entries						
Proceeds from sale of long-term investments				____	____	____
Gain on sale of long-term investments				____	____	____
Total (net cash flow)			====	====	====	

17-2. Using the form that appears below and the indirect method, determine Ingall Company's net cash provided by operating activities.

Net income	$_______
Adjustments to convert net income to a cash basis:	
Depreciation charges	_______
__________ in accounts receivable	_______
__________ in inventory	_______
__________ in prepaid expenses	_______
__________ in accounts payable	_______
__________ in accrued liabilities	_______
__________ in taxes payable	_______
__________ in deferred taxes	_______
Gain on sale of long-term investments	_______
Net cash flow provided by (used in) operations	$_______

17-3. (Appendix 17A) Using the form that appears below and the direct method, determine Ingall Company's net cash provided by operating activities.

Sales	$ 230	
Adjustments to convert sales to a cash basis:		
__________ in accounts receivable	_____	$_____
Cost of goods sold	$ 120	
Adjustments to convert cost of goods sold to a cash basis:		
__________ in inventory	_____	
__________ in accounts payable	_____	_____
Operating expenses	$ 70	
Adjustments to convert operating expenses to a cash basis:		
__________ in prepaid expenses	_____	
__________ in accrued liabilities	_____	
Depreciation charges	_____	_____
Income taxes	$ 14	
Adjustments to convert income taxes to a cash basis:		
__________ in taxes payable	_____	
__________ in deferred taxes	_____	_____
Net cash provided by (used in) operating activities		$_____

17-4. Prepare a statement of cash flows for Ingall Company for the year. (It is not necessary to show the details for the "net cash provided by operating activities" figure.)

INGALL COMPANY
Statement of Cash Flows

Operating activities

Net cash provided by (used in) operating activities .... $______

Investing activities

______________________________ .... $______

______________________________ .... ______

Net cash provided by (used in) investing activities .... ______

Financing activities

______________________________ .... $______

______________________________ .... ______

______________________________ .... ______

Net cash provided by (used in) financing activities .... ______

Net increase (decrease) in cash .... ______

Cash balance, beginning .... ______

Cash balance, ending .... $______

17-5. **Critical thought writing exercise:** An article in a prominent business magazine stated: "During the last year, depreciation has been one of X Company's biggest sources of cash." Do you agree that depreciation is really a source of cash? Explain your answer

....

....

....

....

....

....

....

....

Answers to Questions and Exercises

True or False

1. F Cash equivalents consist of investments in short-term, highly liquid investments. Stocks and bonds do not fall in this category, since they represent long-term investments.

2. T Dividends received enter into the determination of net income and therefore are not included in investing activities.

3. F Interest paid on amounts borrowed would be included in operating activities since interest enters into net income.

4. F Lending money to another entity would be classified as an investing activity.

5. T Dividends do not affect net income and therefore are not considered to be an operating activity.

6. F Transactions involving accounts payable are included among operating activities—not financing activities.

7. T Only transactions involving operating activities are presented in net amounts.

8. F The two methods will yield exactly the same figure for the net cash provided by operating activities.

9. F Changes in all noncash accounts, current as well as noncurrent, are analyzed in preparing a statement of cash flows.

10. F The cash account could decrease during the year even if a company is profitable, and the opposite could also be true (it could increase even if the company is unprofitable). Changes in the cash account hinge on cash management—not on whether a company is profitable or unprofitable.

11. T See Exhibit 17A-1 for an example.

12. T This may seem strange, but subtracting depreciation from an expense when the direct method is used is equivalent to adding it to net income when the indirect method is used.

Multiple Choice

1. b Inventory is a current asset. Increases in current assets are classified as uses. (Cash might have to be used to acquire inventory.) Changes in current assets are considered to be the result of operating activities.

2. a Accounts payable is a current liability. Increases in current liabilities are classified as sources. (An increase in accounts payable indicates that the company essentially saved some cash by using its credit.) Changes in current liabilities are considered to be the result of operating activities.

3. c Bonds payable is a noncurrent liability. An increase in a noncurrent liability is considered to be a source. (An increase in bonds payable occurs when a company borrows more money, which is certainly a source of cash.) A change in a noncurrent liability is considered to be a financing activity unless it enters into net income.

4. b Long-term investments is a noncurrent asset account. An increase in a noncurrent asset is considered to be a use. (Investing in a long-term asset requires the use of cash.) A change in a noncurrent asset is considered to be an investing activity unless it directly enters into the determination of net income.

5. d Dividends are considered to be a use. They are classified as a financing activity since they do not enter into the determination of net income.

6. c An increase in the common stock account is considered to be a source and a financing activity.

Exercises

17-1. The completed worksheet for Ingall Company appears below:

	Change	*Source or use?*	*Cash Flow Effect*	*Adjust-ments*	*Adjusted Effect*	*Classi-fication**
Assets (except cash and cash equivalents)						
Current assets:						
Accounts receivable	+6	Use	-6		-6	Operating
Inventory	+7	Use	-7		-7	Operating
Prepaid expenses	-4	Source	+4		+4	Operating
Noncurrent assets:						
Plant and equipment	+50	Use	-50		-50	Investing
Long-term investments	-20	Source	+20	-20	0	Investing
Liabilities, Contra-assets, and Stockholders' Equity						
Contra-assets:						
Accumulated depreciation	+11	Source	+11		+11	Operating
Current liabilities:						
Accounts payable	+1	Source	+1		+1	Operating
Accrued liabilities	-2	Use	-2		-2	Operating
Taxes payable	-5	Use	-5		-5	Operating
Noncurrent liabilities:						
Bonds payable	+10	Source	+10		+10	Financing
Deferred income taxes	+5	Source	+5		+5	Operating
Stockholders' equity:						
Common stock	+10	Source	+10		+10	Financing
Retained earnings						
Net income	+31	Source	+31		+31	Operating
Dividends	-18	Use	-18		-18	Financing
Additional entries						
Proceeds from sale of long-term investments				+25	+25	Investing
Gain on sale of long-term investments			___	-5	-5	Operating
Total (net cash flow)			+4	0	+4	

Note: The hardest part of this worksheet is the adjustment for the sale of the long-term investments. Basically, it has the effect of moving the gain on the sale from the operating activities section to the investing section. It would be wise to pay particular attention to this entry and what effects it has on the subsequent statement of cash flows.

17-2. The operating activities section of the statement of cash flows constructed using the indirect method appears below:

Net income	$31
Adjustments to convert net income to a cash basis:	
Depreciation charges	11
Increase in accounts receivable	(6)
Increase in inventory	(7)
Decrease in prepaid expenses	4
Increase in accounts payable	1
Decrease in accrued liabilities	(2)
Decrease in taxes payable	(5)
Increase in deferred taxes	5
Gain on sale of long-term investments	(5)
Net cash flow provided by operations	$27

Note that the gain on sale of long-term investments is deducted from net income. This removes the gain from the operating activities section of the statement of cash flows. The gain will show up implicitly in the investing activities section of the statement of cash flows. See the solution to 17-4 below.

17-3. The direct method can be used to arrive at the same answer as in 17-2 above.

Sales	$230	
Adjustments to convert sales to a cash basis:		
Increase in accounts receivable	(6)	$224
Cost of goods sold	$120	
Adjustments to convert cost of goods sold to a cash basis:		
Increase in inventory	7	
Increase in accounts payable	(1)	126
Operating expenses	$ 70	
Adjustments to convert operating expenses to a cash basis:		
Decrease in prepaid expenses	(4)	
Decrease in accrued liabilities	2	
Depreciation charges	(11)	57
Income taxes	$ 14	
Adjustments to convert income taxes to a cash basis:		
Decrease in taxes payable	5	
Increase in deferred taxes	(5)	14
Net cash provided by operating activities		$ 27

17-4.

INGALL COMPANY
Statement of Cash Flows

Operating activities		
Net cash provided by operating activities		$ 27
Investing activities		
Proceeds from sale of long-term investments	$25	
Increase in plant and equipment	(50)	
Net cash used for investing activities		(25)
Financing activities		
Increase in bonds payable	$10	
Increase in common stock	10	
Dividends	(18)	
Net cash provided by financing activities		2
Net increase in cash		4
Cash balance, beginning		10
Cash balance, ending		$14

17-5. Depreciation isn't really a source of cash. Adding back depreciation charges to net income to compute the net cash provided by operations creates the illusion that depreciation somehow generates cash. Actually, any cash provided by operations comes as a result of sales revenues, not as result of depreciation charges. A company could double or triple its depreciation charges on its external reports and there would be no effect on the amount of cash provided by operations. The increase in depreciation charges would be precisely offset by decreases in net income or by changes in other accounts, so that the net effect on cash flow would be zero. (This would not be true if depreciation were changed on reports to the tax authorities. In that case, depreciation could have a real effect on cash flows. The effect does not occur, however, because depreciation is added back to net income on the statement of cash flows!)

Chapter 18

"How Well Am I Doing?" Financial Statement Analysis

Chapter Study Suggestions

The chapter is divided into two parts. The first part discusses the preparation and use of statements in comparative and common-size form. Your study time in this part should be focused on Exhibits 18-1 through 18-4 in the text. These exhibits show how statements in comparative and common-size form are prepared and used to assess the well-being of the firm.

The second part of the chapter deals with ratio analysis. Altogether, seventeen ratios are presented in this part of the chapter. You should memorize the formula for each ratio since it is likely that you will be expected to know these formulas on quizzes and examinations. You should also learn how to interpret each ratio. Exhibit 18-7 in the text provides a compact summary of the ratios.

CHAPTER HIGHLIGHTS

A. Financial statement analysis is concerned with assessing the financial condition of the firm and its future prospects.

1. To be most useful, financial statement analysis should involve comparisons.

a. Comparisons should be against other periods, as well as against other firms within the industry.

b. Differences in accounting methods may make comparisons difficult.

2. The analyst must be careful not to rely just on financial statement analysis in making a judgment about a firm.

a. The ratios should be viewed as a starting point for analysis rather than as an end in themselves. They indicate what should be pursued in greater depth.

b. The analyst should also look at industry trends, technological changes, changes in consumer tastes, and so forth.

B. Three common analytical techniques for financial statement analysis are: 1) dollar and percentage changes on statements; 2) common-size statements; and 3) ratios.

1. Horizontal analysis uses dollar and percentage changes to highlight trends. Horizontal analysis involves placing two or more yearly statements side by side and analyzing changes between years.

a. Showing changes in dollar form helps identify key factors affecting profitability or financial position.

b. Showing changes in percentage form helps the analyst gain perspective and a feel for the significance of the changes that have taken place.

c. Horizontal analysis can also be done by computing trend percentages. Trend percentages state several years' financial statements in terms of a base year.

2. A common-size statement shows items in percentages rather than in dollars. Preparation of common-size statements is known as vertical analysis. Showing the balance sheet and the income statement in common-size form helps the analyst see the relative importance of the various items.

3. In addition to the above analytical techniques, ratios can assist stockholders, short-term creditors, and long-term creditors in assessing the well-being of a firm. Ratios that are designed to meet the needs of these three different groups are discussed in sections C, D, and E below.

C. Several ratios provide measures of shareholder well-being.

1. *Earnings per share* is an important measure of the annual earnings available for common shareholders. The formula is:

$$\frac{\text{Net income} - \text{Preferred dividends}}{\text{Common shares outstanding}} = \text{Earnings per share}$$

a. If net income includes extraordinary gains or losses, two earnings per share figures must be reported. First, earnings per share must be shown for normal operations; and second, the effect of extraordinary items on earnings per share must be shown.

b. By showing the effect of extraordinary items on earnings per share, the distorting influence of the extraordinary items on net income is highlighted. In addition, the trend of normal earnings can be evaluated by the analyst.

c. When reporting extraordinary items separately, they must be shown "net of their tax effect."

2. If a company has convertible securities, the earnings per share figure must again be computed in two ways. First, it must be computed assuming no conversion of the convertible securities into common stock; and second, it must be computed assuming full conversion of the convertible securities into common stock. The latter is referred to as fully diluted earnings per share and is computed using the following formula:

$$\frac{\text{Net income}}{\text{Common shares outstanding} + \text{Common stock equivalent of convertible securities}} = \text{Fully diluted earnings per share}$$

For example, if there are 10,000 shares of preferred stock outstanding and each of them can be converted into 2.5 shares of common stock, then the "Common stock equivalent of convertible securities" is 25,000 shares.

3. The *price-earnings ratio* shows the relationship between the market price of a share of stock and the stock's current earnings per share. The price-earnings ratio is computed as follows:

$$\frac{\text{Market price}}{\text{Earnings per share}} = \text{Price–earnings ratio}$$

Companies have differing price-earnings ratios. One of the biggest factors affecting the price-earnings ratio is the prospects for future earnings growth. If investors believe high future earnings growth is likely for a particular company, they will tend to bid up the price of its stock and hence it will have a high price-earnings ratio.

4. The *dividend payout ratio* gauges the proportion of current earnings being paid out as dividends. The formula is:

$$\frac{\text{Dividends per share}}{\text{Earnings per share}} = \text{Dividend payout ratio}$$

5. The d*ividend yield ratio* provides the investor with a measure of the cash yield on his or her investment. The ratio is computed as follows:

$$\frac{\text{Dividends per share}}{\text{Market price per share}} = \text{Dividend yield ratio}$$

Investors hope to profit from both dividends and increases in the market value of the stock they own. The dividend yield measures only the contribution of the dividends. The current market price per share is used in this ratio.

6. The *return on total assets* is a measure of how well assets have been employed by a firm. It is a measure of operating performance. The formula is:

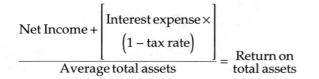

$$\frac{\text{Net Income} + \left[\begin{array}{c}\text{Interest expense} \times \\ (1 - \text{tax rate})\end{array}\right]}{\text{Average total assets}} = \begin{array}{c}\text{Return on} \\ \text{total assets}\end{array}$$

a. Notice that the interest expense is placed on an after-tax basis before being added back to net income.

b. The reason for adding the interest expense back to net income is to derive a net income figure that shows earnings *before* any distributions have been made to either creditors or stockholders. This adjustment results in a total return on assets that measures operating performance independently of how the assets were financed.

7. The *return on common stockholders' equity* is a measure of a company's ability to generate income for the benefit of common stockholders. The formula is:

$$\frac{\text{Net Income} - \text{Preferred dividends}}{\begin{array}{c}\text{Average common} \\ \text{stockholders' equity}\end{array}} = \begin{array}{c}\text{Return on common} \\ \text{stockholders' equity}\end{array}$$

a. The return on common stockholders' equity is usually higher than the return on total assets because of financial leverage.

b. *Financial leverage* involves purchasing assets with funds obtained from creditors or from preferred stockholders at a fixed rate of return. If the assets in which the funds are invested earn a greater return than the fixed rate of return required by the suppliers of the funds, then financial leverage is *positive*. Leverage is *negative* if the assets earn a return that is less than the fixed rate required by the suppliers of the funds.

c. Sources of leverage include long-term debt, preferred stock, and current liabilities.

d. Long-term debt is usually a more effective source of positive leverage than preferred stock since interest on long-term debt is tax-deductible, whereas dividends on preferred stock are not.

e. Because of leverage, the prudent use of debt can benefit the common stockholder.

8. The *book value per share* measures the net assets per share of common stock. The formula is:

$$\frac{\text{Common stockholders' equity}}{\begin{array}{c}\text{Number of common} \\ \text{shares outstanding}\end{array}} = \begin{array}{c}\text{Book value} \\ \text{per share}\end{array}$$

The book value per share is usually less than the market value per share. Market value is geared toward future earnings and dividends; by contrast, book value reflects the past. Generally speaking, book value measures financial effects of already completed transactions. Because of this, book value is of limited usefulness.

D. Short-term creditors are concerned with being paid on time. As such, they are more interested in cash flows and in working capital management than in how much accounting net income is being reported by a company.

1. *Working capital* measures the excess of current assets over current liabilities. Working capital is computed by the following formula:

$$\text{Current assets} - \text{Current liabilities} = \text{Working capital}$$

2. The *current ratio* is also a widely used measure of short-term debt-paying ability. The formula is:

$$\frac{\text{Current assets}}{\text{Current liabilities}} = \text{Current ratio}$$

a. Although widely regarded as a measure of debt-paying ability, the current ratio must be interpreted with a great deal of care. The *composition* of the assets and liabilities is very important. For example, there may be very little cash in the current assets.

b. The general rule of thumb calls for a current ratio of 2 to 1. However, this general rule is subject to many exceptions, depending on the industry and firm involved.

3. The *acid-test* or *quick ratio* is designed to measure how well a company can meet its short-term obligations using only its *most liquid* current assets. The formula is:

$$\frac{\text{Cash + Marketable securities + Current receivables}}{\text{Current liabilities}} = \text{Acid–test ratio}$$

The current receivables in this ratio includes accounts receivable and short-term notes receivable, but not inventories or prepaid assets since these latter assets are relatively difficult to convert into cash.

4. The *accounts receivable turnover* ratio measures the relationship between sales on account and accounts receivable. The formula is:

$$\frac{\text{Sales on account}}{\text{Average accounts receivable balance}} = \text{Accounts receivable turnover}$$

By dividing the turnover rate into 365 (the number of days in a year), the *average collection period* for accounts receivable can be computed. Its formula is:

$$\frac{\text{365 days}}{\text{Accounts receivable turnover}} = \text{Average collection period}$$

5. The *inventory turnover* ratio measures how many times a company's inventory has been sold during the year. The formula is:

$$\frac{\text{Cost of goods sold}}{\text{Average inventory balance}} = \text{Inventory turnover}$$

The number of days required to sell the entire inventory one time (called the *average sale period*) can be computed by dividing 365 by the inventory turnover figure. Its formula is:

$$\frac{\text{365 days}}{\text{Inventory turnover}} = \text{Average sale period}$$

E. Long-term creditors are concerned with both the near-term and the long-term ability of a firm to repay its debts.

1. The *times interest earned ratio* gauges the ability of a firm to meet its near-term commitments. The formula is:

$$\frac{\text{Earnings before interest expense and income taxes}}{\text{Interest expense}} = \text{Times interest earned}$$

Interest expense has a claim on earnings *before* any income taxes are paid. Therefore, earnings before income taxes is used in the computation rather than earnings after taxes.

2. The *debt-to-equity ratio* indicates the relation of debt to equity financing. The formula is:

$$\frac{\text{Total liabilities}}{\text{Stockholders' equity}} = \text{Debt–to–equity ratio}$$

Creditors generally prefer a low debt-to-equity ratio since this provides a large cushion of protection.

REVIEW AND SELF TEST
Questions and Exercises

True or False

For each of the following statements, enter a T or an F in the blank to indicate whether the statement is true or false.

___ 1. Horizontal analysis uses dollar and percentage changes from year to year to highlight trends.

___ 2. Common-size statements are statements of companies of similar size and operations.

___ 3. The current ratio is current assets less current liabilities.

___ 4. Trend percentages in financial statements would be an example of vertical analysis.

___ 5. A common-size statement shows items in percentage form, with each item stated as a percentage of some total of which that item is a part.

___ 6. The earnings per share figure is computed after deducting preferred dividends from the net income of a company.

___ 7. In computing the earnings per share figure, extraordinary gains and losses should be included with ordinary income and expense items.

___ 8. If earnings remain unchanged and the price-earnings ratio goes up, then one would expect the market price of a stock to go down.

___ 9. Dividing the market price of a share of stock by the dividends per share gives the price-earnings ratio.

___ 10. Book value per share is not a good predictor of either earnings potential or debt paying ability.

___ 11. The acid test ratio excludes inventories from current assets.

___ 12. When computing the return on total assets, the after-tax interest expense is subtracted from net income.

___ 13. Inventory turnover is computed by dividing sales by average inventory.

___ 14. If a company's return on total assets is substantially higher than its cost of borrowing, then the common stockholders would normally want the company to have a high debt-to-equity ratio.

Multiple Choice

Choose the best answer or response by placing the identifying letter in the space provided.

___ 1. Artway Company's net income last year was $200,000. It paid dividends of $50,000 to the owners of the company's preferred stock. There were 10,000 shares of common stock outstanding at the end of the year. What was the company's earnings per share for the year? a) $20; b) $5; c) $15; d) $25.

___ 2. Refer to the data in question 1 above for Artway Company. Assume that in addition, each of the company's 2,000 shares of preferred stock can be converted into 3 shares of common stock. What was the company's fully diluted earnings per share for the year? a) $12.50; b) $9.375; c) $15; d) $20.

___ 3. Carston Company's earnings per share last year was $3.50 and its market price per share at the end of the year was $28. There were 1 million shares of common stock outstanding. What was the company's price-earnings ratio? a) 43.75; b) 4.375; c) 80.0; d) 8.0.

___ 4. Refer to the data for Carston Company in question 3 above. Assume in addition that the company paid a dividend of $2.17 per share last year. What was the company's dividend payout ratio? a) 62%; b) 7.75%; c) 217%; d) 8.9%.

___ 5. Refer again to the data for Carston Company in questions 3 and 4 above. What was the company's dividend yield ratio? a) 62%; b) 7.75%; c) 217%; d) 8.9%.

___ 6. Darsden Company's net income last year was $800,000; its average assets were $4,000,000; its interest expense was $200,000; and its tax rate was 30%. What was the company's return on total assets? a) 23.5%; b) 25%; c) 16.5%; d) 30%.

___ 7. Kristal Company's net income last year was $600,000. The company paid preferred dividends of $200,000 to the owners of its preferred stock. The average common stockholders' equity was $5,000,000. What was the company's return on common stockholders' equity? a) 12%; b) 4%; c) 10%; d) 8%.

___ 8. Harrison Company's common stockholders' equity is $24 million. There are 6 million shares of common stock and 2 million shares of preferred stock outstanding. What is the company's book value per share? a) $3.00; b) $4.00; c) $6.00; d) $2.40.

___ 9. J.J. Company's current assets are $6 million and its current liabilities are $2 million. What is the company's working capital? a) $6 million; b) $2 million; c) $4 million; d) $8 million.

___ 10. Refer to the data for J.J. Company in question 9 above. What is the company's current ratio? a) 3.0 to 1; b) 2.0 to 1; c) 0.33 to 1; d) 0.50 to 1.

___ 11. Refer to the data for J.J. Company in question 9 above. Assume in addition that the company as $1 million in cash and marketable securities and $1.2 million in current receivables. What is the company's acid-test ratio? a) 0.8 to 1; b) 1.0 to 1; c) 1.2 to 1; d) 1.1 to 1.

___ 12. Proctor Company had $25 million of credit sales last year and its average accounts receivable balance was $5 million. What was the company's average collection period? a) 73 days; b) 5 days; c) 20 days; d) 84 days.

___ 13. Larimart Company's cost of goods sold last year was $750,000 and its average inventory balance was $300,000. What was the company's average days to sell inventory? a) 2.5 days; b) 5 days; c) 146 days; d) 912.5 days.

___ 14. Bresser Company's earnings before interest and taxes last year was $48,000 and its interest expense was $6,000. What was the company's times interest earned? a) 12.5 times; b) 1.25 times; c) 80 times; d) 8.0 times.

___ 15. Nupper Company's total liabilities are $320,000 and its stockholders' equity is $400,000. What is the company's debt-to-equity ratio? a) 0.2 to 1; b) 1.25 to 1; c) 0.8 to 1; d) 5 to 1.

___ 16. The acid-test ratio: a) can be expected to be less than the current ratio; b) can be expected to be greater than the current ratio; c) could be either greater or less than the current ratio; d) none of these.

Exercises

18-1. The financial statements of Amfac, Inc., are given below:

AMFAC, INC.
Balance Sheet
December 31

Assets	
Cash	$ 8,000
Accounts receivable, net	36,000
Merchandise inventory	40,000
Prepaid expenses	2,000
Plant and equipment, net	214,000
Total Assets	$300,000

Liabilities & Equities	
Current liabilities	$ 40,000
Long-term liabilities (10%)	60,000
Preferred stock (8%)	50,000
Common stock, $10 par	30,000
Retained earnings	120,000
Total liabilities and equity	$300,000

AMFAC, INC.
Income Statement
For the Year Ended December 31

Sales	$450 000
Cost of goods sold	270,000
Gross margin	180,000
Operating expenses	129,000
Net operating income	51,000
Interest expense	6,000
Net income before taxes	45,000
Income taxes (30%)	13,500
Net Income	$ 31,500

Accounts receivable and inventory remained relatively constant during the year. There are no convertible securities. Assets at the beginning of the year totaled $250,000, and the stockholders' equity at the beginning of the year totaled $180,000. Preferred stock did not change during the year.

Compute the following:

a. Current ratio.

b. Acid-test ratio.

c. Debt-to-equity ratio

d. Accounts receivable turnover in days

e. Inventory turnover

f. Times interest earned.

g. Return on total assets.

h. Return on common stockholders' equity

i. Is financial leverage positive or negative? Explain

....

....

....

....

....

18-2. Cartwright Company has reported the following data relating to sales and accounts receivable in its most recent annual report

	19x5	*19x4*	*19x3*	*19x2*	*19x1*
Sales	$700,000	$675,000	$650,000	$575,000	$500,000
Accounts Receivable	$ 72,000	$ 60,000	$ 52,000	$ 46,000	$ 40,000

Express the data above in trend percentages. Use 19x1 as the base year.

	19x5	*19x4*	*19x3*	*19x2*	*19x1*
Sales	______	______	______	______	______
Accounts Receivable	______	______	______	______	______

Comment on the significant information revealed by your trend percentages:

....

....

....

....

18-3. Consider the following 19x1 and 19x2 income statements of Eldredge Company:

ELDREDGE COMPANY
Income Statements
For the Years Ended December 31, 19x1 and 19x2

	19x2	*19x1*
Sales	$600,000	$500,000
Cost of goods sold	420,000	331,000
Gross margin	180,000	169,000
Operating expenses:		
Selling expenses	87,000	72,500
Administrative expenses	46,800	51,000
Total operating expenses	133,800	123,500
Net operating income	46,200	45,500
Interest expense	1,200	1,500
Net income before taxes	45,000	44,000
Income taxes (30%)	13,500	13,200
Net Income	$ 31,500	$ 30,800

a. Express the income statements for both years in common-size percentages. Round percentages to one decimal point.

	19x2	*19x1*
Sales	______	______
Cost of goods sold	______	______
Gross margin	______	______
Operating expenses:		
Selling expenses	______	______
Administrative expenses	______	______
Total operating expenses	______	______
Net operating income	______	______
Interest expense	______	______
Net income before taxes	______	______
Income taxes (30%)	______	______
Net Income	______	______

b. Comment briefly on the changes between the two years.

Answers to Questions and Exercises

True or False

1. T This is true by definition.

2. F A common-size statement is one that shows the separate items appearing on it in percentage form rather than in dollar form. Each item is stated as a percentage of some total of which that item is a part.

3. F The current ratio is current assets *divided* by current liabilities.

4. F Trend percentages would be an example of horizontal analysis.

5. T This point is discussed in connection with question 2 above.

6. T The earnings per share figure is computed for common stock, and the portion of net income belonging to the common stockholders is the amount that remains after paying preferred dividends.

7. F Extraordinary gains and losses should not be included in earnings per share; however, the per share effect of extraordinary gains and losses should be computed and reported to stockholders.

8. F The opposite is true. If the price-earnings ratio goes up, then the stock is selling for a higher market price per dollar of earnings.

9. F Dividing the market price of a share of stock by the earnings per share gives the price-earnings ratio.

10. T Book value per share is the balance sheet carrying value of completed transactions—it tells little about the future.

11. T Inventories are excluded when computing the acid-test ratio since they are relatively illiquid; that is, they are relatively difficult to quickly convert to cash.

12. F When computing the total return on assets, the after-tax interest expense is *added back* to net income to remove its effect.

13. F The inventory turnover is computed by dividing cost of goods sold by average inventory.

14. T If a company's return on total assets is higher than its cost of borrowing, then financial leverage is positive. Common stockholders would want the company to use this positive financial leverage to their advantage by having a high amount of debt in the company.

Multiple Choice

1. c The computations are:

$$\frac{\text{Net income} - \text{Preferred dividends}}{\text{Common shares outstanding}} = \text{Earnings per share}$$

$$\frac{\$200{,}000 - \$50{,}000}{10{,}000} = \$15$$

2. a The computations are:

$$\frac{\text{Net income}}{\text{Common shares outstanding} + \text{Common stock equivalent of convertible securities}} = \text{Fully diluted earnings per share}$$

$$\frac{\$200{,}000}{10{,}000 + (20{,}000 \times 3)} = \$12.50$$

3. d The computations are:

$$\frac{\text{Market price}}{\text{Earnings per share}} = \text{Price–earnings ratio}$$

$$\frac{\$28}{\$3.50} = 8.0$$

4. a The computations are:

$$\frac{\text{Dividends per share}}{\text{Earnings per share}} = \text{Dividend payout ratio}$$

$$\frac{\$2.17}{\$3.50} = 62\%$$

5. b The computations are:

$$\frac{\text{Dividends per share}}{\text{Market price per share}} = \text{Dividend yield ratio}$$

$$\frac{\$2.17}{\$28.00} = 7.75\%$$

6. a The computations are:

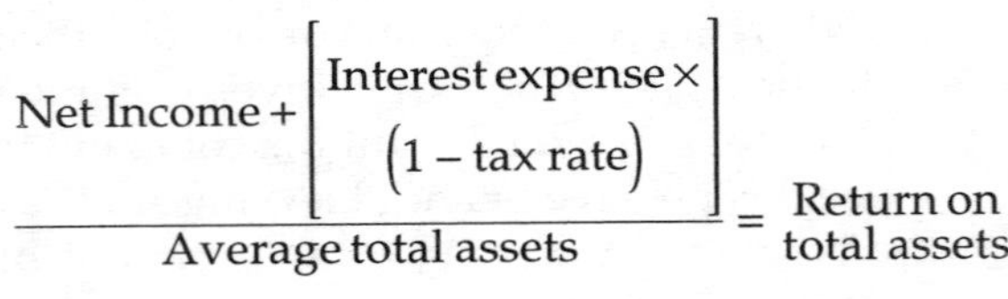

$$\frac{\text{Net Income} + \left[\text{Interest expense} \times (1 - \text{tax rate})\right]}{\text{Average total assets}} = \text{Return on total assets}$$

$$\frac{\$800{,}000 + \left[\$200{,}000 \times (1 - 0.30)\right]}{\$4{,}000{,}000} = 23.5\%$$

7. d The computations are:

$$\frac{\text{Net Income} - \text{Preferred dividends}}{\text{Average common stockholders' equity}} = \text{Return on common stockholders' equity}$$

$$\frac{\$600{,}000 - \$200{,}000}{\$5{,}000{,}000} = 8\%$$

8. b The computations are:

$$\frac{\text{Common stockholders' equity}}{\text{Number of common shares outstanding}} = \text{Book value per share}$$

$$\frac{\$24{,}000{,}000}{6{,}000{,}000} = \$4.00$$

9. c The computations are:

$$\text{Current assets} - \text{Current liabilities} = \text{Working capital}$$

$$\$6{,}000{,}000 - \$2{,}000{,}000 = \$4{,}000{,}000$$

10. a The computations are:

$$\frac{\text{Current assets}}{\text{Current liabilities}} = \text{Current ratio}$$

$$\frac{\$6{,}000{,}000}{\$2{,}000{,}000} = 3.0 \text{ to } 1$$

11. d The computations are:

$$\frac{\text{Cash} + \text{Marketable securities} + \text{Current receivables}}{\text{Current liabilities}} = \text{Acid–test ratio}$$

$$\frac{\$1{,}000{,}000 + \$1{,}200{,}000}{\$2{,}000{,}000} = 1.1 \text{ to } 1$$

12. a The computations are:

$$\frac{\text{Sales on account}}{\text{Average accounts receivable balance}} = \text{Accounts receivable turnover}$$

$$\frac{\$25{,}000{,}000}{\$5{,}000{,}000} = 5.0 \text{ to } 1$$

$$\frac{\text{365 days}}{\text{Accounts receivable turnover}} = \text{Average collection period}$$

$$\frac{\text{365 days}}{5.0} = \text{73 days}$$

13. c The computations are:

$$\frac{\text{Cost of goods sold}}{\text{Average inventory balance}} = \text{Inventory turnover}$$

$$\frac{\$750{,}000}{\$300{,}000} = 2.5 \text{ to } 1$$

$$\frac{\text{365 days}}{\text{Inventory turnover}} = \text{Average sale period}$$

$$\frac{\text{365 days}}{2.5} = \text{146 days}$$

14. d The computations are:

$$\frac{\text{Earnings before interest expense and income taxes}}{\text{Interest expense}} = \text{Times interest earned}$$

$$\frac{\$48{,}000}{\$6{,}000} = 8.0 \text{ to } 1$$

15. c The computations are:

$$\frac{\text{Total liabilities}}{\text{Stockholders' equity}} = \text{Debt–to–equity ratio}$$

$$\frac{\$320{,}000}{\$400{,}000} = 0.8 \text{ to } 1$$

16. a The acid-test ratio will always be less than the current ratio because it contains fewer assets in its computation but the same amount of liabilities.

Exercises

18-1.

a. $\frac{\$86{,}000}{\$40{,}000} = 2.15 \text{ to } 1$

b. $\frac{\$44{,}000}{\$40{,}000} = 1.10 \text{ to } 1$

c. $\frac{\$100{,}000}{\$200{,}000} = 0.50 \text{ to } 1$

d. $\frac{\$450{,}000}{\$36{,}000} = 12.5 \text{ times (accounts receivable turnover)}$

$$\frac{365}{\text{Accounts Receivable Turnover}} = \frac{365}{12.5} = 29.2 \text{ days}$$

e. $\frac{\$270{,}000}{\$40{,}000} = 6.75 \text{ times}$

f. $\frac{\$51{,}000}{\$6{,}000} = 8.5 \text{ times}$

g. $\frac{\$31{,}500 + [\$6{,}000 \times (1 - 0.30)]}{\frac{1}{2}(\$250{,}000 + \$300{,}000)} = 13.0\% \text{ (rounded)}$

h.

	Beginning of Year	*End of Year*
Total stockholders' equity	$180,000	$200,000
Less preferred stock................................	50,000	50,000
Common stockholders' equity	$130,000	$150,000

$$\frac{\$31{,}500 - (8\% \times \$50{,}000)}{\frac{1}{2}(\$130{,}000 + \$150{,}000)} = 19.6\% \text{ (rounded)}$$

i. Financial leverage is positive, since the return on the common stockholders' equity is greater than the return on total assets.

18-2.

	19x5	*19x4*	*19x3*	*19x2*	*19x1*
Sales	140%	135%	130%	115%	100%
Accounts Receivable	180%	150%	130%	115%	100%

Sales grew by 15 percent per year through 19x3, and then dropped off to a 5 percent growth rate for the next two years. The accounts receivable grew at a 15 percent rate through 19x3, but then rather than dropping off to a 5 percent rate, the accounts receivable grew at an even faster rate through 19x5. This suggests that the company may be granting credit too liberally and is having difficulty collecting.

18-3.

a.

ELDREDGE COMPANY
Common-Size Income Statements
For the Years Ended December 31, 19x1 and 19x2

	19x2	*19x1*
Sales	100.0	100.0
Cost of goods sold	70.0	66.2
Gross margin	30.0	33.8
Operating expenses:		
Selling expenses	14.5	14.5
Administrative expenses	7.8	10.2
Total operating expenses	22.3	24.7
Net operating income	7.7	9.1
Interest expense	0.2	0.3
Net income before taxes	7.5	8.8
Income taxes (30%)	2.2	2.6
Net Income	5.3	6.2

b. Cost of goods sold and administrative expenses were the two primary areas affecting the percentage decrease in net income. Cost of goods sold increased from 66.2 percent of sales in 19x1 to 70.0 percent of sales in 19x2—an increase of 3.8 percentage points. On the other hand, administrative expenses dropped from 10.2 percent of sales in 19x1 to only 7.8 percent of sales in 19x2—a decrease of 2.4 percentage points. The net effect was a decrease in net income as a percentage of sales, which fell from 6.2 percent of sales in 19x1 to only 5.3 percent of sales in 19x2.

Appendix A

Pricing Products and Services

Appendix Study Suggestions

This appendix contains two major topics, both of which relate to pricing issues. The first topic deals with cost-plus pricing. Exhibits A-l through A-5 contain the essential computations involved in cost-plus pricing under both the absorption and contribution approaches. Also study the section titled *Determining the Markup Percentage* with care, and memorize the two formulas in this section.

The second topic deals with time and material pricing. Carefully study Exhibit A-7 and the accompanying text, which illustrates how the time component and material component are computed.

APPENDIX HIGHLIGHTS

A. Many companies sell products in markets where they have some latitude in the prices they can charge. The most common approach to product pricing in such situations is to employ some type of cost-plus pricing formula. Under this method, a markup is added to a cost base to arrive at a target selling price. The formula is:

$$\text{Target selling price} = \text{Cost} + \text{Markup percentage} \times \text{Cost}$$

Cost-plus pricing can be used to compute a target selling price under either the absorption approach or the contribution approach.

1. The absorption approach uses unit manufacturing cost as the cost base. Selling, general, and administrative (SG&A) expenses are not included in cost base, but rather are provided for through the markup. The format is:

Unit manufacturing cost	$50
Markup to cover SG&A expenses, and desired profit—40%	20
Target selling Price	$70

2. The contribution approach uses unit variable cost as the cost base. A markup designed to cover fixed costs and to provide the desired profit is added to this variable cost base. The format is:

Variable production costs	$35
Variable SG&A expenses	5
Total variable costs	40
Markup to cover fixed costs and desired profit—75%	30
Target selling price	$70

3. In both cases above, the term "cost plus" is a misnomer, since part of the cost is buried in the "plus" or markup part of the formula. For the absorption approach, the SG&A expenses are included as part of the markup—for the contribution approach, the fixed costs are included as part of the markup.

B. Managers often base the markup on their costs and desired return on investment (ROI). They reason that the percentage markup added to the cost base must be large enough to cover a portion of the costs of the firm, and to provide for the desired profit element.

1. If absorption costing is being used, the markup formula is:

$$\text{Markup percentage on absorption cost} = \frac{\text{Desired return on assets employed} + \text{SG\&A expenses}}{\text{Volume in units} \times \text{Unit manufacturing cost}}$$

2. If the contribution approach is being used, the markup formula is:

$$\text{Markup percentage on variable cost} = \frac{\text{Desired return on assets employed} + \text{Fixed costs}}{\text{Volume in units} \times \text{Unit variable costs}}$$

3. However, it is very important to note that *the target ROI will be attained only if the budgeted sales volume is attained.* There is absolutely no guarantee that the company will earn its desired profit or even breakeven simply because it uses these formulas. The company must sell the budgeted volume at the price it has computed to earn the desired return.

C. Target costing is used by some companies when a new product is being developed. Managers estimate how much the new product can be sold for and then deduct the desired profit per unit to arrive at the target cost figure. The formula is:

$$\text{Target cost} = \text{Anticipated selling price} - \text{Desired profit}$$

It is then the responsibility of the product development team to produce and market the product for no more than this target cost. This approach is radically different from the cost-plus approach in which costs are determined and then the price is based on those costs. In highly competitive markets, target costing is often the better approach.

D. Some organizations—particularly in service industries—use a variation on cost-plus pricing called time and material pricing. Under this method two pricing rates are established—one based on direct labor time and a second based on direct material used.

1. The time component is typically expressed as a labor rate per hour. The rate is computed by adding together three elements: (1) the direct costs of employee time, including salary and fringe bene-

fits; (2) an allowance for the SG&A expenses of the company; and (3) an allowance for a desired profit.

2. The material component is determined by adding a material loading charge to the invoice cost of the materials used on the job. This charge is designed to cover the costs of ordering, handling, and carrying materials in stock, plus a profit margin on the materials.

REVIEW AND SELF TEST
Questions and Exercises

True or False

For each of the following statements, enter a T or an F in the blank to indicate whether the statement is true or false.

___ 1. In cost-plus pricing, the cost base is generally the same under either the absorption or the contribution approaches.

___ 2. The contribution approach to cost-plus pricing defines the cost base as consisting of a product's variable costs, including variable selling, general, and administrative expenses.

___ 3. If a company has a 20% desired rate of return on investment, then it should add a 20% markup to its products.

___ 4. In time and material pricing, the material loading charge includes a profit element.

___ 5. The markup in cost-plus pricing consists solely of the desired profit of a firm.

___ 6. Under target costing, a firm knows how much a product will cost and efforts are directed toward determining an appropriate selling price.

Multiple Choice

Choose the best answer or response by placing the identifying letter in the space provided.

___ 1. Lerner, Inc. has provided the following data for one of its products:

Direct materials	$8
Direct labor	7
Variable manufacturing overhead	2
Variable SG&A expenses	3

The company produces and sells 15,000 units of this product each year. Fixed manufacturing overhead cost totals $15,000 per year and fixed SG&A expenses total $30,000 per year. If the company uses the absorption approach to pricing and desires a 50 percent markup, the target selling price per unit would be: a) $34.50; b) $31.50; c) $27.00; d) $23.00.

___ 2. Refer to the data in question 1 above. If the company uses the contribution approach to pricing and desires a 35 percent markup, the target selling price per unit would be: a) $29.70; b) $22.95; c) $20.00; d) $27.00.

___ 3. Justin Corp. estimates that an investment of $800,000 would be needed to produce and sell 20,000 units of a new product each year. At this level of activity, the unit manufacturing cost would be $100. Selling, general, and administrative expenses would total $500,000 per year. If a 25 percent rate of return on investment is desired, then the markup for the new product under the absorption costing approach would be: a) 35%; b) 25%; c) 62.5%; d) 100%.

___ 4. Kares Ltd. produces and sells 10,000 units of a particular product each year. The following data concerning this product are available:

Variable production cost per unit	$45
Variable SG&A expense per unit	$10
Fixed production cost per year	$600,000
Fixed SG&A expense per year	$300,000

The company's total investment in the product is $1,000,000 and the company's required rate of return on investment is 20%. If the company uses the contribution approach to cost-plus pricing, what markup would it use? a) 20%; b) 50%; c) 100%; d) 200%.

___ 5. Vintage RR, Inc. is considering introducing a new line of model railroad engines. To compete effectively, the engines would be priced at $45. The company expects to be able to sell 2,000 engines a year at this price. The company requires a rate of return on investment of 20%. The new product line would require an investment of $150,000. The target cost per engine is: a) $30; b) $45; c) $15; d) $60.

___ 6. Larry's Downtown Motors uses time and material pricing in its service shop. The shop charges $35 per hour for repair time and uses a material loading charge of 55% of invoice cost. An electrical repair required two hours of repair time and $40 of materials. The total charge for the repair was: a) $70; b) $132; c) $92; d) $75.

Exercises

A-1. Costs relating to a product made by Mackey Company are given below:

Direct materials	$10
Direct labor	12
Variable manufacturing overhead	1
Fixed manufacturing overhead ($210,000 total)	7
Variable SG&A expenses	2
Fixed SG&A expenses ($90,000 total)	3

Assume that the company uses the absorption approach to cost-plus pricing and a 50% markup. Compute the target selling price for the above product.

______________________________	$ ________
______________________________	________
______________________________	________
______________________________	________
Unit manufacturing cost	________
Markup—50%	________
Target selling price	$ ________

b. Assume that the company uses the contribution approach to cost-plus pricing and a 80% markup. Compute the target selling price for the above product.

______________________________	$ ________
______________________________	________
______________________________	________
______________________________	________
Total variable cost	________
Markup—80%	________
Target selling price	$ ________

A-2. Speckart Company has determined that an investment of $800,000 is needed to produce and market 30,000 units of a particular new product each year. The company's cost accountant estimates that the unit manufacturing cost will be $50 at this level of activity, and that SG&A expenses will total $400,000 per year. Compute the markup percentage for the product, assuming that the company uses the absorption approach to costing, and has a 25% desired rate of return on investment.

$$\text{Markup percentage on absorption cost} = \frac{\text{Desired return on assets employed} + \text{SG\&A expenses}}{\text{Volume in units} \times \text{Unit manufacturing cost}}$$

$$\text{Markup percentage on absorption cost} = \frac{\_\_\_\_\_\_ + \_\_\_\_\_\_}{\_\_\_\_\_\_ \times \_\_\_\_\_\_} = \_\_\_\_\_\_\%$$

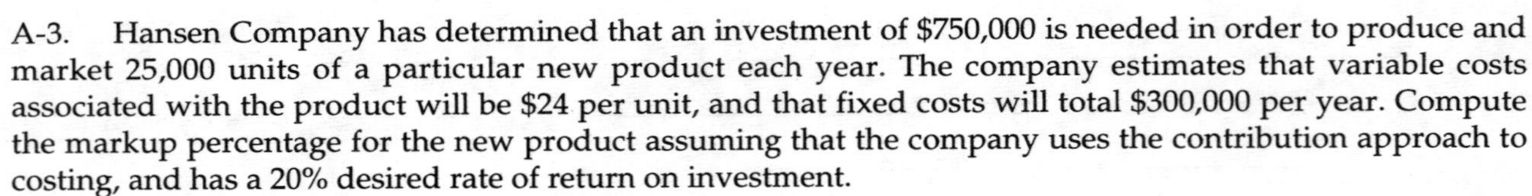

A-3. Hansen Company has determined that an investment of $750,000 is needed in order to produce and market 25,000 units of a particular new product each year. The company estimates that variable costs associated with the product will be $24 per unit, and that fixed costs will total $300,000 per year. Compute the markup percentage for the new product assuming that the company uses the contribution approach to costing, and has a 20% desired rate of return on investment.

$$\text{Markup percentage on variable cost} = \frac{\text{Desired return on assets employed} + \text{Fixed costs}}{\text{Volume in units} \times \text{Unit variable costs}}$$

$$\text{Markup percentage on variable cost} = \frac{\_\_\_\_\_\_ + \_\_\_\_\_\_}{\_\_\_\_\_\_ \times \_\_\_\_\_\_} = \_\_\_\_\_\_\%$$

Answers to Questions and Exercises

True or False

1. F The cost base is different under the two approaches, as shown in Exhibits A-2 and A-4 in the text.

2. T This is true by definition.

3. F The markup includes some element of cost under both approaches.

4. T The material loading charge consists of two elements: (1) the cost of ordering, handling, and carrying materials in stock, and (2) a profit margin on the materials.

5. F The markup consists of the desired profit plus some element of cost. Under the absorption approach, this element is the selling and administrative expenses; under the contribution approach it is the fixed costs.

6. F The opposite is true; a firm knows what price to charge, but it does not know what the product will cost to manufacture and sell.

Multiple Choice

1. c The computations are:

Direct materials	$ 8
Direct labor	7
Variable manufacturing overhead	2
Fixed manufacturing overhead ($15,000 ÷15,000 units)	1
Unit manufacturing cost	18
Markup—50%	9
Target selling price	$27

2. d The computations are:

Direct materials	$ 8
Direct labor	7
Variable manufacturing overhead	2
Variable SG&A expenses	3
Total variable expenses	20
Markup—35%	7
Target selling price	$27

3. a The computations are:

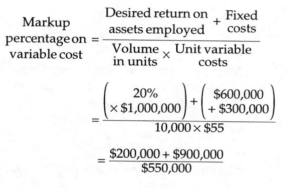

$$\text{Markup percentage on absorption cost} = \frac{\text{Desired return on assets employed} + \text{SG\&A expenses}}{\text{Volume in units} \times \text{Unit manufacturing cost}}$$

$$= \frac{25\% \times \$800{,}000 + \$500{,}000}{20{,}000 \times \$100}$$

$$= 35\%$$

4. d The computations are:

$$\text{Markup percentage on variable cost} = \frac{\text{Desired return on assets employed} + \text{Fixed costs}}{\text{Volume in units} \times \text{Unit variable costs}}$$

$$= \frac{\left(\begin{matrix}20\% \\ \times \$1{,}000{,}000\end{matrix}\right) + \left(\begin{matrix}\$600{,}000 \\ + \$300{,}000\end{matrix}\right)}{10{,}000 \times \$55}$$

$$= \frac{\$200{,}000 + \$900{,}000}{\$550{,}000}$$

$$= 200\%$$

5. a

Projected sales ($45 × 2,000)	$90,000
Less desired profit (20% × $150,000)	30,000
Target cost for 2,000 units	$60,000

Target cost = $60,000 ÷ 2,000 units = $30 per unit

6. b

Labor time (2 hours × $35)	$ 70
Parts used:	
Invoice cost	40
Material loading charge (55%)	22
Total price of the job	$132

Exercises

A-1. a.

Direct materials	$10
Direct labor	12
Variable manufacturing overhead	1
Fixed manufacturing overhead	7
Unit manufacturing cost	$30
Markup—50%	15
Target selling price	$45

b.

Direct materials	$10
Direct labor	12
Variable overhead	1
Variable SG&A expenses	2
Total variable costs	$25
Markup—80%	20
Target selling price	$45

A-2.

$$\begin{aligned}\text{Markup percentage on absorption cost} &= \frac{(25\% \times \$800{,}000) + \$400{,}000}{30{,}000 \times \$50} \\ &= \frac{\$600{,}000}{\$1{,}500{,}000} \\ &= 40\%\end{aligned}$$

A-3.

$$\begin{aligned}\text{Markup percentage on variable cost} &= \frac{(20\% \times \$750{,}000) + \$300{,}000}{25{,}000 \times \$24} \\ &= \frac{\$450{,}000}{\$600{,}000} \\ &= 75\%\end{aligned}$$